THE
TABLE
I LONG
FOR

Learning to Participate
in the Mission and
Family of God

SHAWN
BRACE

SIGNS
PUBLISHING®
Established 1885

"*The Table I Long For* is beautifully written, compelling and biblical. It doesn't just talk about mission, it demonstrates it through stories and personal experience. Inspiring and practical, this book could forever change the way you approach your life and church. Although there's a point or two I could dispute with Shawn, the book gave me a deep breath of fresh mission air that we all so desperately need."

—*Gary Krause, Director, Office of Adventist Mission, General Conference of Seventh-day Adventists*

"Shawn Brace offers a refreshingly candid reflection on his journey of discovering how Christian mission and discipleship are inextricably bound up with ordinary life, the joy of mutual relationships, the pursuit of justice, and learning—simply yet profoundly—to love one another well. One need not share all of Brace's assumptions and convictions to benefit from the stories and insights he offers because the book itself reflects the open posture of missional church that he proposes."

—*Nicholas Zork, PhD, Minister for Worship and the Arts, Church of the Advent Hope, New York City*

"In a time where so many things seem to either be changing too fast or stuck in the past, Shawn Brace brings a biblical, fresh and intentional perspective to the ecclesiology conversation. I can't wait to recommend this book to every pastor in our field. Adventist to the core and incredibly timely—pick this book up!"

—*Roger Hernandez, Ministerial and Evangelism Director, Southern Union Conference of Seventh-day Adventists*

"*The Table I Long For* traces Brace's journey as he leads his congregation away from program and performance to people and community. The main stage of the book is not a church building, but homes, parties, barbeques, recovery groups and coffee shops. Brace weaves experiences of joy, meals, broken hearts, addiction and local life into the story of God's continuous action in the world. He paints a beautiful picture of what it might look like when Christians commit to be a faithful, loving presence in our local communities. He does not shy away from the missteps of the project, or his own mistakes, pulling the veil back to reveal a pastoral heart ignited by love for people."

—*Andreas Beccai, Lead Pastor, Walla Walla University Church*

"Shawn Brace's *The Table I Long* For is the 'must read' book of the year for anyone interested in the church and its mission—especially in our secular age. Shawn writes with clarity, conviction and a depth that keeps you engaged page by page. He challenges our assumptions about church and takes us back to the Bible over and over again with an invitation to settle no more for what is, but to pursue with holy abandon, what can be. I could not recommend this book enough. Two thumbs way up from me."

—*Marcos Torres, Pastor, Perth, Australia*

Unless otherwise indicated, all Bible quotations are from the *New King James Version®*. Copyright © 1982 by Thomas Nelson. Used by permission. All rights reserved.

Bible quotations marked "CEV" are from the *Contemporary English Version*. Copyright © 1995 by American Bible Society.

Bible quotations marked "HCSB" are from the *Holman Christian Standard Bible*. Copyright © 1999, 2000, 2002, 2003, 2009 by Holman Bible Publishers, Nashville Tennessee. All rights reserved.

Bible quotations marked "KJV" are from the *Holy Bible, King James Version*.

Bible quotations marked "*The Message*" are from *The Message*, Copyright © 1993, 2002, 2018 by Eugene H Peterson.

Bible quotations marked "NIV" are from the *Holy Bible, New International Version*, copyright © 1973, 1978 by the International Bible Society. Used by permission of Zondervan Bible Publishers.

Bible quotations marked "NLT" are from the *Holy Bible, New Living Translation*, copyright © 1996, 2004, 2015 by Tyndale House Foundation. Used by permission of Tyndale House Publishers, Inc., Carol Stream, Illinois 60188. All rights reserved.

Proudly published and printed in Australia by
Signs Publishing
Warburton, Victoria.
This book was
Edited by Lauren Webb
Proofread by Nathan Brown
Cover design by Shane Winfield
Cover image by Rawpixel, Getty Images
Typeset in Berkeley Book 11/14 pt

ISBN (print edition) 978 1 922373 42 7
ISBN (ebook edition) 978 1 922373 43 4

To Camden, Acadia and Winnie:

May you always remember that you are not just welcome at the table, but desperately and fiercely wanted here.

And may you continuously invite others to it as well.

CONTENTS

Preface...ix

STARTING

1. Re-imagining Church..3

MISSION

2. Why I'm Always Hanging Out at Bagel Central...........13
3. Life-on-Life..23
4. Life Is the Bible Study...32
5. The Way Up Is Down 41
6. Skin-to-Skin..51
7. Drive-by Evangelism 59
8. The Same, but Different 67
9. Losing My Religion 78
10. Becoming a Functional Pluralist...............................87
11. Not All Who Wander Are Lost..................................97

FAMILY

12. Together at the Table..111
13. Better Together...120
14. The Allure of Pseudo-community 127
15. Fully Known and Yet Fully Loved.............................136
16. Wounded Healers 146
17. Why It Isn't Enough to Be "Not Racist"....................156
18. God Has Left the Building 167

RESTARTING

19. Raising the Dead...181

Appendix A: Finding a "Person of Peace"...191
Appendix B: Thirteen Practical Ways to Be
  Missional In Your City or Town...193
Appendix C: How to Start a Missional Community........................195
Appendix D: Ellen White on Being Missional...............................198
Appendix E: Further Reading...205
Endnotes..208
Acknowledgments...212

PREFACE

A word to readers: you're about to read about one person's journey. My journey. Though the chapters are mostly topical in nature, they follow a trajectory. Back in 2016, my whole paradigm of what it meant to be a pastor and Jesus-follower came crashing down. My understanding of what church is, on a fundamental level, toppled.

In some ways, this is a story about deconstruction, which is a popular genre these days. But it is also a story about a beautiful reconstruction— of learning what it means to truly understand the gospel, at least as I've come to see it, and to live it out in ways that are vibrant, embodied and contextualised. This is a story about what it means to stop "doing" church and to instead start "being" church.

To that end, you will read lots of stories from my life over the past few years. That is a little outside my comfort zone. I am always self-conscious about talking about myself too much. And yet I decided to include all these stories because the concepts and ideas I share came as a result of my journey of self-discovery. I also find that it is so much better, and more inspiring, to see how these theories and concepts work in real life. It gives them flesh and makes them practical. So I share them to that end—not presuming that everyone has to do it the way I've done it, but as an example of what it has looked like for one person.

You will also read many stories that involve other people. All of the stories are true. All of the people are real. Most of the names are accurate—except where people specifically requested I change their names or where it was obvious that I needed to. I am appreciative to all those who graciously allowed me to include parts of their stories as I shared mine.

I am a pastor in the Seventh-day Adventist Church and this is the context I am writing from. However, I have tried to write in a way that makes relevant aspects of my faith community accessible to anyone who is interested in the mission of the church. I also hope that writing in this way will help readers from my own faith community reflect on how we explain and invite others into the doctrines, practices, traditions and assumptions of our particular church community.

Lastly, this book details an ongoing journey. Neither I nor my church have completely arrived. It's one of the reasons why I chose the title I did: it's the table I *long* for. It's always a work in progress. One of my favourite chapters of Scripture of late has been Hebrews 11, where the author notes how all the great heroes of faith died having never received the promises, "but having seen them afar off were assured of them, embraced them and confessed that they were strangers and pilgrims on the earth" (Hebrews 11:13). That is the story of the Jesus-way: this side of eternity, we are always on the journey, feeling a certain restlessness and incompleteness, and never quite arrive. And yet we press on.

So you will read about a part of my journey: about how in 2016 my whole paradigm of church came crashing down, and how since then I've continued to learn what it means to be the church and what it means to be a disciple of Jesus. We replanted our church in 2018—what we called a "restart"—but in many ways, we continuously experience mini-restarts (especially when we crashed into an unprecedented worldwide pandemic), as we learn to more faithfully align ourselves with and embody the gospel.

I hope this humble story can captivate your imagination and propel you into new heights as you reconsider the much larger vision God longs for his church to experience—the table *He* longs for us to sit at and invite others to.

STARTING

1

RE-IMAGINING CHURCH

To the casual observer it wouldn't have appeared very significant, but my whole world began to shift that fateful Friday night in March, 2016. A small group of us were sitting around the living room at my in-laws' house, singing, sharing, studying Scripture together. I'd invited them to embark on a journey that was a long time in the making.

The results would prove cataclysmic.

For many years, I'd led a pretty traditional ministry. Pastoring was preaching, visiting my church members and trying to maintain doctrinal integrity. There were certainly the typical stresses of church attendance and financial challenges, but overall life was good.

But then I started noticing a crack in the dam. I became overwhelmed with a sense that something wasn't right. Something was missing, but I couldn't put my finger on what it was. The traditional pastoral formula—preach good sermons, visit your parishioners—just didn't seem to be working for me. I felt like a glorified manager—that my job was to keep the saints happy, pursuing the status quo at all costs.

I began seriously wrestling with my calling. It wasn't that I doubted I should be in ministry. I was struggling with what *type* of ministry.

Eventually, I landed on the idea of academia. I'd always been passionate about deeper study and had harboured the idea of someday pursuing a doctorate in Old Testament studies. Just as significantly, I couldn't shake my ambivalence about what I was supposed to be doing as a pastor.

So for the next two years, I prepared to apply to various PhD programs at top universities. It quickly became everything I breathed and dreamed about—all the while doing just enough in pastoring to get by. I was obsessed with the thought of someday walking the hallowed grounds of Harvard, not too far from where I grew up, debating the nuances of Hebrew with classmates and professors.

But spoiler alert: I didn't get accepted—not into Harvard, not into Duke, not even into Boston University. One by one, the rejection letters came, and each time I crashed to my knees, confused about what God was doing.

A couple of days after the last rejection letter, something really strange happened though: I felt peace—like a heavy burden had been lifted from my shoulders. And instead of preparing to apply again the following year, I sensed that God had something else in mind. I didn't know what exactly, but I'd soon find out it was something far better—and far different—than I could ever imagine. I was about to discover what my friend Ben Lundquist has tweeted, that "God often uses our deepest pain as a launching pad for our greatest calling."[1]

My wife Camille and I initially assumed it involved moving. We'd been anticipating a change of scenery anyway if I got into a doctoral program, so even though that didn't work out, we were already halfway out the door emotionally. It had been one of the snowiest winters in Maine and despite being hardy New Englanders, we were ripe for a move to a warmer location.

"I think I could live in Maryland," Camille said one day, a week or two later.

When a well-positioned friend in ministry randomly called me the next week, asking if I'd ever consider pastoring in Maryland, we figured it was a sure sign. So for the first time in my ministry, I threw my hat in the ring for a church far away from the land I loved.

And then I waited. And waited. And waited—occasionally getting updates, telling me my name was slowly making its way to the top.

But then I waited some more.

And then something mysterious happened: while waiting and wrestling, I became overwhelmed one morning during prayer with the sense that I was not done in Maine. God still had more for me to do in Bangor. I didn't know what exactly, but I knew it was something.

I suddenly felt incredible peace. And by the time I finally heard back from the church a couple of months later, telling me they'd chosen someone else, I didn't care anyway. I was where God wanted me.

But I also knew this: if I was staying in Bangor, it wasn't simply to do more of the same thing. I knew God had gifted me with abilities and passions to do more than simply maintain the status quo. In fact, I knew if I was going to survive ministry and maintain my sanity, I'd have to start following a different path.

Little did I know it would actually be more like blazing an entirely new trail, with no road map, and many harrowing twists and turns.

At that point, the only thing I could think that meant was to plant a new church. Which makes some sense. I'd grown up in the home of a man, one of my great heroes, who'd experienced his own ministry crossroads three decades earlier and come to the same conclusion. Similarly dissatisfied with traditional ministry, my dad left the comforts of a sizeable church in rural Massachusetts to start new churches in secular Boston, arguably the least-religious city in America.

His family, with me the youngest of three, went from the luxuries of traditional rural religious life to worshipping in dingy basements of rented Lutheran churches in poor Boston neighbourhoods. Many times, my dad's eyes welled up with tears as he peeked into the children's classrooms on Saturdays, seeing little me there all by myself with only the teacher for companionship, wondering if he'd made a mistake by pulling his family away from the large Christian community he'd left behind.

I guess the upshot of it was that somehow, unknowingly, it had gotten into my DNA. I somehow knew that status quo church is no church at all—that the Christian faith is one of movement, refusing to ever feel too content in one's station.

And so I felt the strong conviction that if we were going to stay in Bangor, it would be a creative venture. It couldn't be business as usual. Through a series of conversations, I roped my church into apprehensively agreeing to plant a new church.

Which is what led to that Friday night.

The church had formed a planting team to plot the course, venturing into the unknown. And that's exactly what it was—the unknown. Despite being raised by a man who'd started three churches, the nuts and bolts had somehow eluded me. And my one seminary course on church planting was a faint memory also, leaving it all a black box to me.

So I started consuming everything I could. I listened to podcasts, read books and spoke with experts, including my dad, trying to crack the code. The best I could come up with was that we needed to form a planting team, which would prepare to launch the church a few months later. We'd need to get organised to start off with a bang—finding a place to rent, recruiting a great music team, preparing a killer children's program. We'd have to send out flyers, inviting our city to the first service, hoping to draw in lots of strangers. It all sounded exciting, if not a little stressful.

When we met that first night, a dozen or so of the church's finest, there was a buzz in the air. We sensed something epic was happening, at least in our minds. But little did we know just how epic.

We were there to organise ourselves to launch a new church, but the Spirit had another agenda altogether. We thought our task was figuring out how to put on the best program we could put on, but the Spirit started the process of making us the best people we could be.

As we sat around the living room, reclining on couches and overstuffed chairs, laughing, sipping hot drinks, praying, studying Scripture together, sharing our hearts with one another, suddenly it hit me like a bolt of lightning, seemingly out of nowhere: *Why does church have to be more than this?*

The question wrecked me.

And I've never been the same.

I'd come upon an idea—not original to me—that was revolutionary. It was one that had never occurred to me before, mainly because I'd never experienced it before.

To that point, church—faith, religion—had been about putting on a program. It had been about showing up at the right time to the right holy building, sitting quietly in a pew, listening to one person talk. It had been about organising complicated committees and worrying about budgets. It had been about spending hours each week carefully crafting sermons and practising catchy ditties or elaborate arias, hoping to dazzle with our performances. It had been about strictly policing dogma, thinking that was the church's primary mission. It had been about spending thousands of dollars on maintaining a building, all because we called it "God's house."

But what I began to realise that night is that we'd really overcomplicated this whole church thing. Somewhere along the way we began thinking church was about putting on programs and maintaining buildings—when it's really about being with and investing in people.

I went to bed that night with my head in the clouds and my heart captivated. My imagination ran wild and I couldn't sleep.

That night, in that living room, something profound had happened: I started falling in love with what church really is.

THE CHURCH OF ACTS

The irony, of course, is that this vision had been staring at me all along in the pages of Scripture. But I'd somehow missed it.

I couldn't miss it this time though as I read the book of Acts afresh. It was there as plain as day. Soon after Pentecost, when the fledgling group of Jesus-followers were launched by the Spirit into cosmic-sized mission, Acts shares this insight about the life of the church:

> They spent their time learning from the apostles and they were like family to each other. They also broke bread and prayed together.... All the Lord's followers often met together, and they shared everything they had. They would sell their property and possessions and give the money to whoever needed it. Day after day they met together in the temple. They broke bread together in different homes and shared their food happily and freely, while praising God. Everyone liked them, and each day the Lord added to their group others who were being saved (Acts 2:42–47, CEV).

It's pretty simple, really. There's no mention of buildings that needed renovating, committees to nominate nominating committees, introits, benedictions or Personal Ministries leaders. There's nothing about elaborate mission statements or organisational flow charts. Church wasn't a fancy program one attended but a community one belonged to.

The New Testament church spent a lot of time together—they ate together, learned together and prayed together. They became family. And amazingly, astoundingly, awesomely, the result was explosive growth! "*Each day* the Lord added to their group others who were being saved."

This was actually what God's vision for His people had always been. When He created the world, He created a family—Adam and Eve, together reflecting His image. When they turned their backs on God, they also turned their backs on each other, fracturing the family, ultimately leading to a scattering of all peoples across the earth. Togetherness became separation.

It was for this reason God called Abraham out of Ur, away from his family. God wanted to create a new family—a family that would bless all the families of the earth, displaying God's glory to the world. That's what Israel was to be—the family of God, reflecting the God-family—Father, Son and Spirit. They were to be a picture of how God could restore togetherness to the world, how people from all nations could join in fellowship and community, becoming one people again.

Ultimately, Jesus came to earth to do what Israel failed to do. He gathered to Himself a group of disciples "that they might be with Him" (Mark 3:14), demonstrating what the family of God was to be. The disciples ate with Him, walked with Him, went everywhere with Him. He invited them to leave their own families, promising they would experience family a hundredfold. He called them His own brothers and sisters and mother, sending them into the world to announce that everyone was a child of God, all invited to sit at the same table together, experiencing God's kingdom of love.

It didn't take long for our church-planting team to catch this vision. We'd tasted something intoxicating and wanted more, not quite sure where it would lead. What we did know was that Scripture was inviting us to keep it simple. Instead of putting on fancy programs and starting complicated ministries, we were going to simplify and focus on the core scriptural principles of church—being family, encouraging one another and inviting others in.

Over the next few years, what that all looked like came into greater focus, slowly and messily and beautifully unfolding.

TC, THE SEVENTH-DAY AGNOSTIC

No-one epitomises this early part of our journey more than TC, someone we quickly came to love and adore. TC was married to Avery, one of our planting members, but was himself not a Christian. Raised in a Catholic family, he left religion behind when he went to college, with a stop along the way in Judaism. Through medical school, he ultimately landed on an agnosticism that seemed to at least admire Jesus.

For 30 years, Avery prayed for TC but never pushed her faith on him. He respected her religious commitments and even occasionally showed up to church, but it ultimately wasn't for him—the dogma, the sitting quietly in a pew, the rituals, the preacher preaching at him.

That first night Avery came to our meeting, TC curiously asked her where she was going. When she told him, he asked her why he couldn't go, and she promptly said it was because he wasn't invited. As she later recounted the exchange to us, we immediately burst out in unison: "Avery, tell him he's invited! This is why we're meeting. We want people like him."

The next week TC showed up.

He never stopped coming.

He quickly endeared himself to us and we to him. Despite having a ton of religious baggage, he realised something was different about our group. We weren't there to peddle religion; we were there to be God's family. We were there to talk about Jesus, whom he'd loved all along, to listen to each other's hearts and stories, and encourage one another.

This didn't mean we were interested in a Scripture-light experience. Not at all. We were never more serious about pursuing the heart of Scripture, wrestling deeply with what it meant to be Scripture-informed people in the present world. And TC loved all of it, offering incredible theological insights that left us all baffled, wondering how a self-proclaimed agnostic could have such a rich and beautiful grasp of concepts that had eluded many life-long Christians.

We soon realised that TC was a poignant example of someone who hadn't really rejected *church*; he was someone who'd rejected our *version* of church, which wasn't even scriptural. When we implicitly define church as a program that takes place in a building, full of rituals and traditions that have little scriptural basis, rather than the dynamic family of God, we leave behind a bunch of people who are attracted to Jesus and His mission but have no interest in sitting quietly in a pew for an hour, being talked at with dogma.

Pretty soon, our connection with TC turned into more than just a weekly thing. We started spending holidays together, watching football together, travelling together, crying together. When TC and Avery's youngest daughter, whom we'd met just a few times before, got engaged and needed someone to perform her wedding in Ohio, TC didn't hesitate. "Shawn will do it," he said, without even consulting with me. He knew because I was his pastor—but even more significantly, I was his family.

It all really started sinking in that this journey had seriously reshaped TC's understanding of church when one day Avery delightfully reported what he'd said to her extended family as they sat around a table one day. Avery had trained them to never bring up religion with TC for fear of offending him, so it came as a shock when out of nowhere, TC, with a gleam in his eye and in his endearing way, casually announced to everyone, "Well, I've become a church planter."

You could have blown everyone over with a feather, Avery told us, including herself.

We all had a good laugh when she recounted the story to us. But we knew: TC had been drawn into the orbit of God's love and into His family. He was a testament to what I've heard Eric Pfeiffer say: people today aren't looking for a church—at least as we've wrongly defined church—they're looking for family.

So in our own clumsy and bumbling way, putting one foot in front of the other without much visibility beyond the next step, we started on a new and exciting journey—a journey to become the family of God, inviting others into the ever-widening circle.

MISSION

2

WHY I'M ALWAYS HANGING OUT AT BAGEL CENTRAL

Not long after that fateful Friday night in March, I found myself at Bangor City Hall one evening, attending a city council meeting. I had recently become friends with Ben, who was the mayor of Bangor at the time, and he'd invited me to attend a meeting. Having never attended before, and being somewhat intimidated by stepping into the public square—which I was largely unaccustomed to doing, having lived my whole life in an insular religious environment—I sheepishly slid into the back row of the meeting and settled in.

It was eye-opening to see the inner workings of public life, to hear the issues that mattered to my neighbours and fellow residents. It was sobering to realise not everyone in the world was debating the religious minutiae I'd devoted much of my life to studying and arguing about.

One particular agenda item stood out to me the most. A measure was proposed that would give the city's first responders the ability to use Narcan when responding to individuals who'd overdosed from opiates, thus effectively saving their lives.

Though it was obvious the proposal would pass, Ben shared a gripping story about one of his young neighbours, William, who'd died from an overdose a few days before—a tragedy that could have been easily prevented if first responders had Narcan. As he shared the story, I noticed a few people in the audience in tears and I later learned they'd known William quite well.

William's story was not isolated, of course. I soon learned that Maine had the highest rate of prescription opiate addiction in America—a point that had caught the attention of many citizens. It was a huge epidemic that had acutely affected many within the state of Maine in general and the city of Bangor particularly.

I left the meeting with a heavy heart, wondering what I could do to come alongside people in my city to help address the life-or-death needs many faced. I also wondered what my church could do.

A few days later I partly got my answer.

I attended another meeting, this time with folks from my church, that was just as paradigm-shattering as that Friday night in March. I was about to get a big lesson in what it means to truly be the church, with the city council meeting acutely juxtaposed with the church meeting we held.

As we started down the path of church planting, some of my parishioners became increasingly anxious about the idea, worried what it would all mean going forward. And I didn't blame them. Not only is such a venture stressful and risky in itself, but I don't always help to ease others' concerns due to my own character flaws. I can be independent and sometimes insensitive, and I often don't finish what I start, which can be pretty frustrating.

So when a few people approached me about holding a meeting to update the church on our progress, I somewhat reluctantly agreed and scheduled the meeting. Within no time, the handful of people who attended started asking questions about our plans, urging me to explain what exactly I was trying to accomplish.

And then the question came—the question that would turn another light on for me about how we "do" church. Someone noted that our planting team had two persons who played the piano, leaving one person in the existing church to shoulder the load. "What happens if that one person can't come to church?" the person asked. "Do you know what it's like to be at church with no piano player?"

I could definitely sympathise. It's painful to fumble through a song without an accompanist to carry the melody. It doesn't make for a riveting church service, encouraging attendees to return each week.

But as my sympathies lingered, another thought suddenly dawned on me and I couldn't help but blurt it out. "Let me ask you a question," I hesitantly started, "did Jesus have a piano player?"

The question hung in mid-air, not fully appreciated by all. But it was clarifying for me. And as I reflected on the meeting later, the juxtaposition dawned on me with tragic clarity: the church was worried about losing piano players while our city was worried about losing lives.

Of course, in all fairness, nobody consciously pitted the two against each other—pianists or lives. But what clicked with me that day was the realisation that church for many of us—I'd say nearly *all* of us—is this event we put on and invite people to attend. And we essentially judge the effectiveness of a church by its ability to put on a good program.

In fact, some of us will drive miles and miles, passing other churches along the way, because the things that take place in that specific building are executed in a more attractive way than in the other buildings we pass to get there. Many of us base our entire investment in a church on the return it brings us. We are consumers in the church marketplace, looking for the best or most biblical preaching, the most compelling music or the best fellowship.

None of us explicitly thinks this way of course. But we have implicitly thought the church's mission is to put on good programs and exciting events. I've observed many churches that, for decades, seemingly thought they were one good piano player away from fulfilling their mission and impacting the world. They were just waiting for their ship to come in: the right speaker, enough money, a better building.

But I started to wonder if there was a better way—a more scriptural way.

THE MISSIONARY GOD

One of the simplest yet most significant words in Scripture is a word that pops up frequently, especially in the mouth of Jesus. It's the word *send*. It's the mission Jesus gave His disciples after His resurrection when He met them in the upper room. Unaware that Jesus had come back to life, they'd barred the doors, locking themselves away from the world—which is a poignant illustration of what many churches do today.

Mysteriously, Jesus suddenly stood before them, giving them their marching orders. "As the Father has sent Me," He commissioned them, "I also send you" (John 20:21).

There's that word *send*. Jesus made it clear to His disciples: their task was not to remove themselves from the world, remaining holed up in their safe upper room. He sent them *out into* the world to be His agents, announcing and demonstrating God's kingdom of love.

This was merely a reminder, of course. Jesus had repeatedly told His disciples this throughout His ministry. "I don't pray that You should take them out of the world," He petitioned His Father shortly before His crucifixion. "As You *sent* Me into the world, I also have *sent* them into the world" (John 17:15, 18). Elsewhere, He told His disciples that He was sending them out as "sheep in the midst of wolves" (Matthew 10:16). Theirs was not to be a play-it-safe religion, cautiously tucked away from the bad influences of the world. They were to be the salt of the earth, shot out of the salt-shaker into the world as the *sent-ones*, showing the ways of God.

This is the definition of the word *apostle*. In the original Greek, an apostle was one who was *sent out*. The primary posture of the early church was that of *sentness*. Eventually, the word "apostle" morphed through Latin, giving us the more familiar term "missionary." Someone who is a missionary is one who is *sent out* to live the ways of Jesus before an alienated people, inviting them to join God's family.

The apostles weren't the first missionaries though. Far from it. Jesus clued us in on this when He told them that the basis for their sentness was the fact that He, Himself, was first sent. "*As the Father has sent Me,*" He told them, "I also send you."

Many have rightfully noted that the God of Scripture is a missionary God. Mission—*sentness*—is at the heart of all God does. He saw a world in need and He *sent* Jesus to demonstrate and proclaim His character. Everything God does stems from this singular focus. And just as the Father sent Jesus to demonstrate His character, Jesus sent the Spirit to aid us as we join with Him in this mission.

It's for this reason that some have observed it's not accurate to say the church has a mission. It's more accurate to say that *the mission has a church*. Mission is why the church exists. It's not one thing among many the church does, squeezing it in amid all the other programming the church offers. We don't have a "missions department." The only reason the church exists at all is to participate in the mission God has already started. Nothing more, nothing less.

As Lesslie Newbigin boldly states, "There is no participation in Christ without participation in his mission to the world. . . a church that is not 'the church in mission' is no church at all."[1]

We have been *sent out* into the world to participate in God's mission. This is true for the church as a whole and it's true for each of its members. The church is not primarily in the event business or in the real estate business. The church is in the business of joining up with God in His mission, wherever or whenever that might be.

Unfortunately, we seemed to have taken a wrong turn.

WILL THE REAL CHURCH PLEASE STAND UP?

All these concepts started making sense to me when I came across a clarifying dichotomy about the way we "do" church. To be clear, this dichotomy is overly simplified and ignores nuance, but I've found it to be extremely helpful in clarifying how God wants us to participate in His mission.

Many have observed that churches "do" church one of two ways. The first way is what some have called the *attractional* approach. When a church is attractional, its life revolves around a program it puts on in a building each week. In fact, we even use the term "church" this way, referring to the event we put on each week ("When does church *start*?") or the building the event takes place in ("Should we build a new church?"), neither of which are ways Scripture ever uses the word "church." We then try to *attract* people to the event we hold in our building with the hope that these people will commit to coming to the event again each week.

So under the attractional model, church is essentially events, ministries and programs, with the hope of attracting more people to participate in our events, ministries and programs.

Of course, it doesn't take much reflection to recognise that churches have to compete with each other to be the most appealing and attractive church on the block. In a world of limited religious interest, every church has to raise its game, competing for a limited number of consumers. Churches therefore find themselves hustling to have the best music, the most attractive facilities, the most compelling and inspiring speakers.

It also needs to be mentioned here that not every attractional church is a contemporary church, replete with fog machines and designer coffee. So long as a church operates from a paradigm that places its emphasis on a weekend program, even if that program is poorly executed or old-fashioned, it's basically an attractional church. With an attractional church, members are consumers whose primary participation with the church is attending events and programs where they receive religious goods and services from others who are doing the ministry. In my experience, this is the vast majority of churches, across all denominations or non-denominations.

My particular community of faith has also perfected the art of *attractional evangelism*. We set up proclamation meetings in a particular location, either renting out a neutral site or holding them in our church building, then we rely on the postal service to be the missionary. Instead of sending out our *people* to live God's mission, we send out *handbills*, hoping to attract strangers to our prophecy meetings, advertised with dragons and promises to explain what the mark of the beast is. We're usually successful in drawing a small percentage of people in, but rarely are they discipled in the mission of God—at least from my observation.

What's more, especially in more traditional faith communities like my own, not only are churches *attractional* but they are *extractional*. That is, when someone joins the church from the outside, they're essentially *extracted* from their previous existence and thrust into a parallel society that rarely intersects with the outside world in any meaningful way. Suddenly, their lives become cluttered with attending Christian events and programs, and they hang out almost exclusively with other Christians.

In more extreme cases, they may adopt a downright adversarial posture towards what is broadly labelled and yet vaguely defined as "the world." This is the definition of the term "Pharisee," that group of religious elites who spent so much time criticising Jesus for contradicting their man-made rules and traditions. A Pharisee is literally a "separatist," one who separates himself from those who threaten his sense of religious security. Holiness to them is separation, rather than togetherness, as God intended. It quickly becomes an "us versus them" dynamic.

All this reflects the church's failure to disciple people in God's mission and in what it means to be a part of His family. As someone has said, what you win them with is what you win them to.

So if we win them through the consumption of religious programming, or if we win them through the message that the world is all wrong and the church is all right, we're setting them up to extract themselves from the very mission God has called them to participate in.

The second way of "doing" church—or more accurately, the second way of *being* church—is the *missional* way. Church in this understanding is not a what, where or when. It's a *who*: God's people sent out into the world to participate in God's mission in everyday life. The church is not concerned with putting on good programs and exciting events and then inviting people to *come to us* to consume them. The church *goes out* into the world, seeking to bring the healing ministry of Christ to a world that desperately needs it. The church doesn't have a mission; the mission has a church, with all of church life revolving around and participating in that mission.

This is all founded on the church's understanding of the good news of what God has done in Christ. Recognising the beautiful reality of God's self-giving, self-emptying, other-centred love, the church follows God into the world to spend and be spent for those who don't know what true love is. As Stacy L Sanchez puts it, "We aren't called to fill the pews with members. We are called to fill the world with disciples."[2]

To be sure, a missional church still meets together regularly—but it meets more as a family and less as an event, seeking to encourage, edify and equip one another to live out "love and good works" in everyday life (see Hebrews 10:24). Gathering together is more like a football huddle, rather than an end zone, where God's people receive the plays and then go out to execute them throughout the week.

Jesus shows us the way. He lived a *missional life* as He sought to form a *missional people*. He didn't confine Himself to an upper room and then wait for the masses to come to Him. He was on the road all the time, travelling to Bethany and Jericho and Jerusalem—and even to Samaria, to the Jews' hated enemies. Everywhere He went, He brought "church" with Him.

He didn't have a piano player and yet He turned the world upside-down, showing us the simplicity of what it means to be His family—a family sent into the world to participate in God's mission.

It's not complicated. A church's effectiveness is not dependent on the homiletical skills of the pastor or the musical talent of the worship leaders; it's based on the willingness of its members, empowered by the Spirit, to live out the gospel in everyday life. It's based on their willingness to press into the beautiful and messy togetherness of being God's family, showing the world His fullness and sufficiency.

This distinction between attractional church and missional church really clicked for me when I saw it illustrated with a graphic.

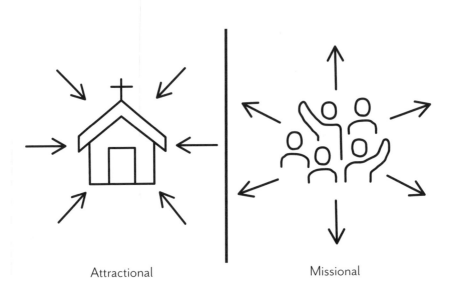

Attractional   Missional

MY NEW OFFICE

It didn't take long for our planting team to get excited about this new paradigm of church. We didn't want to be an attractional church anymore, merely putting on programs, trying to draw people in. That sounded like too much work and overly complicated, and even somewhat self-serving. More significantly, it didn't look like the beautiful picture Scripture paints of what it means to be the sent family of God. We instead wanted to participate in God's mission in everyday life, making a tangible difference in our city.

For some, this came easy. In fact, they began to realise they were already being missional but hadn't known it was a legitimate expression of church. They had never been told.

I specifically remember the look on my sister-in-law Ellie's face when the light turned on. It suddenly occurred to her that the little acts of kindness she'd already been doing for her friends and neighbours were every bit a part of "doing" church, every bit as much an act of worship, as singing a hymn or listening to a sermon. "Oh," she said, "you mean baking bread for my neighbours is being the church?"

Others also recognised they were already living lives of sentness as they went to work every day, took their kids to the library for story time, or ran with their running club. It was all God's mission, even if they failed to have a gospel conversation each time. They were still doing a gospel work, demonstrating what God's love looks like in the flesh.

For others, like myself, it required a little more creativity and courage. Not only does a traditional pastor's work typically keep her or him inside the boundaries of the fold, focused on the needs of the flock, but, quite frankly, I was not at all used to living a life of sentness.

Through no fault of my parents, I grew up with a Christian existence that didn't often traffic in the world's highways. We did have a few friends who didn't share our religious beliefs, and we spent lots of time with them. But whenever we stepped out of the safety of the nest, it wasn't long before we quickly retreated. Together with the fact that I attended Christian schools from the womb to graduate school, then got hired to work for the church, I was wholly ill-equipped and unsettled about how to even tackle my own sentness.

Camille was the same exact same way. One day, it occurred to her that she hadn't had a friend outside her faith community until she was in her late 20s. It was a sobering realisation for her.

So what was I to do? I felt this overwhelming sense that God was inviting me into a life of sentness, but I literally had no idea where to go or what to do.

And then an idea came to mind—one that was not original to me, nor all that profound, yet ultimately trajectory-altering. Instead of cloistering myself up in my home office when I had menial ministry tasks, why not do them in a public space? It would put me in the rhythms of everyday life with people in my city, providing opportunity for me to keep God's mission before my mind.

So that's what I resolved to do. I would move my "office" from my home to Bagel Central, a bagel shop in downtown Bangor, which serves as a hub for many people in the city. After much planning and plotting, I made my way there, lugging my computer and a few books—and a lot of optimism.

Yet when I showed up for the first time, I was strangely nervous, unsure of what I would do. What was my real purpose there? What was I trying to accomplish? Should I just try to strike up awkward conversations with random strangers?

21

It took me a few visits but eventually I caught on. God hadn't sent me there to really do much. He was just calling me into a humble ministry of presence as I listened to how the Spirit was already present and working there.

Eventually, I started noticing many of the same people showing up regularly and would occasionally strike up conversations with them since we had become recognisable to one another in a natural and unforced way. Then I started seeing friends I already knew who were there visiting with other friends, and they'd introduce me to those friends.

It wasn't long before I couldn't go there without running into people I'd come to know, and we'd get into conversations about a whole host of things—from Immanuel Kant to the Boston Red Sox to family struggles—and yes, Jesus quite frequently.

I don't wish to imply that this was all some magical missional bullet or even all that terribly profound. It's rather quite simple and hardly revolutionary. In fact, I feel funny that a basic behaviour—hanging out at a city crossroads, seeking to become a part of the fabric of one's community—was something that felt so foreign and awkward to me. All these years later, it now feels strange to think how utterly intimidating and unnerving it was when I first started going there. It's hard to believe I was ever so apprehensive.

Now it feels like home.

I can honestly say the simple decision to move my office to Bagel Central transformed me from feeling like someone who was standing on the outside of my city, looking in, to a person who became fully enmeshed in it. It was nothing profound and wholly intangible. But it was real.

It was just one simple way that I decided to participate in God's mission in my city, the effects of which might only become fully evident in eternity.

Quite frequently, when I'm out and about, people will ask me where my church is. The question always amuses me. I know what they're really asking, of course: they want to know where the building is located that my congregation meets in. But the truth is, wherever a follower of Jesus is—at work, in school, walking the neighbourhood—there is God's church, His family.

This is what it means to be the church, faithfully participating in God's mission.

3

LIFE-ON-LIFE

The second time I ran into Jim, I figured God was up to something. A few months before, I was taken aback when I spotted him at a restaurant where my family was eating. I hadn't seen him in probably a decade—although we had only been acquaintances at best then anyway.

All I knew of him at that point was that he had been a Seventh-day Adventist pastor but, for reasons that were unclear, was no longer serving in that capacity. The only other thing I knew about him, based solely on his long salty hair and beard, was that he seemed to style himself as a hippy of sorts.

Recovering from the shock at seeing him, I called out, "Jim!" Somehow, he also recognised me. After exchanging pleasantries and finding out that he'd been living in Bangor for a while, working as a drug and alcohol abuse counsellor, he gave me his phone number and I vowed to call him to get together.

And like any good pastor, I immediately lost his number and never called him.

But there I was a few months later, sitting in Bagel Central, and in walked Jim. Again shocked, I yelled his name, apologising profusely for failing to call him before. But he gave me his number again, humorously muttering under his breath about how irresponsible I was.

This time, however, I did call—the first Seventh-day Adventist pastor to reach out to him since being nudged out of ministry, and the church, some 15 years earlier.

And the rest is history.

We got together, again at Bagel Central, a week or two later, unsure about what God was doing with the relationship. But we decided to meet again the next week, and the next week, then the week after that. Since running into him that second time, we've gotten together at least weekly to encourage one another, pray for one another, mentor one another.

It also wasn't long before he started joining our planting team each Friday night, and then he eventually worked up the courage to start participating in our larger church each Saturday morning. Unlike his previous experiences with our denomination, he found our church family to be a safe and healing community. It restored some of his belief in a faith community whose theology he'd never abandoned, despite the church abandoning him.

The whole journey with Jim has been extremely life-giving and also enlightening. I've learned a lot.

Perhaps what stood out to me the most was a profoundly simple idea: these types of relationships—meeting regularly together one-on-one to mentor and encourage each other—were the building-blocks of church.

I had previously imagined church to largely revolve around me standing up and talking to a mass of people, often wondering if anything was really sinking in. It also felt like most of the pastoral care I provided was of the emergency variety—visiting a member in the hospital, or providing temporary crisis care for a couple whose marriage was struggling. I would drop in and then drop out, struggling to build any momentum.

Ministry was five miles wide but one inch deep—no way to really build relationships or truly impact people, which requires repeated attention over a long period of time.

But my journey with Jim was different and it gave me a taste of how life-giving participating in the mission and family of God could be. Through our weekly visits, as well as the other organic touchpoints we'd regularly have, God was helping me see that church consists of the slow, committed, life-on-life journey of people He's brought together.

Scripture has a word for this that's a trendy topic these days. The word is this: *discipleship*.

GO, THEREFORE, AND…

Tucked in the middle of the Great Commission is a nuance that many people miss to their own peril. If you've been a Jesus-follower for any length of time you're likely familiar with this course-setting mandate that Jesus left His disciples before His ascension. But you might have missed its full import.

After reminding His followers that He possessed all authority in the universe, He then gave them their commission. "Go therefore and make disciples of all the nations," He instructed them, "baptising them in the name of the Father and of the Son and of the Holy Spirit, teaching them to observe all things that I have commanded you; and lo, I am with you always, even to the end of the age" (Matthew 28:19, 20).

In my experience, the church has done a great job of taking seriously the invitation to baptise people, and we sure like teaching them up on the doctrines we deem important. We take great pride in reporting the hundreds or thousands of people who were baptised as a result of the latest proclamation meeting we conducted somewhere around the world.

The great challenge with this is that counting baptisms doesn't tell the whole story. Baptism doesn't automatically make a person a follower of Jesus any more than putting on a tie makes one the president of the United States. To be sure, there's a place for baptising people—just as there's a place to have a wedding ceremony—but we too often exchange form for substance.

Of course, everyone knows this and agrees. But we keep doing it— mostly because we like to have *something* we can point to that convinces ourselves and others that our efforts were successful, the money spent was justified.

We do the same thing with attendance numbers. We always want to know how many people attended an event—assuming that the more people who attended the better. We pastors like to boast of how many people attend our church, especially if it is more than when we arrived.

I've identified in my own heart that my sense of self-worth is often tied up in how many people attend the events I put on. We implicitly believe that only things we can count actually count—and that *we* only count when we out-baptise or out-draw others in ministry.

But the only command Jesus gave in the whole commission is the part we largely ignore.

It's hard to detect in English, but in the original Greek, the words "go," "baptise," and "teach" are not in command form. The only part that is written as a command? "Make disciples."

When Jesus commissioned His followers, He didn't command them to baptise people, to put on events, to provide services or to even grow the church. He simply told them to make disciples—nothing more, nothing less.

25

Our failure to follow this command has been to our great detriment. I remember hearing Bill Hull once say that we've come to this troubling place where a person can be a Christian but not a follower of Christ.

Think about that paradox.

Somewhere along the way, we got the idea that attending a 90-minute church service each week, sitting passively in a pew as someone talks at us, is somehow a significant reflection of our spirituality. And if we're extra sanctified, we might even participate in "ministry" by performing up front occasionally or serving as a greeter or usher.

It leaves me wondering, as Caesar Kalinowski humorously asks, if that's the height of Christian aspiration for many of us. "[Is] this the highest goal," he wonders, "to become an usher in the church building... to someday *ush* with the best of them?"[1]

But I've yet to find a single line in Scripture that indicates that attending a religious service is any reflection of one's spirituality. To be sure, occasionally, Scripture encourages God's family to gather for mutual edification (as in Hebrews 10:25). But that in no way resembles the type of passive spectating we tend to use as the barometer of spiritual maturity today.

It reminds me of conversations I've had with friends who've lamented the perceived lack of spiritual commitment in their adult children. I've listened as they've cried that their children are no longer "going to church," as though that somehow provided more insight into their spirituality than the selfless humanitarian work I knew those same children were doing.

Honestly, if I had to choose between having my children participate in God's mission every day of the week but never "going to church," or having them fill a pew each Saturday but ignoring the mission of God the rest of the week, it's a no-brainer what I'd choose.

As Jeff Vanderstelt so poignantly says, "Jesus didn't live, serve, suffer and die so we could just attend a Christian event....Jesus doesn't just want your afterlife. He wants your present life."[2] God is not looking for fans but followers—those who will truly commit to participating in His mission to the world not just once a week but every day.

TRUE RELIGION

The truth is, God isn't doling out points for attending religious events. We don't impress Him with our participation in church programs. In fact, in the Old Testament, one of the most repeated refrains is God rebuking His people for thinking their worship services had any value while their lives contradicted the praise on their lips. He even said their convocations wore Him out.

"Quit your worship charades," He declared through Isaiah (as rendered incisively by *The Message*). "I can't stand your trivial religious games: Monthly conferences, weekly Sabbaths, special meetings— meetings, meetings, meetings—I can't stand one more! Meetings for this, meetings for that. I hate them! You've worn me out! I'm sick of your religion, religion, religion, while you go right on sinning" (Isaiah 1:13, 14, *The Message*).

The sin that so bothered God wasn't some arbitrary form of personal piety or their failure to sing the right songs with the right syncopation— as I used to believe. What wearied Him was Israel's failure to pursue relational integrity and justice—failing to provide for the oppressed, widowed and orphaned, instead taking advantage of them.

The results were catastrophic. Nearly 200 years later, God pointed out the missional fallout through Ezekiel. He declared He would have to step in to save His own name because His people had "profaned" His name wherever they went. They made God look bad to the surrounding nations through their relational and social violations (see Ezekiel 36:20–23).

This is the real downside of our failure to make disciples, prioritising drawing a crowd and baptisms over mentoring people to bear relational fruit. As Brennan Manning famously said decades ago, "The greatest single cause of atheism in the world today is Christians, who acknowledge Jesus with their lips, then walk out the door, and deny Him by their lifestyle. That is what an unbelieving world simply finds unbelievable."[3]

But the gig is up for many people—especially among the younger generations. I know many who love Jesus, who love Scripture, who love helping people, and even love being with God's family—but they can't take the hypocrisy and they can't take another church service. They certainly can't take being told that if they don't "go to church" that they somehow love Jesus less than those who do. Believe it or not, sitting in a hard pew trying to fight off boredom, or shushing one's children every three seconds while the pastor preaches a 45-minute sermon, isn't everyone's idea of a productive or edifying time.

This is why the ministry of Jesus is so attractive to many. He didn't just talk the talk, He walked the walk—living only by love. He also spent three-and-a-half years investing in and mentoring a small group of people to do the same. He did this so the love could spread, the family of God could get bigger, so that more and more and more people could encounter this other-worldly love.

It's interesting: Jesus had only a few decades on earth to achieve His mission and yet He spent the first 30 years in complete obscurity and then much of the last three focused on only 12 people. He certainly drew and spoke to big crowds—though not as much as we think—but most of His time was spent with His small group of disciples and audiences of one. Thus, we read of Him talking to Nicodemus at night, a Samaritan woman by a well, a paralytic by a pool.

If I had been Him, with only a short time to change the world, I would have tried to speak to as large an audience as possible. I would have gone on satellite TV or held the largest Facebook Live event, preceded by the biggest advertising campaign, blasting my message to every corner of the globe.

But that wasn't His agenda. He wanted to go deep rather than wide, knowing that only quality could turn the world upside-down.

In short, He wanted to make disciples.

BUT WHAT IS A DISCIPLE?

Of course, we need to define terms. We need to define the term "disciple" and how we go about making them.

Jesus implicitly defined discipleship when He explained what the greatest commandment was. "You must love the Lord your God with all your heart, all your soul, and all your mind," He said, adding that loving one's neighbour as one's self is equally important. "The entire law and all the demands of the prophets are based on these two commandments" (see Matthew 22:37–40).

So check this out: Jesus said we must love God with our all—heart, mind and soul—and love and treat our fellow humans with the same regard we have for ourselves. Loving God with our all means bringing every corner of our lives into loving submission to Him, developing every nook and cranny, by His Spirit, to His glory.

This is a wholistic venture, treating the entirety of our being. We endlessly pursue growth—motivated by Christ's love—in emotional, spiritual, mental, intellectual, physical and relational health. It's an all-encompassing, all-of-life thing.

Which means it can't happen by sitting passively in a pew, listening to a 45-minute sermon once a week, or loading our head with Bible knowledge. Discipleship is not about learning how to make theological arguments or how to give killer Bible studies. It definitely includes learning Scripture—in personally transformative ways—and discovering how to share those life-changing insights with others. But that's just one aspect of being a disciple.

The Pharisees knew their Bibles but persecuted and killed the Son of God.

This is why Christ wants us to learn to love Him with our all, submitting and developing *every* aspect of our being, not just our intellect. He wants us to learn how to love others wholly and completely, bringing His healing grace to a hurting world.

Jesus wants us to learn how to live in the same way He would if He were walking in our shoes, living our life. In essence, discipleship is about learning to love well—which sounds incredibly attractive to a world starving for love.

I had a conversation with a Jewish friend about this very idea recently. We get together regularly to talk about a myriad of topics—philosophy, science, Judaism, Jesus—and one day he indicated that he'd stumbled onto our church website, curious about what we were all about. He said he loved everything he saw, especially the statement of our core values, but there was one value that made him uncomfortable. "What's this thing about 'disciple-making'?" he wondered. "That sounds like you're just trying to convert people." It was not a posture he'd perceived in me during our friendship.

Jews are especially sensitive to the idea of Christian attempts at conversion, with a long history of forced conversions during various Inquisitions. Likewise, in our increasingly secular world, many people are understandably sceptical of zealous Christians focused on trying to rescue souls they perceive to be on the road to hell.

So as he asked the question, I shifted in my chair, sympathetic to his concerns. But then I offered him this explanation. "It's like this," I said to him. "I think you would agree that people in this world need to experience love." He nodded his head cautiously. "So disciple-making is simply the process of spreading this love. If you and I decided that we wanted to bring love to the whole world, we could only reach so many people because we are only two people. But if I can love a person in such a way that they learn to love someone else, the love can expand and grow and take in more people."

Somewhat to my surprise, I saw a little smile come across his face and his head nod in agreement. "That makes a lot of sense. I like that," he said.

My response wasn't simply a clever sleight of hand. While he and I might not fully agree on some of the details—at least at this point—that is truly the whole crux of the matter. That's what discipleship is about. It's about having our entire being transformed by God's love in such a way that we learn to love others as Jesus loves, so those others can learn to love others as Jesus loves, so those others can learn to love others as Jesus loves—and the circle keeps growing.

It's about multiplying God's kingdom of love.

That's why I like to remind my church that our goal is not just to be a church that loves people. As admirable as this goal is, it falls short of who God is calling us to be and what He's calling us to do. Instead, our goal is to love people in such a way that those people will be transformed enough to love others in the same way.

This is what it means to make disciples.

BUT IT TAKES TIME

But all this takes time. Discipleship is not simply information transfer. It has to be modelled and seen and processed and discussed—and modelled and seen and processed and discussed all over again. It's an all-of-life thing, not something that can be accomplished by showing up to a building once a week.

That's why Jesus invested time in His small group of disciples. He invited them into His life. They watched everything He did, heard everything He said, went everywhere He went. And He did the same with them. They had full access to His life and He had full access to theirs.

Jesus knew it would take time, intentionality and ongoing mentorship to prepare His disciples to carry His banner after He went back to heaven. He understood that the world wasn't going to be turned upside-down by a large crowd of half-committed consumers. This is why the Gospels are saturated with stories of people who sadly turned away from following Jesus—like the rich, young ruler—frustrated that the cost was too high and that Jesus wouldn't lower it.

Pursuing the hard work of learning to love well requires our all. There are no shortcuts. As we well know, love hurts. But it's also the most rewarding and fulfilling thing we can do.

What Jesus recognised while He walked the earth is no less true today. God isn't looking for a crowd, He's looking for the committed. As Alan Hirsch has aptly said, "You can do more with 12 disciples than you can with 12,000 religious consumers."[4]

This all started making sense to me the more I met with Jim. We were investing in each other, learning how to apply the gospel to every aspect of our lives, trying to become more like Jesus. This required more than one-off visits. It required life-on-life discipleship.

There was one articulation of this dynamic that really brought it home for me. I heard it while attending a church-planting conference in Florida, the largest of its kind in the world. I don't remember who exactly said it, but it was equally course-setting in its effect. "When most people talk about planting a church," the person proposed, "what they really mean is they are planting a worship service."

Talk about clarity!

As I started explaining these concepts to our church-planting team, they fully agreed. We wanted to be on God's mission in everyday life. The hustle of putting on the most polished worship experience just didn't seem to be our calling. The time cost—hours taken away from walking alongside people—seemed too steep.

And it didn't take long for us to realise that, in some ways, our calling wasn't to plant a new church—at least at that point—but to focus on the simple task of making disciples in all of life. Eventually it would lead to us replanting our existing church—or restarting it, as we called it—but that would come later.

In the meantime, we decided to transition away from being a "planting team," instead becoming a missional small group—what we called a "missional community." We decided to focus on being the family of God together and making disciples who would embrace the beautiful and scriptural reality of Christ's kingdom of love.

4

LIFE IS THE BIBLE STUDY

I was rounding Norway Road and onto Hammond Street when it suddenly hit me.

I had been running with my neighbour, Dan, and the conversation was flowing. Dan is what I'd call a "blissful agnostic." He was raised in a mixed religious home, his mum some stripe of Protestant and his dad Jewish, and he came out the other end unsure about his religious beliefs, seemingly not too worried about any of it. But he was somewhat curious, and our conversations as we ran covered a wide range of topics—work, music, parenting, marriage, religion.

On this particular day, we got to talking about the movie *Hacksaw Ridge*, which both of us had recently seen. "Tell me," he started, "I noticed that Doss made a big deal about this Sabbath thing. What's that all about?"

Dan knew I shared a faith with Desmond Doss, who the movie was about, and that I kept the Sabbath too. Despite my surprise that someone who had a Jewish father wasn't up to speed on the Sabbath, I nevertheless quickly explained the scriptural basis for it.

His next question could have been easily anticipated. "So why do people today go to church on Sunday?" he asked.

Over the next quarter-mile, between huffs and puffs, I gave him a brief synopsis of how I understood it. And then, just like that, Dan moved on to the next topic, curious about some other pressing issue.

He wasn't trying to avoid any sort of conviction that I could tell; it just wasn't the time for an altar call.

But as I rounded that corner, I realised what had just happened: our run together had turned into a Bible study of sorts. I didn't go looking for it, nor did Dan, I'm quite sure. I didn't have my Bible on me, nor did I prepare any notes. It just happened.

And I suddenly realised this: *life is the Bible study*.

Indeed, it occurred to me that as we talk about the important task of making disciples, the reality is that we are never *not* discipling people. This doesn't only apply to when we are explicitly talking about Jesus or Scripture; we are literally *never* not discipling people, no matter what we're doing or talking about.

AS YOU GO . . .

There is another interesting dynamic at play in the Great Commission that Christ gave His disciples before His ascension. When He commanded His disciples to go out and "make disciples," He didn't actually command them to baptise or to teach. He assumed that baptising and teaching would be a part of the discipling process.

Similarly, Jesus didn't command His disciples to "go" at all. Instead, in the original Greek of the passage, the way the verb is constructed *assumes* they would be going. A better translation would actually be something like, "*As you go*, make disciples . . ."

So Jesus didn't tell the disciples to go anywhere specific—at least not in this instance. He encouraged them to see that *all of life* was the stage for discipleship. Wherever they went, whatever they did, they were making disciples.

This realisation elevates every act. Everything we do has the ability to communicate the gospel. Every act implicitly disciples people in something or someone. Indeed, we are never *not* discipling people.

Often when people hear they're supposed to "make disciples," they get a little uncomfortable and start thinking about all the extra time and effort it will require. Most people are already overworked and highly stressed. So when a well-meaning pastor tells them they're supposed to add disciple-making to their lives, it doesn't evoke excitement. In their minds, it means going door-knocking or helping out at a seminar five nights a week for months at a time.

It also means awkward religious conversations with strangers, which is a daunting thought. Many of us struggle to talk about Jesus with people we know—never mind the stranger we sit next to on the plane or the co-worker we barely know in the cubicle next to us.

Don't get me wrong: being a disciple and making disciples requires everything of us—our time, our money, our devotion, our conversations. God isn't asking us to fit mission into our lives when it's convenient for us. He's inviting us to submit all of our life for His glory. We build our lives around mission instead of squeezing it in if we have time. And when we understand and appreciate the gospel—when we grasp the depths to which Christ has gone to rescue us—we'll want to fully participate in God's kingdom of love and widen His family circle.

But all this is a whole lot easier than we've thought. And God doesn't grade us based on the degree of difficulty. He's not more impressed if we stand on a street corner, announcing to strangers passing by that they're going to hell if they don't repent, than if we invite our neighbours over for dinner. We don't get any extra credit for going door-knocking, when just being a kind co-worker or neighbour goes a long way.

Instead, people like Jeff Vanderstelt frame it this way: making disciples is not about putting any *additional* stuff into your schedule; it's about simply being *intentional* about what you're already doing. It's about being aware that "as you go" you are inevitably making disciples—and choosing to be intentional about making disciples in the image of Jesus.

This makes it very practical and extremely simple. Instead of thinking that God is sending you *somewhere else* to be on His mission, He already has you right where He wants you.

One of the ways we began living this out was simply by inviting our friends and neighbours to do activities with us that we were already doing. If we were planning to go hiking as a family, we would ask ourselves who we could invite. When we went to the indoor pool every Sunday during the winter—as we did for a number of years—we would reach out to friends and ask them to join us. And many did—with some showing up every Sunday. When I'd go out for a run, I'd see who was interested in joining me—which is what led to my neighbour Dan going on several occasions.

Of course, one thing everyone does repeatedly throughout the week is eat. Everyone eats. We eat at least two or three times a day, which is 14 to 21 times a week, and these are times that are ripe for connection.

It occurred to us that if we were going to be eating anyway, why not invite others to join us? Even if we just took one meal a week and invited others to sit at the table with us—whether in our home or at a restaurant or in the lunchroom—it might go a long way in communicating to people that they have value and dignity. All it takes is throwing in a little extra pasta than you normally would or sitting at a table in the lunchroom with other people, rather than by yourself.

These are simple things that don't take a lot of extra effort, money or time. It's being *intentional* about the things you're already doing, inviting people into your life, which inevitably leads to gospel opportunities and conversations—in organic and natural ways. The more that people hang out with us, the more love rubs off on them and the more Jesus gets into their system.

To be clear, even if they never become Jesus-followers, the time we spend together is not in vain. We connect with people *regardless* of whether they ever buy into the values we embrace. People are worth being loved and invested in for *their* sake—not for *ours*. We enter into life with others because they are *already* children of God, reflecting His image, not so that they can become children of God by joining our team.

The reality is, if we believe that the knowledge of God will someday cover the whole earth, "as the waters cover the sea" (Habakkuk 2:14), it won't come as the result of a couple of great evangelists getting on TV or YouTube. As wonderful as that is, it is simply information transfer and not disciple-making. Instead, it will require us to roll up our sleeves and make space in our lives for our friends and neighbours and co-workers.

The truth is, it takes all kinds of people to reach all kinds of people. It takes just precisely what I've heard Jeff Vanderstelt say—ordinary people doing everyday things with gospel intentionality.

MISSIONAL RHYTHMS

One of the best ways that we can live an intentional life is by doing the same things over and over again in the same places. When we show up to the same places at the same time, it gets us into rhythms with others. It puts us alongside the same people day in and day out, opening up organic opportunities to connect.

It's quite remarkable how simply *seeing* a stranger over and over again builds up a certain level of trust—without even speaking a word to each other. I run the same route just about every day and I often see the same people along my route. Camille does the same thing and has met quite a few people who live in our neighbourhood. Lately, we've gotten to know an older gentleman on the street next to ours quite well, and Camille and I have talked about inviting him over for dinner sometime.

This whole idea hit home last year when a kindly older woman at the pool we used to go to every week stopped Camille to tell her something. "It's quite amazing how big your littlest one has gotten," she said of our six-year-old, Winslow. "I remember when she was just born."

It floored us. We had been going there every Sunday for more than six years and had seen this woman from a distance as she swam laps on the other side of the pool, but we'd never said a word to her. But she spoke to Camille as though she was an aunt we hadn't seen in a while.

More than any other way, this has manifested in Camille's life through her regular routine of taking the kids to story times at the library each week—sometimes multiple times a week in various towns. It was initially a survival tactic for Camille. She is an extroverted person and the idea of staying cooped up in our house all day long with little kids and minimal adult interaction was not her idea of a good time. So she started going to a bunch of story times.

Inevitably, this brought her together with the same parents week after week, leading to natural conversations about being a stay-at-home parent, followed by playdates and birthday parties—and occasionally cries with new friends who were going through divorce.

This is what it means to step into the natural rhythms of a community and share love. It is intentional, "as you go" discipleship.

JOSE, THE FRIENDLY ATHEIST

For me, the most dramatic example of the power of intentional rhythms is my friend Jose, who we met at one of our local Mexican restaurants. A few years earlier, my brother-in-law Cameron and I had started a book club and invited a few guys to join us. The books covered various topics—some religious in nature, others not—and provided a time for us to have good conversation and enjoy mutual support.

Over time, more and more guys joined the group, invited by the various members, and we started searching for a new place to meet during the lunch hour on Wednesdays. That led us to Las Palapas, where Jose was our server the first week. He had a big smile, a warm heart, and was very friendly, cracking jokes in his broken English.

When we returned the next week and sat down at the same table, we were delighted to see Jose walk over again. The same thing happened the week after that and the week after that and the week after that. For two years, Jose served us almost every week, letting us into his world a little through cordial conversation.

And then one day, having noticed we brought a book every time, he sheepishly asked us, "You know, my English is not very good and I'd like to get better at it. I'm wondering if you would let me join your group some time so I can practise my English." Without hesitation, we excitedly declared he'd be more than welcome to join us.

After Jose left, my friend Ben spoke up and reminded us that summer was looming and we were going to be taking a little break just as Jose was leaning in. "Maybe you should offer to meet with him on your own over the summer," Ben said to me. "You can explain to him what's going on."

And so that's what we did. Jose and I met a few weeks later at Bagel Central, enjoying great conversation. When he discovered I was a pastor, he was a little taken aback. "Oh, I don't believe in God," he quickly responded. "Is that a problem?" I laughed a little and assured him that it wasn't a problem for me. Of course, I believed in God and would love for everyone to embrace His love, but I had no interest in trying to argue him into my beliefs. My only agenda, I told him, was to be in his life and to support him however I could.

We began to meet weekly at Bagel Central and he started sharing more of his story. He'd been born and raised in Mexico and bounced between his relatives' homes. And with each new home came a new religion. First it was the Catholicism of his father, then the Pentecostalism of his mother, and finally the Mormonism of his grandmother. It all left him confused, especially in the light of his pain. "How can there be a god," he asked, "when so many people experience so much hurt?"

I didn't pull out my Bible or my stock theological answers. I just listened and sympathised and encouraged.

As the weeks turned into months, Jose's heart became more troubled by the pressures he felt from the political climate in America. He was undocumented and he started sharing with me about how he felt limited in his opportunities because of his status. He was thinking about returning to Mexico, wondering what advice I could give him. And then he shocked me one day when he announced that he had quit his job at

Las Palapas and bought a one-way ticket to return to Mexico a month later.

I had mixed emotions about his decision. I understood his dilemma but also knew that I would probably never see him again after he left and that made me sad. I had come to really love and appreciate him. He was such a kind-hearted, funny, intelligent and thoughtful guy, and our conversations always left me the better for them.

And I guess he felt the same way about me, which became clear after he started telling me about one thing he planned to do when he moved back to Mexico. "You know," he said, "because of our meetings, I've been feeling impressed that I should start going back to church when I return to Mexico."

His statement totally caught me off guard. My heart burst with gratitude.

And then I got an idea—one that was a little uncomfortable for me. "Jose," I said, "I really don't do this very much, but I'm wondering if you would have any interest in coming to worship with my church sometime before you move back. We meet on Saturdays."

It's not usually my style to invite people "to church" before inviting them to one of our missional community gatherings or to my kitchen table, but we had just restarted our church the week before, including the way we gather on Saturday mornings, and I had finally come to a place where I felt comfortable inviting people into that circle. So I extended the invitation to him.

Without deliberating over the question very long, he delightedly accepted my invitation.

A few days later, I drove to his house, a few miles away from mine, and picked him up. We drove together to the gathering, with me trying to prep him as much as I could to what he was about to experience, trusting that the Spirit would ultimately do what the Spirit does.

And not surprisingly, that's precisely what the Spirit did.

The family of God embraced Jose and made him feel welcomed and loved. He listened curiously as we sang songs he'd never heard and people shared stories of God's love. And he was fascinated by my teaching, which he wanted to talk about later.

But what really captivated his imagination was a key feature of every gathering we have—in whatever circle we're in. One person shares their story, through whatever twists and turns it takes. We don't expect everyone's story will be tied up in a neat bow by the end. We expect it to be raw and authentic and honest—and that whoever shares will feel validated that their story deserves to be heard, which is very healing and affirming.

As I drove him home after the gathering, I could see the wheels turning in his head, and then he came out with it. "I have a question," he started. "Could I share my story next week?" It caught me off guard and I took a big gulp, not completely sure if my people were yet fully prepared to have an atheist share his story up front. "Ah, sure," I said to him somewhat reluctantly.

The next week, Jose stood up and shared his story, with all its twists and turns. He spoke of what led him to become an atheist, and how he had found a renewed spirituality by spending time with our church family. He said he felt embraced and loved like never before by being with us—and he knew he wanted to find a church when he returned to Mexico.

It was all so amazing and powerful and heart-warming. And the next two weeks Jose faithfully returned, eagerly feeling the embrace of the family of God and learning more about the mission of Christ.

But then the day came. It was time for him to leave. I picked him up at his house to bring him to the bus station. He informed me that he never usually cried, but he couldn't fight back the tears as he shared with me how incredibly grateful he was that we had journeyed together. "My only regret," he said, "is that I wish I had started coming to your church a long time ago." But then he thought about it a little more and added, "But truthfully, I don't think I would have attended if you had invited me before. I think the timing was just right."

He then shared with me that he was so excited about what our church was trying—unlike any other church he had seen or been a part of—and how he thought all of his friends in the area should know about it and join.

I said a prayer with him, wished him goodbye, then watched him walk out of my life. I felt joy and I felt sadness—grateful for the time we had shared but longing for much, much more.

I wonder what would happen if every Jesus-follower recognised that everything we do is either nudging people closer to God's kingdom or pushing them farther away; either building people up in love or tearing them down. *Everything* we do—even the humble act of sitting at a restaurant table or going to the pool. The life we live is the Bible study we give.

This is not at all to deny the important place of explicit Bible study. I spend a *lot* of time studying Scripture with people.

But if we understood that every moment is pregnant with gospel-possibilities—that the people around us are reading our lives before they'll ever read Scripture—I'm quite sure we would elevate all of life to the level of mission and worship.

The knowledge of God will someday cover the earth as the waters cover the sea. The whole earth will be ablaze with God's glory—as Revelation 18:1 predicts. But that won't come through sleek video presentations or mega-Facebook Live events. It will come when ordinary people live everyday lives with gospel intentionality.

5

THE WAY UP
IS DOWN

A couple of years ago I had an enlightening experience at our city's annual Christmas parade, which is one of our favourite city events. We usually invite as many of our friends to join us as we can, and on this particular night, Camden had invited his friend, Matty, who lived a few houses down from us.

It was really cold that night, as December nights usually are in Maine, and as we tried to stay warm, waiting for the parade to start, Matty slipped away. He returned a few minutes later with a cup of hot chocolate in his hand and excitedly announced he'd gotten it for free. I'm not a fan of hot drinks, but it sounded good on that frigid night, so I asked Matty where he got it and he pointed to a line a little way up the street.

Making my way there, I reached the line, and a man handed me a cup, saying, "Merry Christmas," which I gladly reciprocated. As I excitedly made my way back, I raised my hand to take my first sip when something caught my eye. Examining it closer, my heart sank. There, on the side of the cup, was the name of a local church—one of the bigger churches in Bangor.

And just like that, it felt like the whole experience had been cheapened. I felt like I had been taken advantage of. What went from an act of altruistic kindness quickly turned into a transaction with strings attached—and religious ones at that.

I don't know. Maybe I'm making too big a deal of it. But I have become familiar enough with the unchurched mind to know that there are many who would resonate with the gospel of love but get turned off when churches shove religion in people's faces, even if it's done with a smile. This is especially true when religion is presented within the guise of so-called service.

This hot chocolate giveaway was a classic example of what some call "service evangelism," where a church provides some type of material service to a specific community for a few hours.

I don't doubt this church's sincerity, but for many who are the recipients of such "service," it feels gimmicky at best and a little predatory at worst. When we pass out bottles of water at beaches on hot summer days or hot chocolate at cold Christmas parades and the name of our church is plastered all over everything, it can feel like the only people we're truly serving are ourselves.

My own faith community seems to excel at this as well in our own way. It feels like we frequently utilise times of crisis to gain a hearing, trying to leverage people's fears to gain an audience with them and to push our religious beliefs and prophetic interpretations. Again, perhaps this is just me, but despite our best intentions, which I know are often sincere, it feels a bit predatory, and off-putting to many people who don't know Jesus.

Of course, there are many unchurched people who don't seem bothered by such efforts. And some people do join the mission and family of God through such approaches. But I'm not sure the ends justify the means.

As our missional community continued to explore what it means to participate in the mission of God, we found ourselves feeling a tension. On the one hand, we knew we had been invited to live out our missional calling—to enter into life with people and to make disciples. But we didn't want to get into the icky space where it felt like we were coming at people with an agenda, pursuing life with them for the sake of converting them.

We discovered that no matter how well-intentioned we tried to be, any time "conversion" or growing the church became our agenda, it undermined our ability to be fully present with people for their sake, rather than our own. And that's not what we wanted to be about.

Fortunately, the Spirit began teaching us how to walk that narrow line of making disciples from a place of genuine, disinterested love. Not that we've arrived. But pursuing this balance is critical in our attempts to participate in the mission and family of God.

DISINTERESTED LOVE

When one examines the life and ministry of Jesus, one can't help but notice that He acted from a place of self-emptying, other-centred love. His was not an acquisitive love. He acted out of His desire for the best interests of others, seeking no personal gain from any encounter.

In the book of Philippians, Paul enunciates this reality, presenting one of the most powerful and compelling explanations of the gospel in Scripture. He describes the great "emptying" of God in the Person of Christ, as Jesus descended to meet us in our weakness. "Christ was truly God," Paul writes, "but he did not try to remain equal with God. Instead he gave up everything and became a slave" (Philippians 2:6, 7, CEV). He "emptied Himself," the NRSV says, making "Himself of no reputation" (NKJV).

Jesus repeatedly demonstrated this throughout His ministry. When He described His kingdom of love, He compared it to mustard seeds and to yeast (see Luke 13:18–21), which were underwhelming analogies for people who were used to thinking in terms of might and power. When He spoke of greatness, He said that it did not come from "lording over" others like the people of the world believed (see Luke 22:25). It came through humbling oneself and serving, taking the posture of a slave, just as He demonstrated when He stooped down and washed the disciples' feet, and just as He would wait on them in the coming kingdom (see Luke 12:37).

Of course, the greatest manifestation of all this, and the precise reason for which Jesus came, was the experience of the cross. He suffered eternal agony on Calvary, feeling His existence was being crushed out forever. When He cried out "My God, My God, why have You forsaken Me?" (Matthew 27:46), He felt truly forsaken. He genuinely "poured out His soul unto death" (Isaiah 53:12) as the prophet Isaiah proclaimed, "enduring the cross [and] despising the shame" (Hebrews 12:2).

The life and death of Jesus demonstrate with unequivocal clarity that everything God does is for the benefit and uplifting of others. There is no self-interest involved, no personal benefit He seeks to acquire. Jesus didn't try to build His brand or grow His platform. He didn't hire a marketing firm or pay for Instagram followers. Jesus is truly, as Matthew records, "meek and lowly in heart" (Matthew 11:29, KJV).

With God, the way up is down.

These gospel truths challenge what is buried within my heart. They cut deep. I don't want to make myself of no reputation. I don't want to give up all for the mission of God. I don't want my ministry to be small. I want it to be big. I want my methods to be vindicated. I want to be a megastar pastor, with the largest church, the most successful mission and the glitziest branding. I want to acquire more and more converts and followers, and I want my church to get bigger and bigger and bigger.

But the church's glory comes not in power or in growth but in weakness and in service. It comes by losing our lives, by laying them down and emptying ourselves, by spending and being spent for God's glory and the world's uplifting. "The church must lose itself," Lesslie Newbigin writes. "The reign of God is present under the form not of power, but of weakness."[1]

In taking such a posture, we are acting as a signpost to God's character of service and love, demonstrating that He is a God of self-emptying, other-centred grace.

All this challenges the modern emphasis on "church growth," which seems to be an all-pervasive concern among so many of us. It's accepted as self-evident that our primary task as God's people is to grow our churches, to gain as many converts and followers as we can. In my community of faith, we even talk about "soul-winning," as though people are objects of conquest or prizes to be acquired.

Nowhere do we find this emphasis in Scripture, however. Jesus never told His followers to grow the church. In his letters, Paul never set out numerical benchmarks for the churches in Galatia or Philippi or anywhere else to determine if their ministry was successful.

Of course: we want the family of God to expand and grow and to embrace ever more people. We want everyone to encounter the living Christ and to have their lives transformed by His grace. And we rejoice when this takes place and worry when it doesn't—and we worry about those who would deny the important place for this concern. There is no need for a false dichotomy.

But as followers of the self-emptying, other-centred Christ, our *primary* concern is not in growing our kingdom but in advancing His— which may or may not result in more people joining our team.

Lesslie Newbigin has gone so far as to put it in this way. "A church that exists only for itself and its own enlargement is a witness against the gospel."[2] The first time I read that statement my jaw dropped. I was cut to the heart, feeling extremely convicted. We cannot accurately portray the self-emptying gospel by emphasising a self-serving and self-promoting mission. We cannot give a coherent picture of the God who willingly made Himself small in the babe of Bethlehem by obsessively chasing after big and large.

When the latter is our chief aim, we commit violence against the gospel, rendering it incoherent.

Newbigin isn't done though, adding:

> We have to ask whether the church is most faithful in its witness to the crucified and risen Jesus and most recognisable as the community that "bears about in the body the dying Jesus," when it is chiefly concerned with its own self-aggrandisement. When numerical growth is taken as the criterion of the judgment on the church, we are transported with alarming ease into the world of military campaign or commercial sales drive.[3]

The challenge here for me, as I'm sure it is for many, is recognising and admitting that the shoe fits. We can talk ourselves into believing that our motives are pure, that our desires to grow our churches and gain more converts are completely altruistic. But I have seen so often in my own heart that even the slightest desire of wanting to convert others and grow my church neutralises my ability to serve them with selfless love.

This happened to me just the other day with my next-door neighbour. Camille and I discovered that his girlfriend and her children had moved out, leaving him alone. A few days later, as I was about to go for a run, he called out to me, wanting to chat. We ended up talking for a while as he poured out his heart, speaking of his loneliness and his longing to experience true love. My heart was moved deeply as he shared, wondering how we could better serve him and alleviate his loneliness.

Very quickly though, I also noticed the wheels starting to turn in my brain, imagining him as a member of my church with a conversion story to be paraded about—a conquest to be celebrated. It's quite alarming how quickly my mind can go from zero to 60. To be sure: it would be troubling if I didn't want him to ultimately know Jesus and join the mission and family of God. But the more I dwell on such a thought, the more liable I am to turn our relationship from one where I'm serving him to one where he's serving me.

The same is true of my friend, Mike, whom I met a few years ago. He played for nine seasons in the National Football League before settling down in Bangor, where his wife is originally from. Mike is an awesome guy who loves Jesus and wants to do His will. He's also a bright guy and is now pursuing a PhD in philosophy.

When we first met, Mike, who has a Pentecostal background, told me point blank that I better do everything I could to try to convert him to my brand of Christianity. "If I'm going to hell because I don't keep the Sabbath," he said to me, "then you'd better tell me." Talk about an opportunity served on a silver platter! And, of course, one could get a lot of mileage by parading such an accomplished and famous "trophy" around.

But that is not my calling. Mike and I have certainly spent many hours studying Scripture together and exploring the beautiful truths I appreciate. But I have assured him that my primary posture in his life is one of service and blessing. God brought me into his life to support and encourage and disciple him. If that means that someday he officially joins my church, I wouldn't complain. But if that doesn't happen, my ministry to him will not have been in vain nor my time wasted.

We are primarily called to demonstrate and proclaim God's kingdom of love—not to acquire more and more people for our team.

WITH, NOT *TO*

The truth is, our cities are littered with giant churches that seemingly think our primary calling is to get bigger and bigger. But one wonders if our communities are any better for us having been there. Sometimes, all we accomplish is annoying people, pushing them farther away from God.

I remember a conversation I had with my brother-in-law's mother, Elaine, a few years ago along these lines. She's a kind-hearted atheist who grew up in England but now lives in Florida. She loves to share her views about God and church with me whenever I see her. Among other things, she's mentioned her frustration with the megachurch near her house. The ever-expanding campus is huge, which creates a headache-inducing traffic-jam for people like her each Sunday. That's about the only impact they've had on her, which doesn't exactly breed good will.

She also mentioned that she attended the Christmas program they put on annually one year, which left her even less impressed. After she got through the maze of Starbucks-inspired coffee stands and found her seat in the 5000-person auditorium, she was left wondering what their mission truly was. Elaine is someone who would love to sit in a living room each week, talking about God with a small group of open-minded seekers, but she doesn't have much interest in religious organisations who seem to be focused on building their kingdom rather than God's.

And I don't blame her. One is sometimes left with the impression that we are converting people to our church brand but failing to connect them to Jesus and His mission.

It all leaves me wondering: what does it matter if our churches are growing but the communities in which they reside are dying? Is the purpose of the gospel simply to enlarge our territory but ignore anything else that doesn't help accomplish this goal? What would happen if we helped build up the community for the community's sake and not simply to advance ours?

Of course, even when we start ministries to address the community's needs, we can still fail to take on the full posture of servanthood, leaving the impression that these ministries are ultimately pipelines to grow our churches. We often think we need to come up with our own ministries instead of just joining ones that already exist within our cities, practicing an anonymous, disinterested and humble Christianity that genuinely helps others pursue their agenda to improve the world with no strings attached.

I like how Bob Roberts Jr put it in a tweet he shared about being on God's mission in the world. We should seek to bring value to the *whole* community, he said, and not just look to have another worship gathering. And in seeking to do this, we should do it *with* the community and not *to* the community.[4]

With, not *to*. That's a revolutionary thought. When we join *with* the community in pursuing its good, we demonstrate an attitude of true humility and service, communicating that we come without agenda and for the benefit of all. When we instead minister *to* the community, we come as self-appointed heroes who have all the answers, which isn't very attractive anyway.

This is not to say we ignore the call to make disciples or proclaim the gospel. As Tim Chester and Steve Timmis say, "Social action without proclamation is like a signpost pointing nowhere."[5]

When we are part of God's family, we truly want to bear witness to the hope that gives context to our lives and mission. We are not merely nice people, apart from God's grace. And as we live lives of generous, self-emptying love, it naturally produces a curiosity in the minds and hearts of those who witness it. As Jeff Vanderstelt says, we should "live in such a way that it would demand a 'Jesus explanation.'"[6]

But the point is that our *primary* objective is *not* to grow our church, convert people to our beliefs or bolster our church rolls. Our primary objective is to bring "healing [to] the nations," as Revelation 22:2 puts it, surrendering our agenda to the Spirit's capable hands and humbly living out God's kingdom of love in all places and among all people, hoping to nudge them closer to His heart.

The irony is that a posture of humble, self-emptying love is an attractive and counter-cultural force in the world, drawing people into the mission and family of God of their own initiative.

Speaking of the power of disinterested love, Ellen White puts it in these mind-boggling terms. "Our influence upon others depends not so much upon what we say as upon what we are," she writes. "Men may combat and defy our logic, they may resist our appeals; but a life of disinterested love is an argument they cannot gainsay. A consistent life, characterised by the meekness of Christ, is a power in the world."[7]

LILLI'S SHOES

This is all acutely illustrated in my mind through an experience we had with our friend Sandra and her daughter Lilli. They had recently moved to Bangor from Germany and through a series of events, Sandra started teaching me German in preparation for a trip I was due to take to Switzerland.

The first time Sandra and I met, the conversation turned to what I did for work. She was shocked to hear that I was a pastor. "Just last week I was telling my husband I wanted to talk to a pastor," she declared. She was confused by the many different flavours of churches in America and wanted help navigating this new religious world.

We had a good chat about it, with religion inevitably coming up each time we met to go over German. Over time, our family invited theirs increasingly deeper into our lives, trying to help them navigate life in America.

Sandra eventually expressed a desire to check out our church, and so one Saturday she brought her two younger children along and participated in this strange new religious experience. It was all fascinating to her, wholly different from the pomp and circumstance of the Catholic church she had been part of in Germany. But after attending a few times, she settled into a level of comfort with our approach and with our community and started making our church her home.

Not long after, something interesting happened. Her daughter Lilli, who was a senior in high school, went back to Germany for Christmas. When she returned to the United States, she flew into Boston and then took a bus to Bangor. Sadly, her luggage was misplaced by the bus company and likely stolen, leaving her without clothes and the personal Christmas gifts she'd received. She was absolutely heart-broken.

I was heart-broken too as Sandra shared the story. I immediately wanted to do something to help. I knew many of the personal items couldn't be replaced, but I felt that some small gesture could go a long way in cheering Lilli's heart.

I immediately contacted our church family and explained the situation, wondering if we could raise $500 to help buy a new wardrobe. It might help put a better taste in Lilli's mouth for Americans and embody God's love to a young lady who wasn't quite sure about Him. Within a few hours, the church pledged $1200 to help her.

Not surprisingly, when I tried to present the idea to Sandra, she absolutely refused to accept the gesture. The generosity of our church community overwhelmed her and brought her to tears, but she said there was no way they could take our money.

A few weeks later, we were again talking and she happened to mention how one present Lilli was most sad about losing was a pair of shoes she'd received. She had wanted them for a long time. "Look," I said to Sandra, "would you at least let us buy Lilli those shoes? We already collected a little bit of the money that people pledged, so we can use that for the shoes." Reluctantly, she agreed.

Later that night, I went to order the shoes and was amused to discover they were the exact amount we'd already collected. Thinking that was more than a coincidence, I ordered them and had them shipped to Lilli.

A few days later, I got a text message from an unknown number. It was Lilli. "The shoes arrived today," she shared, "and I just wanted to take the opportunity to say thank you." She said when her mother told her who gave her the gift, she was speechless. "I have never experienced such kindness from people that don't know me well," she explained. And then her text took an unexpected turn. "I would like to come by the church on Saturday to say thank you."

I immediately responded to her text, thanking her for her kind words but assuring her that she didn't need to come to church. "We gave them to you without any strings attached," I told her. "We simply want to bless others the same way God has blessed us."

She said she understood there were no strings attached, for which she was thankful, but still wanted to come to church to express her gratitude and to check out what an American church was like anyway.

It is fascinating. We bless others because we've been blessed. That's our only agenda. We seek to live lives of disinterested love—not to gain converts or to grow our churches, but because every child of God has inherent value and worth and deserves to be loved.

But such a life is inevitably attractive, standing in sharp relief to the way the world operates.

Interestingly, that's not the end of the story. A few weeks later, the bus company called Lilli and told her they had located her bag. She quickly made her way down to the bus station, expecting everything to be missing. Amazingly, every item was still there. Every item, that is, except one.

The shoes.

Needless to say, this turn of events grabbed the attention of both Lilli and Sandra.

When we participate in God's mission, seeking to live lives of disinterested love, He works in strange and mysterious ways.

6

SKIN-TO-SKIN

It is probably no surprise that one of the most amazing, awe-inspiring and surreal moments of my life was when my first child was born. The birth of my second two were also sublime, of course, but as any parent can attest, there is just something about becoming a parent for the first time, seeing that child making the longest trip of his life, though only a few inches out of the birth canal, into the big, wide, scary world.

There are simply no words.

But at 9.59 pm on Sunday night, May 24, 2009, Camille and I welcomed our first child—Camden Shawn Brace—into our family. It had been a long time coming. He was two weeks overdue and the delivery was slow and hard. But then there he was, in all his tiny glory and infinite vulnerability—his little fingers, his harrowing cry, his utter confusion. It inspires worship.

The first things the nurses did were wash him, weigh him and wrap him in a towel. They then did something that is simple in its scope but awe-inspiring in its effect. They took Camden and placed him on Camille's bare chest—the sight of which is indelibly seared into my mind. He remained there for quite a while, connecting with Camille and establishing the critically important bond between mother and baby.

Throughout the night I was able to join in the experience as well, taking my shirt off and laying him on my hairy chest. We snuggled for a bit, as I smelled his smells, held him close and bathed in the marvel of new life.

This whole thing, this skin-to-skin connection, is quite remarkable. Cultures the world over have instinctually known there is something beneficial about the practice, but modern science has recently begun to understand there is a physiological basis for it. It's not just a cute thing a mother does to establish an emotional bond with her child. Getting skin-to-skin with her baby literally alters the child's physiology and brain structure. It helps stabilise the baby's heart rate, as well as his or her oxygen levels, and significantly impacts a child's brain development. Researchers know that frequent contact with a parent's skin is a great predictor of a child's emotional, physical, psychological and intellectual wellbeing later in life.

Truly, the human body is a wondrous thing.

But the body's ability to affect and regulate other bodies is even more wondrous.

And it's not just with infants. In their book *A General Theory of Love*, three psychiatrists note how science has discovered that our bodies need other bodies to operate and survive.[1] We humans are "open loop" systems rather than "closed loops" systems, requiring other humans to help regulate our physiological and emotional equilibrium. The body cannot operate in isolation from other bodies.

It's well-established, for example, that a baby will die within 12 months of birth if it has no skin-to-skin contact or social interaction with other humans, even if it's being fed, clothed and changed. And even with limited social contact or poor parental connections, a child's physical growth can be stunted and his or her ability to stave off sickness can be seriously compromised. Scientists call it "failure to thrive."

Although it is less dramatic the older we get, when it comes to our physical wellbeing, humans never graduate from needing other humans for survival, especially emotionally. Adult bodies still need other bodies in order to regulate. We need to be in physical proximity to other humans—to be able to see, smell, touch and hear them. In fact, there is an element of emotional growth and healing that can only take place in the human psyche through what is called "limbic revision," which is wholly unrelated to a person's cognitive faculties.

A person's limbic system is the part of the brain that experiences emotions and processes feelings. It is not necessarily governed by a person's reasoning capacities. And when damaged or distressed, logic can go only so far. A healthy limbic system requires in-the-flesh experiences with other safe humans. We need to walk through life with others, mediating grace in intangible yet beautiful ways and reconstructing the psyche through committed, unrelenting, fully embodied love.

What this all means is that there are ways for humans to communicate and transfer the gospel to other humans that don't involve logic and words. In fact, the gospel cannot be fully transferred through logic and words alone. It must be embodied.

And this is why the Word had to become flesh.

ANALOG CHURCH

For the follower of Jesus, everything begins and ends with the incarnation—everything hinges on God becoming flesh. Perhaps no passage in Scripture more succinctly and yet beautifully communicates this astonishing thought than how John describes it in the beginning of his Gospel. Referring to the pre-incarnate Jesus as the "Word" who was both "with God" and yet was also "God" (John 1:1), John establishes the full divinity of Jesus as well as the relational nature of the godhead, then transitions to describe the mind-blowing descent of God into human flesh.

"And the Word became flesh," he writes, "and dwelt among us" (John 1:14). This is the incarnation—a word which literally means "enfleshment." This is God taking on the human condition and meeting us in our frailty and need. It is the most staggering thought the mind can ponder—that the God of the universe would lower Himself to take such a position inspires worship and awe.

This affirms our humanity, telling us that God believes we are full of potential and value and are worth rescuing. It also tells us, of course, that we humans couldn't rescue ourselves from sin, so God had to step in and become one of us to elevate us to our full potential.

Interestingly, the word John employs for "Word" is *logos*, from which we get the word "logic." He was primarily addressing a Greek audience that denigrated the body in favour of spirit and logic. Many of the Greek philosophers believed the great goal of humanity was to escape the material world and become disembodied souls. And this perspective was starting to find a home in the church as well. This is why John emphasised that God affirmed the material world—including the flesh—even later saying that anyone "that does not confess that Jesus Christ has come in the flesh is not of God" (1 John 4:3).

We have our own ways of subtly falling into the same trap. We prioritise logic over embodiment, right-thinking over right-living. We think truth is primarily a list of doctrines on a page, a set of propositional ideas one mentally ascribes to.

But Jesus came to show us that the Word had to take up residence in humanity in order to be fully communicated and understood. The Word had to be seen, felt and heard—in the flesh.

That's why I love the way John opens his first letter as well, denoting the tactile nature of truth. "That which was from the beginning," he writes, "which we have heard, which we have seen with our eyes, which we have looked upon, and our hands have handled, concerning the Word of life—the life was manifested, and we have seen, and bear witness, and declare to you that eternal life which was with the Father and was manifested to us" (1 John 1:1, 2).

He notes how his encounter with Jesus was a full-bodied experience—the disciples heard Jesus with their ears, they saw Him with their eyes, they touched Him with their hands. He was a real Person who didn't simply proclaim a message. He lived it out and showed it.

I think this is why the Gospel writers went to such great lengths to note that Jesus touched people when He went about His ministry of healing. Think about it: He touched the lepers, the lame, the blind. Over 30 times between the four Gospels, the writers specifically mention that Jesus "touched" these people when He healed them.

There were certainly times when He simply spoke a word, but often the writers point out that He touched them when carrying out this act. I think this was just affirming their humanity, affirming their dignity and worth—and perhaps using a little "limbic revision" of His own as He went about His work of healing. To be sure, these were supernatural miracles but maybe they partly had a limbic basis as well. Maybe the real miracle in the minds and hearts of those He healed was that the perfect God was willing to touch their imperfect lives, thus communicating His unmerited and unrelenting favour and love. That would be enough to bring healing!

"FOR GOD SO LOVED THE WORLD THAT HE SENT A HANDBILL..."

We can't overstate this point. The humanity of Jesus not only serves as the foundation of our faith in general but also our missional calling specifically. This is the single most important idea to wrap our minds around if we are going to fully participate in the mission and family of God. Mission begins and ends with God's incarnation in the Person of

Jesus. It tells us that our work is one of embodiment and presence, not simply the transfer of ideas.

This is affirmed in the most famous passage of Scripture, also penned by John. "For God so loved the world that He gave His only begotten Son" (John 3:16), he reveals. Compelled by His love to rescue a world in need, God sent His Son in the flesh to reach those who were in the flesh. He didn't send a handbill, He didn't write a tweet. Jesus *came to us* in the frailty of a human baby. He then lived and walked and touched people throughout His life—ultimately revealing the gospel in all its climactic glory by laying down His life on the cross.

Too many times, we have thought our missional calling was to do a giant information dump. We put on seminars and send out tracts. We blitz a city with strange religious books. To be sure, a small percentage—a *very small* percentage—responds positively to such efforts. But when others don't buy into our doctrines after they've encountered them through the page or the airwaves, we write them off and say they've "rejected truth," satisfied that we've done our part in spreading "the truth."

But have people *fully* encountered truth if they've merely heard ideas spoken or read lifeless words on a page? When Jesus defined "truth," He didn't present people with a syllogism or point to a list of abstract doctrines. He unequivocally declared, "I am…the truth" (John 14:6). Truth is a Person—in all His beauty, mystery and relational dynamism.

This is not to say that concepts, ideas and logic aren't needed. I wouldn't be writing this book if I wasn't convinced of their importance. It's simply to say that when we think of our calling, we should primarily think of it as something we *do*—or perhaps even more accurately, as who we *are*—rather than something we say. We are not trying to *argue* people into truth so much as lovingly living out that truth before their eyes.

When I meet people now, I'm not trying to figure out how to invite them to my church or how to invite them to do Bible studies. I'm trying to figure out how I can invite them deeper into my life—where they will hopefully, despite my imperfections, encounter truth in all its dynamic and lived-out beauty.

I came across this same idea in a book written 125 years ago by Ellen White. The whole book, *Thoughts From the Mount of Blessing*, is powerful and potent, but this one paragraph in particular is off the charts:

As Christ is the channel for the revelation of the Father, so we are to be the channel for the revelation of Christ. While our Saviour is the great source of illumination, forget not, O Christian, that He is revealed through humanity. God's blessings are bestowed through human instrumentality. Christ Himself came to the world as the Son of man. *Humanity, united to the divine nature, must touch humanity.* The church of Christ, *every individual disciple* of the Master, is heaven's appointed channel for the revelation of God to men (emphasis added).[2]

What a thought! *Humanity must touch humanity.* We must get skin-to-skin with people, allowing God's grace to flow through us to a hurting world.

This doesn't mean we need to start a "hugging ministry" at our church, though it can certainly include that, as circumstances dictate and allow. It's primarily about sharing life with others, realising that God's kingdom of love is most poignantly communicated through embodied truth.

Simply put, the gospel doesn't make sense either cognitively or emotionally unless we, as God's family, live it out—in the flesh.

HOLDING JIM

My friend Avery, who I mentioned earlier, is a person who has really helped me understand the significance of all this. I had always understood the concept, but she really brought it home to me during our missional community gatherings. As a social worker and a professor at the University of Maine, she understood that there are some people who will never fully understand love and truth apart from our embodiment of them.

I remember her mentioning one experience she had with a friend of ours who happened to overhear Avery talking about God's love to someone else. "You make it sound like this idea that God loves us a good thing," she said. At first, Avery was a little confused by what she meant. After all, in the Christian understanding, it is self-evident that God's love is good news—the *best* good news, in fact.

But then Avery quickly understood: this young lady had been raised in an incredibly abusive home. And the only people who ever told her they loved her abused her. So the word "love" didn't mean much to her. Love was not a good thing; it was the basis for abuse.

As Avery shared this story with me, something suddenly clicked in my mind: the reason the gospel doesn't transfer from the head to the heart for so many of us is because we've not experienced it through the lives of others. I used to think it was because we hadn't *heard* that good news enough, which might be partly true, but I think it's also much more than that. As embodied creatures, we need to *experience* God's love through the lives of others in order for it to penetrate the deepest recesses of our hearts.

I think the church in general has talked about God's love more in recent years, but it has not been accompanied by a proportionally increased embodiment of that love. We go to church and sing songs about that love, hear sermons about that love, and then go home and don't love. We fail to embody what's written on the page or spoken from the pulpit. We fail to prioritise and experience true life-on-life discipleship. And through it all we make love unintelligible.

I got a front row seat with this, in quite an unexpected way, with my friend Jim, who I mentioned earlier. As we spent more and more time together, I gained more access to his life, as he did with mine. And one experience in particular brought it all home.

It was a Friday night in late summer when he frantically called me. He was a wreck. He was going through an acutely painful situation and wondered if I could come to his apartment, a few miles from my house, and offer him some comfort and encouragement.

To be honest, I wavered a little. The next day I was supposed to head to the wilderness of northern Maine with Camden and a few others for a three-day canoe trip, and I wanted to be well-rested as we embarked on the expedition.

But then I remembered that God had called me—just as God has called *all of us*—to not simply proclaim the gospel but to embody it.

When I reached Jim's place, I rapped on the door and walked in without being invited, as was my custom, then climbed the steep stairs to his second-floor apartment. I'll never forget the scene when I got to the top step, which was directly across from his bedroom, the door wide open. Jim was sitting in bed, his hair a mess, crying inconsolably.

I entered his bedroom and looked for a place to sit, amid the scores of records and books that were strewn across the floor. Unable to find a chair, I decided to sit down on his bed beside him. Over the course of the next 15 minutes, he tried to share what was on his heart, but he could mostly just communicate through his tears.

I tried to think of comforting things to say, of course, but no magic revelation came to mind. That's just as well. As limbic beings, words aren't always required to bring comfort and healing—and sometimes logic actually undermines the comforting process.

As time went by, we just sat there, the two of us heart to heart. But eventually my back started tiring as I struggled to sit upright on the bed with no back support. Unable to manage it any longer, I decided to lie back beside Jim, propping my legs up on the bed. It was strange—lying on a bed with a 67-year-old man in a darkened room. But it's what the circumstances called for. And things were about to get even stranger.

A few minutes later we decided to pray, asking God to visit Jim with His comfort. I'll never forget what happened next. As we were lying there praying, I suddenly felt Jim's hand making its way across the bed, reaching out for mine. As soon as I felt his skin connect with mine, I instinctually clutched his hand and held it tight. For the next 30 minutes, we lay there on the bed, side-by-side, holding hands—talking, praying, crying—with me mediating the grace of God to Jim through embodiment.

Upstairs in that tiny apartment, God's love was being communicated and hardly a word came from my lips.

Eventually, our visit ended and I retreated home to rest up for my long trip the next day. When Jim connected with me a few days later, he was a new man with a happier spirit. He thanked me profusely for my presence, and he specifically mentioned how meaningful it was that I held his hand in his time of need. It brought such tremendous healing to his wearied heart.

At the most fundamental level, this is what it means to be on God's mission. This is what it means to make disciples and to be God's kingdom-people.

We must embody love.

We must get skin-to-skin.

7

DRIVE-BY EVANGELISM

One of the most memorable and humorous experiences I've ever had in ministry happened to me when I was pastoring in New Hampshire a number of years ago. I'll never forget it. It was a lesson in how *not* to do mission, served on a silver platter.

It was a Saturday afternoon, right after our worship service had ended, and the whole congregation had filed onto the street. We were all laughing and talking, when suddenly a loud Ford Bronco came screeching to a halt right next to me. The driver rolled down his window, handed me a magazine, and then said, "Can you hold this for me? I'll be right back." Before I knew it, he peeled away and sped down the street, never to be seen again.

Trying to process what had just happened, I looked down at the magazine and it suddenly all made sense. Resting in my hands was my very own copy of *The Watchtower.*

And right then I realised something: I had been the unsuspecting victim of drive-by evangelism.

For those who don't know, *The Watchtower* is a magazine published by the Jehovah's Witnesses. They disseminate it freely, hoping to convince people of their unique views. I have nothing against Jehovah's Witnesses. They seem nice enough. But you may be surprised to hear that I didn't become a Jehovah's Witness as a result of this kind gesture. Very few people would, I'm guessing. Which is not a mystery. Most well-adjusted adults don't respond well to such manoeuvres. It feels predatory and intrusive, and usually does more harm than good, turning many people off.

Jehovah's Witnesses aren't the only ones who employ such tactics. My own faith community gives lots of money to the postal service to disseminate its publications and event invitations. To be sure, many have been brought in this way, but I worry that far more have been turned off as collateral damage.

Other common "evangelistic" activities don't align entirely with the missional vision either. We might go door-to-door in our neighbourhoods, asking if people want Bible studies, or stand on street-corners in city centres calling people to repentance, or even participate in more progressive causes like feeding the hungry or serving the homeless. All of these activities are admirable and reflect considerable courage. But they aren't what it means to be missional in the fullest sense.

Not only is our primary calling embodiment and incarnation, not only is God inviting us to live lives of *sentness* as we join Him on His mission, but we are also called to move into the neighbourhood.

In short, God is not simply calling us to *go*. He's also calling us to *stay* once we get there.

GOD, OUR NEIGHBOUR

I first heard Jeff Vanderstelt share this whole *going* and *staying* idea a few years back. Jeff is a pastor in Seattle who has been a huge missional force and, from all appearances, walks the talk.

He told the story of a church he was consulting with that was seeking to be missional. They excitedly told him about their ministry in the Skid Row neighbourhood of Los Angeles, which has one of the largest homeless populations in America. "That's really awesome," he responded. "So you guys moved into Skid Row and are serving the homeless people there?"

Suddenly, they looked confused. "Moved there?" they asked. "No." They still lived in Simi Valley, an affluent community outside of LA. "But we commute to Skid Row once a week to serve them a meal."

Not wanting to burst their bubble, Jeff tried to let them down gently. "That's great that you're providing a meal for them once a week," he said. "But that's not your real mission. Truly being missional involves living in and among the people you're trying to serve as you disciple them. So your real mission is actually the people you're driving with from Simi Valley to Skid Row each week. Those are the people you're truly doing life with and discipling."

And so it is. Being on God's mission involves not only *going*, it involves *staying*.

This is, after all, what we see in the passage we looked at in the last chapter. John explained that not only did the Word become flesh, He also "dwelt among us" (John 1:14).

I like how Eugene Peterson renders this passage in *The Message*, capturing the nuance John had in mind. "The Word became flesh and blood," he offers, "and moved into the neighbourhood." That really puts some flesh on the concept!

Moving into the neighbourhood is what it means to truly be missional. Being on God's mission doesn't entail dropping in on people, offering them occasional service or love. Being missional means going *and* staying, just as God did in Christ. It means we live a missional *life*, not just take occasional mission *trips*.

While it is certainly admirable to serve once a week, such an approach to mission does not ultimately require too great a sacrifice. It's service of convenience, rather than a *life* of service. We can easily fit it into our schedules and then return to our fortresses of safety. Any of us can carve out an hour or two each week or month to provide services for people and call it a "sacrifice," reassuring ourselves that we've done our part.

But Jesus told the disciples that "*as* the Father has sent Me, so I am sending you" (John 20:21). The same way the Father sent Jesus to be on His mission, Jesus sends us. Just as Jesus moved into the neighbourhood— just as Jesus *came* and *stayed*—He calls us to *go* and *stay*.

Think about it this way: when we *go* but we don't *stay*, it is easy for people to conclude that they are simply projects. When we relate to others as those we serve but not as ones we enter into life with, we leave the impression that they don't possess inherit dignity, value and worth. In many ways, we betray a subtle air of superiority.

Tim Chester poignantly highlights this in his book *A Meal With Jesus*. He recounts a conversation he once had with a woman who reflected on the charity she'd received from others. "I know people do a lot to help me," she said. "But what I want is for someone to be my friend." Reflecting on this sobering response, Chester incisively writes:

> Simply writing a check [cheque] keeps the poor at a distance....What we communicate is that we're able and you're unable....We cloak our superiority in compassion, but superiority cloaked in compassion is patronising.

> Think of how different the dynamic is when we sit and eat with someone. We meet as equals. We share together. We affirm one another and enjoy one another....People don't need to be projects. The poor need a welcome to replace their marginalisation, inclusion to replace their exclusion, a place where they matter to replace their powerlessness. They need community. They need the Christian community.[1]

That's why I like to remind my church that our primary mission is not to put on events, provide services or run ministries. Our goal is to enter into life with people and commit ourselves to their wellbeing *every* day, not just once a week.

This is *not* to say that we ignore people's momentary needs. People still need food, money, clothing and shelter. Addressing these needs is critically important. But our ultimate goal shouldn't be to simply provide occasional services for people, but to instead enter into constant companionship. After all, convincing people that we are safe, that we have their best interests in mind, that we are in it for them and not just in it for ourselves—for the photo ops and Facebook posts—takes time, patience and genuine investment.

This reminds me of a story my friend Avery once shared with our missional community about interactions she had with some of the native people who live nearby. As a professor of social work at the University of Maine, she was tasked with connecting with members of the Penobscot Nation to address issues of poverty and health. The nation is concentrated largely on a reservation in a place called Indian Island, which sits in the middle of the Penobscot River, just 15 minutes up the road from the university, and is accessible only by bridge.

Over the course of her conversations with the leaders, one comment especially pricked her conscience. "You know," the leader said, "everyone always sends us money, but no-one ever crosses the bridge."

What a sombre example of our call to not only *go*, but also to *stay*.

IN LIVING COLOUR

This God-moving-into-the-neighbourhood idea cuts in many directions. Among other things, if God moved into the neighbourhood, so should we. Literally.

When we were originally moving to Maine, I had imagined living on a nice plot of land outside the city, leading a quiet country life, enjoying the beauty of nature. The only place we could find to rent, however, was right in downtown Bangor. And though it's not the largest city in the world, where we landed doesn't have a ton of elbow room, nor is it the wealthiest neighbourhood.

I'm not saying we moved to the projects, by any stretch of the imagination, but we straddle a geographic line that gets quite a bit of traffic from all walks of life. We certainly see our fair share of people who don't seem to be up to much good.

But living a sheltered life is not the Christ-follower's primary calling. We're called to follow Jesus into the neighbourhood and embody God's kingdom of love, which can't be accomplished by taking day trips.

I know this challenges some brands of Christianity. It sounds scary and a bit presumptuous. Sometimes, the "mission" we engage in consists of daytrips, where we visit those in need but then retreat to our shelters of safety beyond the city limits. I get it. There is, in some ways, an appropriate level of sheltering that all of us rightfully engage in, especially when we have impressionable children, and there are certain authors who, from a superficial reading of their work, seem to suggest such an approach.

But is that what we truly see with God, who "moved into the neighbourhood" in the Person of Jesus—living, revealing, and embodying the kingdom of love *in the midst of* the world?

The truth is, incarnation—going into *and staying* in the neighbourhood—is the only way that some people will ever fully encounter true love, true truth. Each house, each family, is an outpost for God's mission, a light in a world that has been darkened by selfishness, abuse, pride and oppression.

The seemingly ordinary stuff of life is God's stage to display His glory. As they observe our lives, see our love, encounter a counter-cultural grace, it stirs up within them a desire for a better life. Seeing love in us, however imperfectly it's displayed, allows them to articulate longings they have felt but never previously been able to express.

This is what happened when people encountered Jesus, in all His incarnational glory.

These longings typically can't be stirred by reading a colour brochure that finds its way into their mailbox, despite our best intentions. They need to see grace in *living* colour—through the everyday love that can only be observed up close and over time.

So after a few years of living in our neighbourhood, we abandoned the thought of moving farther out of town. By then we realised we really liked having neighbours—being able to see people regularly, having them over for a meal at a moment's notice, quickly dropping off cookies when Camille had baked extra.

So we stayed right where we were, realising that in order to take seriously Christ's command to love our neighbours as ourselves, we needed to have actual neighbours.

NEIGHBOURHOOD CHURCH

This is not to say that we always get it right. In fact, more often than not we don't.

A while back, we got an unexpected knock on our door from a neighbour. To be completely honest, I wasn't exactly enthused to see who was standing outside. It was Tony, a man we'd kept at a distance because of his reputation in the neighbourhood. If I was going to do this missional thing, I wanted to do it on my own terms, serving people who met my expectations of respectability, and the rumour was that Tony was a druggie who thought he ruled the street.

Our observations only seemed to confirm this. One evening, Camille had looked out the window and saw him in our backyard—a place he had no logical reason to be. So Camille gingerly walked onto the porch and asked him what he was doing and whether he needed help. "I'm looking for my medication," he said. "I lost it here yesterday as I was walking through."

This is just one example of how he didn't elicit feelings of safety.

But there he was, knocking on our door one afternoon.

When I opened the door, he looked inside my house a little skittishly, asking if my kids were home, which immediately put me on high alert. After telling him they were, he invited me out to the sidewalk. Despite my apprehension, I slowly walked with him to the sidewalk, where he looked at me and said, "You're a minister, right? I heard you're a minister." A little confused by the question, I answered in the affirmative.

Then, in a raspy voice, coughing between words, Tony looked up at me and said, "I need you to really pray for me. I need your prayers. I'm not long for this world." He went on to explain that for the previous few months he had been coughing up blood and deteriorating in health. He was a Christian, he claimed, and he knew my prayers would be helpful.

So I prayed with him there on the sidewalk, asking God to give him peace and give him health and surround him with His love. Then I told Tony I would come by his house soon and pray for him again. He thanked me for that, again coughing, then retreated to his house, just two doors down. As I walked the few steps back to my house, my heart was heavy.

But apparently not heavy enough.

I was anxious about visiting him and put off doing so. One day became two, then 10 and then 30. The truth is, I was mildly intimidated to step into his small house. It might sound silly, but I was honestly afraid of what I might encounter in there. I didn't want to sit in a smoke-infested house, with drug-dealers potentially coming in and out.

Finally, however, I worked up the courage to take the short walk down to Tony's house, resolved to minister to him again, come what may. I slowly approached the door, hearing the sound of his TV blaring out of the windows. Rapping on the door, I anxiously waited, peeking through the windows. No-one came. I knocked again. After a few attempts, and just before I abandoned the mission, a younger woman came to the door and opened it, looking somewhat dazed.

I started to explain to her who I was, how I'd prayed with Tony a few weeks before, and that I was wondering if I could pray with him again. But before I could get it all out, she interrupted, and with a tinge of confusion and despair said, "Actually, Tony died 10 days ago. You hadn't heard?"

I'll never forget that moment and those words. My heart sank. Even now I get a little misty-eyed thinking about it.

I didn't know what to say. All I could muster was a few brief condolences. I then quickly retreated to my house, where I plopped down on my knees and began to weep. This time, my heart was really heavy. And so convicted. I had neglected to incarnate the gospel to Tony. I had gone out to him—I had prayed for him for a moment on the sidewalk—but I hadn't stayed. I hadn't entered into his world, investing in him as a precious child of God who bore His image.

I wasn't sad about his eternity. I know God will sort all that out. I was sad that I had failed to embody God's love when Tony needed it most, offering him continued companionship and assurance.

Because of that experience, I started grappling with an eternally important question that I'd like to pose to you: if you moved tomorrow, would your neighbours miss you? Think about it. Honestly think about it. Would they miss you?

Would they even notice you moved?

Or would they perhaps be glad to rid the neighbourhood of the religious nut who never talked to anyone (which is perhaps only slightly better than talking to them only about religious stuff or in a mean-spirited way)?

Do you even have neighbours?

Or have you chosen to live in a place for the express purpose of getting as far away from people as you can so you can maintain your holiness? If so, I would kindly submit that it's probably not the scriptural variety of holiness, if you think running away from sinners is what God asks you to do.

God invites us to move into the neighbourhood. And then He invites us to participate in His mission in the neighbourhood. Or maybe it's your workplace or classroom. Wherever you find yourself is exactly where God has sent you to live out His love, diffusing His grace and embodying the gospel.

This is what it means to participate in God's mission as followers of Christ.

What would happen if you recognised that your primary calling in life was to serve as a "chaplain" of sorts for your neighbourhood or workplace or classroom—to be present as the embodied representative of God's kingdom? Not to bombard each house or co-worker with religious missiles, engaging in drive-by evangelism. The world doesn't need more people who think they have all the answers but who don't have grace or humility. What the world needs is people who live as the ears of Christ and the hands of the Spirit, listening for the hidden longings of each heart and mediating love to those who need it.

I bet you'd discover your life was never more fulfilling and exciting.

And I bet you'd discover that the neighbourhood is exactly where the Spirit has already been conducting church all along.

8

THE SAME, BUT DIFFERENT

I'm not sure how, but somewhere along the way the word "culture" became a four-letter word to me. I was uncomfortable with religious practices I deemed to be questionable but others described as "cultural" expressions of faith.

What we were called to do, I thought, was to rise above worldly culture—to ascend into heaven and grasp the culture that transcends all human cultures, instilling a sort of *supraculture*. In my mind, that was the goal for any Christian serious about following the ways of God.

But that was then.

As we began to live missionally more, drawing closer to people in our neighbourhood and surrounding community, I slowly started to realise that the "heavenly" culture bore an eerie resemblance to the culture I grew up with and preferred. I noticed that God seemed to like all the music I liked—and *only* the music I liked. He seemed to prefer all the same clothes I thought people should wear. He even wanted us to meet at the precise time our church would meet each week.

It was all quite fortuitous and ironic.

And, of course, not true.

As I reflected on this, I began to realise that every culture is—by definition—"worldly." There is no such thing as a "culture-neutral" expression of life or faith. Everything we do—the suits we wear, the organs we play—derives from "the world." Indeed, everything humans produce is "worldly."

None of us, as far as I know, have ever figured out what exactly beings wear in heaven or discovered sheet music from the angelic choir. Every song ever written on earth and every piece of clothing ever designed was produced by human beings who belong to this world. No instruments have ever fallen down from heaven, no "order of service" has ever been emailed by God.

And this is fine. As we see in the incarnation, Christ fully affirms our humanity—God loves *the world*. The things humans do, the culture we create, are beautiful to God. He delights in them, however imperfect and flawed they may be.

This is not to say, of course, that *everything* humans do brings gladness to God's heart. Sin still exists. Humans engage in behaviours—sometimes even in the name of "culture"—that violate God's law of love.

But I've discovered that there are many things we claim offend God's holiness, when all they really do is offend our cultural sensibilities.

I remember a conversation I once had with a dear friend who was nervous about rumours that I was softening on my insistence that people needed to "dress up" to "go to church." He was worried that allowing people to wear jeans and t-shirts would make us too much like "the world." Not trying to be cute, I asked him where exactly he had bought his suit.

The truth is, we often elevate the traditional to the divine, forgetting that what is traditional was at one time new, with "worldly" origins. Suits—at least to my knowledge—have never been featured in heaven's spring clothing catalogue.

Similarly, back in the 1800s, one member of a prominent Boston church zealously threatened to throw the church's new organ into Boston Harbor, citing its origins in the iniquitous theatre halls and referring to it as an "evil thing." This person's concerns were not at all unique among church people for a long while.[1] Yet here we are 200 years later and somehow the organ has made it through the sanctification process. The truth is that time sanctifies many cultural practices.

Cultural bias has serious missional repercussions. As a people whose primary calling is to join God's mission every day, our cultural biases can alienate people from God, preventing us from getting off the launchpad with them.

This really clicked when I saw a short video from Todd Engstrom talking about what it means to be a missionary people. "A missionary is someone who sacrifices *everything* but the *gospel*, for the *sake* of the gospel," he explained. "Your preferences, your time, your money, the things you love to do—*everything*, but that cherished gospel, for the sake of the gospel." He then added this:

> Who are you expecting to be the missionary? You're expecting somebody who has no hope of salvation to go to places they are uncomfortable going. You're expecting someone who doesn't have the Holy Spirit of God in them to adapt their schedule to yours. You are expecting them to learn a new language and way of interacting; you're expecting them to adapt their entire culture.... [So] who are you expecting to be more like Jesus? Are you expecting the covenant people of God...to go and act like missionaries; or are you expecting your city, who has no hope, to be a missionary people?[2]

It was a mic drop moment for me. I realised that I'd often expected others who didn't consciously know Jesus to adopt a missionary posture in order to access God's kingdom. Instead of laying aside my preferences and cultural commitments, as any good missionary does, I had thought they should be the ones to do so, adopting my language, my dress, my schedule, my culture. I had asked them to be the missionaries instead of me.

Of course, many of us don't even realise just how much we package the gospel in our own cultural wrapping. We think we subscribe to the truth and nothing but the truth. But we all encounter, understand and proclaim the gospel through our own cultural context. As Lesslie Newbigin says:

> Every interpretation of the gospel is embodied in some cultural form. The missionary does not come with the pure gospel and then adapt it to the culture where she serves: she comes with a gospel which is already embodied in the culture by which the missionary was formed.[3]

All this got me wondering what things I was clinging to—often in the misguided name of holiness—that were standing in the way of others encountering God's love through me. What barriers had I created that obscured the face of Jesus?

CULTURAL EXEGETES

When the apostle Paul went about his missionary work, he faced a similar dilemma. He was a "Hebrew of the Hebrews," he once boasted, having perfected the meticulous requirements of Judaism like a good Pharisee (see Philippians 3:5). But the great challenge was that God had called him to share the gospel with the Gentiles—people whose customs and culture were at odds with the peculiar practices of Judaism.

As a good missionary, following in the footsteps of Jesus, Paul knew what he had to do. He had to separate truth from tradition, discarding the latter while contextualising the former. This was what it meant for Paul to embody the mission of God, meeting people where they were, just as God had done in Christ.

"Though I am free and belong to no-one," he thus wrote to the Corinthian church, "I have made myself a slave to everyone, to win as many as possible." He explained that when he was with those who made a big deal of the rules of Judaism, he honoured those rules to gain their confidence. When he was with others who weren't beholden to the traditions of man, he cast off restraint and lived a life of liberty. "I have become all things to all people so that by all possible means I might save some," he declared, doing so "for the sake of the gospel" (see 1 Corinthians 9:19–24, NIV).

Simply put, Paul didn't want anything to distract from the gospel. He wasn't trying to peddle his customs, man-made traditions or even his religion. He was trying let Jesus shine through, refusing to let anything else get in the way. He was willing to lay everything else aside for the sake of the gospel.

Paul was a "cultural exegete." An exegete is one who studies a text to understand and interpret its meaning. Most often we think of exegetes as those who probe sacred texts to flesh out their interpretation. Paul was that, for sure. He knew the ancient Hebrew texts with incredible acuity. But he was also a deep student of the cultures that surrounded him, wrestling with how Scripture and the story of Jesus could intersect with the world in ways that removed any unnecessary distractions or barriers.

One thinks of his visit to Athens, where he held court on top of Mars Hill, waxing eloquent to the philosophers who met there and quoting their poets. He even affirmed their worship of an "unknown god," whose inscription was on a nearby altar, and had the audacity to tell them that this unknown god they worshipped was the God of heaven he proclaimed.

When Paul arrived in Athens, he didn't stay in the safe confines of the synagogue, waiting for the Athenians to find him on his terms. He sought them out, meeting them where they felt most comfortable. And when he observed their customs and familiarised himself with their culture, he didn't mock it or tear them down. He didn't wage a culture war. Paul spoke their language, affirmed their longings and connected it all to Jesus, inviting them into the family of God. As a result, he successfully drew people to join up with God's mission.

Part of what it means to be a cultural exegete is recognising that the Spirit is already working on hearts. God's grace is moving on all people. According to John, "God gives light to every man coming into the world" (John 1:9). And if we listen closely enough, we can pick up on the melodies—however faint—of the Spirit's drawing in sometimes surprising places.

There is a tendency in some circles to assume that all popular culture—music, literature, the visual arts—is nothing more than Satan's sly attempt to lead people away from God. We must therefore run away from it all, lest we become bewitched by the wiles of the devil.

If Paul had taken that approach, he would have never connected the Athenians' poetry to God's heart and he would have missed an opportunity to draw precious people into God's family. While a great deal of pop culture is seemingly mindless entertainment full of gratuitous sex and violence, often employed in pursuit of the almighty dollar, I've also found that a lot of it reveals humanity's shared brokenness and people's sometimes unconscious grasping after God, as they try to make sense of the finite and the eternal the best they know how. To ignore such things prevents us from travelling down the very avenues that could awaken a person's heart to the eternal realities they are unconsciously reaching for.

So if we just spend a little time exegeting the culture—breaking down the symbols and spirit of the age, listening to what makes those around us tick, and what they believe gives them meaning and purpose—we might find that we are better able to incarnate the gospel in ways that make more sense to them. This is more likely to make a difference than insisting that others need to learn our language and culture in order to access God's kingdom of love.

I fear that too many of us Jesus-followers do not understand the full magnitude of our missional task in the 21st century. Making disciples in the West is every bit the cross-cultural exercise that it is for an American who goes to missionise people in the jungles of South America. The forms and cultural expressions we use within Western Christianity today are becoming increasingly unintelligible and foreign to people in the post-Christian contexts around us, as they move further away from and become more unfamiliar with our traditions.

Our failure to understand this has been disastrous, leading to all sorts of tragic results.

THE SAME, BUT DIFFERENT

This intersects with an interesting phenomenon that has puzzled historians of the early church as they've pondered what led to its explosive growth in the first few centuries. Sociologists have long studied religious movements, wondering what ingredients lead to world-altering outcomes. Think about it: why do some religious movements succeed and others fail? Why does Confucianism still exist today, for example, but not Mithraism, despite the fact that both started more than 2000 years ago?

In the case of Christianity, we would, of course, say it was a God-thing—that the Spirit imbued the early church with power and authority to turn the world upside-down. I believe this is unequivocally true, but it doesn't explain how Islam or Buddhism or Taoism have also altered the trajectory of world history to such dizzying degrees. It seems there has to be a sociological basis for this.

In his book *Destroyer of the Gods*, historian Larry Hurtado proposes one explanation for why these things might be so. He notes how religious movements that succeed are both *alike* the surrounding culture and yet also *different*. There has to be a balance of both continuity and discontinuity. This is the strange paradox, the delicate tension.

If a particular religion perfectly mirrors its surrounding culture, then there's no point to join it—it doesn't offer anything unique. As Hurtado asks in the case of Christianity, "If early Christianity essentially affirmed and reflected beliefs, values, and practices commonly shared in the Roman Empire, why would people have bothered to join?"[4]

But then there's the other side of the coin. A particular religion cannot be so *unlike* its surrounding culture that outsiders deem it creepy or cultish. "Distinctiveness is important," Hurtado writes, "but there is a point of diminishing return, and along with being distinctive a movement has to commend itself to its cultural setting."[5]

Think about it this way: if two people knocked on your door tomorrow, inviting you to join their new religion, but it was essentially indistinguishable from your current one, you'd probably be unlikely to join. There would not be sufficient benefit to justify the significant cost it would take to leave your current community and join the other.

Likewise, if the new religion required adherents to paint their faces purple and walk around on their hands all day, you probably wouldn't join either.

This is the balance that early Christianity struck. It offered something different—the incredible invitation into God's family of love—but it did so in relatable and intelligible ways.

This is precisely what we see in the incarnation. Jesus was the *same* as us—He was fully human—but He was also *different* from us—He was fully God. To emphasise one aspect to the neglect of the other proves disastrous—not only in how we understand Christ, but also in the way we relate to the mission He's invited us to participate in.

But somewhere along the way we lost the balance initially present in the early church, with many of us veering into the ditches on both sides of the road. We either emphasise *sameness* or we emphasise *uniqueness*. To stay in either ditch leads to disastrous results.

Exegeting and engaging in the culture around us doesn't mean we sell out to the ever-present idolatry of relevance. Our goal is not to simply be trendy, to put on a cool worship service and wear skinny jeans—or whatever is trending next week. As Jay Y. Kim notes, "Since its earliest days, the Christian church has been marked by its invitation to *transcendence*, not *relevance*."[6] It's easy for people to detect a disingenuous attempt at re-appropriating their cultural values and practices through the slick salesmanship of self-serving church people.

Neither do we want to bury the unique beauty of God's kingdom for the sake of fitting in with a society that has divinised pluralism. We can't compromise when it comes to the core values and teachings of Scripture.

But we also can't live in the past, committed to a culture and to methods that are completely unintelligible to the world around us—all because we've confused tradition for truth. We must learn to adapt, to speak in a language our communities understand, so that people can come into contact with the true substance of the Jesus-message and mission, rather than what we've so often made it to be.

As someone has said, *the medium is the message*. Substance cannot be truly divorced from form. The methods we use implicitly communicate the theology we believe. We can't preach that Jesus' brings liberty and freedom from fear, that in the incarnation God meets us where we are, on the one hand, and then, on the other hand, tell people they have to come to us and adopt our culture and rules—which are so often predicated on fear—in order to access that message.

Our methods become so loud that people can't hear the message we're trying to proclaim.

As Francis Chan has noted, the church is "trying to maintain a Blockbuster video store in the age of Netflix." He clarifies that he's not trying to argue for just keeping up with the times. His invitation is for us to "go back to Scripture and recover what we've lost."[7]

And that's the point: with Paul, we need to *go back to Scripture* and separate truth from tradition, Christ from culture, recognising that, as finite human beings, we will never fully escape our own biases. We need to figure out how to be *the same* but *different*, affirming what we can affirm while inviting people into a better story. We need to recognise that what chiefly separates the church from the world—what makes it fundamentally *different*—is not the unique cultural practices we have deified, like what we wear, sing or watch. What makes the family of God so fundamentally different from the world is the way we love. In a world starving for true, authentic, self-emptying love, *that* is what is *truly* counter-cultural.

After all, as Jesus said, "By *this* everyone will know that you are my disciples, *if you love one another*" (John 13:35, NIV, emphasis mine). It may sound like a cliché, but authentic love is what gets the world's attention, standing in sharp relief to the cultures around us.

COOKOUTS AND CHRISTMAS PARTIES

As our missional community began earnestly grappling with these concepts, we started paying more attention to the cultural values and practices of those we were sent to, wondering how we could serve them in ways that made sense to them. We listened for how the Spirit was already drawing hearts, affirming the things we had in common.

It quickly became apparent that however we pursued God's mission, it probably wouldn't involve inviting people to buildings they weren't familiar with, asking them to dress up in clothes they never wore, conversing in a language they never spoke, listening to songs they'd heard only at funerals.

One way it did play out was through celebration. Every culture and people parties and celebrates—birthdays, holidays, graduations, weddings. Even Jesus' first miracle came at a grand wedding celebration.

So that's one thing we did. We started throwing Christmas bashes and showing up to birthday parties together, being the presence of Jesus in ways that made sense to our friends.

I remember going one time, along with Camille and our sister-in-law Ellie, to a birthday party our friends Sarah and Luke were throwing and meeting all their friends and neighbours. Most weren't Jesus-followers. I'll never forget how Sarah, herself not a Christian, introduced me to people. "This is our friend, Shawn," she'd say. "He's a pastor, but he's actually pretty cool."

Of course, simply being cool isn't the goal, and I can't confirm her assessment of me. But being labelled "cool" is certainly better than the alternative—especially when you're not downing the alcohol like everyone else. This is especially true when one is seeking to enter into life with those who are starting from a different religious place and potentially already have a predisposition against the core beliefs that one holds.

On another occasion, our missional community decided to throw a late-summer cookout at our house, inviting our friends and neighbours to celebrate with us. Admittedly, when we were planning the party, the sticky topic of food came up. Our faith community places considerable emphasis on living and eating healthfully, with many of us vegetarians. It's not a requirement for membership at all, but the emphasis—when presented in a balanced and loving way—makes sense, especially in increasingly secular societies that are catching on to the health benefits.

But we knew that most people who would come to our cookout weren't vegetarians, with some on the opposite end of the spectrum. So we went back and forth on what to do.

Finally, one person spoke up. "Forget this madness!" she said. "*I'm* not a vegetarian, and we don't require our own members to be vegetarian." With great passion, she then declared, "I'm bringing the beef!"

And so she did. We gathered and celebrated, cooking beef burgers alongside tofu burgers.

For some, this might not seem all that revolutionary or profound. It's simply humans relating to other humans in ways that are pretty basic. For others—and I admit I used to be in this category—it's a little more troubling and disturbing. It feels gimmicky and gospel-light. It feels like a betrayal of what makes us fundamentally different, undermining our ability to transfer our core values.

After all, if I serve someone a beef burger today, why will they be convinced there is a better way when I tell them about it tomorrow?

But that's not how life works.

We just set up an adjustable basketball hoop in our driveway for our kids. For now, the hoop is only eight feet high. My willingness to allow our kids to shoot at a hoop that low today doesn't undermine my hope that they'll be able to shoot on a 10-foot hoop tomorrow. In fact, it is a necessary part of their development to be able to start low and work their way up. Insisting that they be where I am right now would discourage them from continuing to try, defeating the very thing I'm trying to accomplish.

And as it relates to food, I can assure you that there are many people who would stop showing up to our table if we only served broccoli and carrots all the time. It would be like cutting our nose to spite our face.

I don't think most church people understand just how dire the situation is. The Western world is moving away from Christianity at a dizzying rate, with very little intention of ever walking through our doors again. If we're going to impact the culture around us, we can't just tweak a few things and think they'll come back. We can't just perfect our doctrines or theology thinking that's the magic bullet—because they aren't listening anyway.

We need an entire paradigm-shift, going out into the world and learning how to engage the culture on its terms, rather than retreating to our empty church buildings and clinging to our traditions in the name of holiness.

Of course, the same applies to the uber-relevant churches, full of fog machines and hipster beards. That ship has sailed as well. They might know how to put on a good show, but most of it doesn't move the needle when it comes to the people outside their doors who will never show up to their events. And it doesn't really make disciples anyway.

We all need a major, earth-shaking paradigm-shift, moving God's people fully into His mission in the world so the knowledge of the glory of the Lord covers the whole earth "as the waters cover the sea" (Habakkuk 2:14).

We all need to learn how to exegete the culture and meet people where they are on *their* terms, as any good missionary does.

This is what it means to be the *same* but *different*.

9

LOSING MY RELIGION

I used to meet weekly at Bagel Central with a group of individuals who were connected with a Jewish synagogue in Bangor. The rabbi, whom I'd become friends with, invited me to join them for "coffee hour" to discuss various topics that had piqued their curiosity.

Six or seven people usually showed up, and we would discuss whatever the topic of the day was. But it usually intersected with Judaism and often connected with issues facing modern Israel.

Not surprisingly, I learned so much each time, helping me become a better person in general and with my walk with Jesus specifically.

But one realisation came in a rather unexpected way.

Quite often, as the group conversed, they'd start talking about religious minutiae, apparently forgetting a Gentile was among them. They would begin to debate, in dispassionate ways, what seemed to be trivial matters of ritual, unrelated to the world outside their faith.

One time, a few people got fairly animated as they discussed whether they should use the name *Adonai* in their prayers each Sabbath at synagogue or whether they should stick to using *HaShem*.

I understood the debate, knowing biblical Hebrew, but for the uninitiated, the discussion revolves around the question in Judaism of how one should refer to God. The original name God revealed to Israel was the name *Yahweh*. But eventually, the people became so deferent to God's holiness they concluded they shouldn't even utter His name—opting instead to use *Adonai*, which is the general term for "Lord."

But even that wasn't enough. Wanting to place even further distance between themselves and God's holiness, many Jews felt it was too risky to even use *Adonai* anymore, instead choosing to use the term *HaShem*, which simply means "the Name."

Some Jews refer to this type of action as *chumra*, which is the act of "building a fence around the Torah," taking extra precautions to make sure one doesn't go anywhere close to violating its strictures.

In the world of rule-centred religion, it's better to be safe than sorry. People must hedge their bets.

And so there they were, debating this critical question in the middle of Bagel Central, wondering how big a fence they had to build.

I sat there quite amused and a little befuddled, grateful I wasn't part of a religion that argued about trivial matters of ritual. I was glad my own faith community never gets hung up on rules and regulations and restrictions, drawing our battle lines and declaring who's in and who's out on their basis.

Actually, I didn't think that at all. As I listened to them debate their religion, it gave me incredible insight into mine. I've found that to be repeatedly true. Nothing causes me to re-examine my own religious assumptions like encountering the bewildering assumptions of another. Those Jewish friends were as certain of the importance of their theological debates as I was of mine.

Pretty soon I started wondering what the things were that I spent so much time fighting about that had undermined my ability to fully participate in the mission and family of God.

Unbeknownst to me, I was about to lose my religion—and find Jesus again.

ANSWERING QUESTIONS NO-ONE IS ASKING

Of course, Jesus had His own journey with Judaism. He knew the Torah backwards and forwards, and He was likely well versed in the ancient debates memorialised in the teachings of the rabbis. If called upon, Jesus could debate with the best of them.

But Jesus wasn't looking to start any debates. He wanted to point people to love.

This often required Him to clear away the rubble, like the fence around the Torah, that had served as a barrier between hurting hearts and a loving God. One of the most poignant examples of this was a run-in with the Pharisees—the *Separatists*—when they accosted Him, asking why His disciples were ignoring the rabbinical rules by refusing to wash their hands before eating (this had nothing to do with hygiene and everything to do with religious sanctimony). "Why do your disciples break the tradition of the elders?" they angrily demanded (Matthew 15:2, NIV).

That's a funny phrase—"tradition of the elders"—but I'll resist the urge to delve too deeply into it. Jesus' response to them is adequate. Referring to a convenient end-around they'd created which convinced them they could ignore the commandment to honour father and mother, Jesus skilfully turned the tables on them, asking, "And why do you break the command of God for the sake of your tradition?" (Matthew 15:3).

The juxtaposition was drawn, the dichotomy exposed. Jesus invited them into a choice: they could either pursue God's heart or man's traditions.

There's nothing inherently wrong with man-made traditions, it must be pointed out. Traditions are great. They add meaning to life and bind hearts together. I participate in *many* traditions, both socially and religiously, and I'd hate to exist in a world without them.

But the great danger with man-made traditions, especially in a religious setting, is when they're presented as universal commands from the almighty God that must be followed by all people in all places, serving as the basis for inclusion within the family of God. And that's exactly what the Pharisees did. They elevated their invented rules and restrictions to a moral status, "teaching as doctrines the commandments of men," as Jesus boldly pointed out.

The trick here is recognising the shoe fits. Few of us probably do. I've discovered that most of us read passages like this and always assume Jesus is talking about someone else's traditions, someone else's rules and regulations. He obviously isn't talking about ours, we conclude.

But as I started noticing afresh passages like this, I humbly asked God if I too was being Pharisaical, clinging to my rules and traditions and judging others on their basis—repelling people from the family of God, rather than drawing them in.

I soon realised that for too long I had had a pretty narrow understanding of the gospel, subtly marked by fear and self-righteousness. Don't get me wrong: I'm fully persuaded I had a healthy *theoretical* knowledge and understanding of God's grace. But looking back now, I'm not sure

I appreciated the depth of its practical implications for how I related to others and to myself.

The gospel hadn't penetrated deep into my heart, delivering me from fear and the belief that my security was ultimately found in keeping the rules—many of which were man-made—and through perfect belief.

I slowly started recapturing the heart of the Jesus-message, recognising how it reaches to every corner of my life and its implications for the way I related to people.

I also began to realise that Christianity in general, and my brand of it in particular, spends a *lot* of time answering questions no-one seems to be asking. We have our own versions of the debates between *Adonai* and *HaShem*, and we waste a *lot* of time, energy, ink and money arguing about them. We *love* to quarrel about theology—mostly because somewhere along the way we got to thinking our primary task was to protect truth, to snuff out heresy and detect deception.

We love to talk to ourselves, argue with ourselves, criticise ourselves, hang out with ourselves—as though we're the only people in the world and our abstract debates are the only topics of significance in the world. But, quite frankly, I started losing my appetite for such things the more I became aware that there is a big, wide world out there where 99 per cent of people are facing *real* life-or-death issues that will never be solved by our insular and myopic theological debates.

This is not to imply that our theological agenda needs to be set by those unfamiliar with or unconcerned about the scriptural values that drive us. It's simply to say that when we lose sight of our primary calling as agents of God's mission in the world, we forget the whole point of our theological task, inventing controversies to argue about and debate. This is why Alan Hirsch reminds us that "mission is, and always was, the mother of good theology."[1]

TRULY ADVENTIST

I want to make something abundantly clear though, if it's not already: I love Jesus so much. I love the Bible. I *really* love the way my particular faith community understands the beautiful story of Scripture—taking in the reality of Creation, the blessing of the Sabbath, the big story of a cosmic conflict, the soon return of Jesus, His desire for us to live healthily, our special mission in the world—all of it. Like Paul, I could boast that I am an "Adventist of the Adventists." I love it all. Full stop.

What I have less patience for these days is when people make that beautiful story about something—*anything*—else.

It was very eye-opening to discover during this journey that many people who think they're the most dogmatically committed Adventists don't actually know what Adventism teaches. This was an ironic and surprising discovery. I recall numerous conversations along the way when people were distraught because they were *sure* our church no longer promoted our doctrines. When I'd ask them which teachings we no longer espoused, they cited a whole list of things nowhere found in our list of beliefs and provided no evidence we no longer believed in the core teachings of our faith community.

One time, a very intelligent gentleman, who I know sincerely loves Jesus, shared that our rhythmic guitar playing and decision to serve refreshments mid-morning at our gatherings each Saturday had caused him to wonder if we were an Adventist church. "Adventists don't eat in between meals," he said, quite appalled.

Don't get me wrong: his concerns might have been perfectly legitimate, containing much wisdom, and we certainly don't claim to have it all figured out. On the other hand, they could have simply been issues his conscience wouldn't allow him to participate in, which is fine. We're all at different places in our journeys.

The real challenge is when we elevate our *personal* convictions to the status of universals and try to "build a fence around the Torah" for everyone else, thinking it's better "to be safe than sorry." It's dangerous to conclude that we're further down the path of spiritual maturity than those who aren't on board with what we're convicted about. I know this is still a risk for me.

But it seems, as we grow as disciples of Jesus, one of the most fundamental ways we start reflecting His image is by extending liberty to others over issues that aren't *clearly* addressed in Scripture. (I recognise, of course, that this is the rub: many people who possess such convictions believe they *are* clearly expressed in Scripture.)

It all reminds me of another confrontation Jesus had with the Pharisees. "You search the Scriptures because you think they give you eternal life," Jesus said to them. "But the Scriptures point to me! Yet you refuse to come to me to receive this life" (John 5:39, 40, NLT).

Imagine that! The Pharisees knew the Scriptures inside and out. They could recite long portions from memory. They had lots of knowledge.

They debated it and argued over it and exegeted it and dissected it and regurgitated it. Yet they don't even really know it! They missed the whole point, revealing they were actually ignorant about their own religion. What a depressing existence!

Jesus was the point of every line in Scripture, yet they somehow missed it. They thought it was about rules and regulations and restrictions. Jesus told them it was about relating to Him—something they were, for whatever reason, entirely unwilling to do.

Again, the trick here is recognising the shoe fits. I started realising we've been blessed with such beautiful and clarifying insights into who God is and what it means to be a part of His mission and family, but, like the Pharisees of old, we've buried those insights underneath a pile of rubble, building a fence around the Torah. We can quote Scripture, quote the revered authors in our own faith community and argue about the finer points of theology, yet totally miss the whole point—totally miss Jesus.

And I wanted out.

Admittedly, such a thought can be scary. When you believe your security comes from subscribing to the exact right beliefs, you feel anxious when you start wondering whether every little belief you once assumed is actually true. When you've elevated everything to the same level—when, say, your views on whether women can be pastors are as significant and important and absolute as the belief that Jesus rose from the dead or the command to love your neighbour as yourself—you start worrying that to question one means you have to question them all. And you begin to fear you're starting down the dreaded "slippery slope."

And those around you start worrying about that as well, especially when you were once an opinionated bastion of black-and-white orthodoxy. *Where will it end?* people wonder. Today it's wearing jeans to church; tomorrow it will be denying Jesus was the Son of God.

Or so the thinking goes, *somewhat* understandably.

LEARNING WHAT IT MEANS TO SABBATH

One occasion particularly stands out that illustrates the wrestling I was doing. One week, in late June, our family, along with Cameron and Ellie's family, were invited by our friends, Manish and Shivani, to spend a day with them at their camp on a beautiful lake. Camille had met

Shivani a few years before at a library story time and they immediately hit it off—as did our kids.

Pretty soon, we all started spending time together, hanging out, celebrating birthdays, becoming family together.

We loved them and they loved us and we enjoyed spending as much time together as we could. Our conversations were always fascinating, as they'd tell us about life in Nepal, where they were originally from, and our discussions about religion—with them being raised Hindu—always gave us a lot to think about. So when they invited our families to a day on the lake, it seemed like the perfect opportunity.

Except for one problem: they invited us to join them on a Saturday.

For those who may not know, traditionally, within our faith community, many people think that Saturdays, as the Sabbath, should be spent participating in strictly religious activities. Growing up, we didn't go swimming and we certainly didn't go boating or waterskiing. It was a day one was supposed to "go to church," spending as much time with other members of the faith community as possible, talking about God, praying, reading Scripture and avoiding "secular" activities.

Even though it was a Saturday I was planning to take off already anyway, I felt conflicted about what to do. The truth is, we'd been heading towards this "iceberg" for a while. The more time we'd been spending with people outside our faith, the more obvious it became that the criteria by which we determined what we would or wouldn't do on Sabbaths wasn't as consistent as we thought. It started to feel like the only thread woven through our decision-making was tradition.

So I began to wrestle in earnest. I desperately wanted to remain faithful to Scripture, having a high regard for its authority, but I also knew I didn't want to needlessly "build a fence around the Torah," thus undermining my ability to participate in God's mission.

As I started sifting through everything Scripture said about Sabbath, I began to realise I had largely missed its true beauty and glory. I had always known *in theory* that it wasn't supposed to be a day about rules and restrictions but a day to rest and rejoice in Jesus. But Jesus had for so long been crowded out by my preoccupation with what I was or wasn't supposed to do.

I went through every single verse in Scripture that talks about Sabbath and I came to an absolutely stunning discovery: literally—and I do mean *literally*—the *only* thing the Bible prohibits on Sabbath is working and having others work on your behalf. That's it. Nothing more, nothing less.*

And then I came to Jesus. It was a revelation to realise, on a real heart level, that Jesus spent *so much time* butting heads with the religious leaders over their strict Sabbath rules and regulations when He repeatedly violated them. Time and again, the Gospels record Jesus challenging the Scribes and Pharisees, who were infuriated that He refused to follow their strict rules and traditions of Sabbath observance.

"The Sabbath was made for man, and not man for the Sabbath," He told them (Mark 2:27). It was a day of restoration, healing, rest, liberation, relationship, justice. They had made it about restrictions, concluding it was better to be safe than sorry.

Again, it's tempting to think the shoe doesn't fit. But I started realising it fit me all too perfectly.

Perhaps no moment in Jesus' ministry better exemplified His vision for the Sabbath than when He announced the beginning of His ministry at the synagogue in Nazareth. Standing up and turning to the book of Isaiah, He read these momentous words:

The Spirit of the Lord is upon Me,
Because He has anointed Me
To preach the gospel to the poor;
He has sent Me to heal the broken-hearted,
To proclaim liberty to the captives,
And recovery of sight to the blind,
To set at liberty those who are oppressed;
To proclaim the acceptable year of the Lord (Luke 4:18,19).

That was Jesus' true intent for the Sabbath—a day to proclaim liberty to the captives, to bring healing to the broken-hearted, recovery of sight to the blind.

---

* One verse people like to cite in dispute of this point is Isaiah 58:13, where God tells Israel that they were to turn away their foot from doing their own "pleasure" on the Sabbath, thus prohibiting any recreational activities, for example, swimming. But two points: (1) This is literally the only verse that goes anywhere close to mentioning a prohibition on pursuing one's own "pleasure," and (2) if we're going to be faithful to the text and its context, we would quickly discover that the "pleasure" God prohibits has nothing to do with "recreation" at all. If we simply read a few verses before, we'd see that the same word—both in Hebrew and even our English versions—is actually in reference to people in Israel exploiting their workers. "You find pleasure, and exploit your laborers," God says (verse 3). Thus, the "pleasure" that God was trying to rectify by giving the Sabbath was the "pleasure" of exploitation, abuse and oppression. It has nothing to do with whether a person goes swimming or rides their bike or goes for a boat ride.

In short, His intent for the Sabbath was not that we would be preoccupied with strict rules of personal piety—of making sure we don't do *this* or we don't do *that*—but that we would extend God's kingdom of love to those who are longing for a better story.

This *doesn't* mean, of course, we bury all boundaries when it comes to how we celebrate the Sabbath. But those boundaries will be more an attempt to make the Sabbath *special*—which is a lot more subjective than many of us care to admit—than it is to measure up to some arbitrary rules in order to make God happy with us.

Needless to say, after much wrestling, we accepted Manish and Shivani's invitation to join the family at their camp. And we had one of the best Sabbaths we've ever had. We swam, we boated, we ate delicious Nepalese food, we talked about God, we widened the family circle. The weather was perfect, the fellowship and conversation even better.

At one point Shivani said, as she had said to Camille a number of times before, that she loved hanging around us because there was just an energy about us that she picked up. She wasn't sure how to describe it or what it was exactly, but she felt so much peace when she was with us.

I didn't say it then, but I had a hunch of what it might be, sharing with her later that it was this thing called the Holy Spirit and the love of Jesus.

It may sound like a cliché or an easy out but here's the beautiful and liberating reality: Jesus is enough. He truly is. It's not about religion. It's not about strict rules or building a fence around the Torah. It's about being with Him and being with His children.

Are we going to opt for our man-made rules and traditions, taking us away from God's mission?

Or are we going to lose our religion and find Jesus?

10

BECOMING A FUNCTIONAL PLURALIST

If I was living during the time of Jesus and had the chance to interact with Him, I think one thing that would frustrate me would be His reluctance to give a straight answer. He evaded questions and answered questions with questions and told stories that left some people scratching their heads.

Think of His encounter with the lawyer in the book of Luke who asked Jesus what he needed to do to inherit eternal life. Jesus could have pulled out His canned gospel pitch and led the man through the sinner's prayer. Instead, He answered His question with a question. "What's written in God's Law?" He asked him. "How do you interpret it?" (Luke 10:26, *The Message*).

To be sure, when the man recited the command to love the Lord with all his heart and to love his neighbour as himself, Jesus affirmed him and told him to go do it. But He led him through the steps of self-discovery, honouring his agency, rather than overpowering him by divine decree.

Or think of the astounding encounter He had with the woman from Canaan, who came to Him because her daughter was demon-possessed, begging Jesus to heal her. Matthew records that He ignored the woman, refusing to acknowledge her. When she finally did get His attention, He said it was "not good to take the children's bread and throw it to the little dogs" (Matthew 15:26).

It's hard to hear these words from the mouth of the perfect Son of God—at least with modern ears that aren't attuned to the cultural context of Scripture. But the woman persisted and ended up astounding Jesus with her faith, which He affirmed. But He made the woman work for it.

It probably doesn't need to be said, but I'll say it anyway: Jesus wasn't being a jerk in these situations. He just wasn't interested in giving pat answers or overly simplified solutions. He didn't want to conquer people with airtight logic or prematurely alienate them with dogma. He wanted to guide them through a journey of self-discovery that would allow for much greater rooting in the story of Scripture.

In some ways, Jesus would have a hard time navigating our modern world, which prioritises quick soundbites and 280-character tweets. In other ways, though, He would be right at home. In a world where no answer is the wrong answer so long as it is offered without the packaging of dogmatism, Jesus would excel.

As our missional community continued to walk through the landscape of post-modern pluralistic society, we realised we needed to take our cues from Jesus. We needed to become functional pluralists.

ARGUING PEOPLE INTO TRUTH

I had an interesting conversation with a Jewish friend a while back that left me both frustrated and enlightened. I don't remember how we got there, but we started talking about the nature of inspiration and whether the Bible held any authority as an inspired document.

As we sat across the table from each other, I decided it was time to break out my secret weapon: Daniel 2. This critical chapter has been a favourite of evangelists the world over in my faith community, serving as a persuasive and nearly airtight argument for the divine origins of the scriptural narrative.

Whipping out the broad outline from memory, I began to expound upon the image that Nebuchadnezzar saw in his dream, speaking of the succession of Babylon, Media-Persia, Greece and finally Rome. I pointed to the feet of iron mixed with clay, identifying them as divided Europe, and then the rock that followed this, cut without human hands, arguing this pointed to the terminus of human empires and the establishment of God's kingdom. My explanation was not perfect, but it would have made any evangelist proud.

I didn't expect my friend to make a beeline for the baptistry, ready to convert to Christ. But I at least expected him to acknowledge my argument was worthy of some consideration.

Instead, without much fanfare, he simply replied, "Yeah, it seems like you're trying really hard to read something into the text."

I was devastated. The plain truth was staring him right in the face, yet what was so obvious to me was apparently anything but to him.

This was just one conversation in a series of many that helped me realise that no matter how winsomely or persuasively I presented my theological arguments to others, they almost never resulted in an epiphany. And that started really frustrating me. I wondered why I apparently couldn't come up with the perfect way to argue my points or overpower people with my logic. I'd heard so many stories of evangelists who had seatmates baptised by the end of airplane rides or preachers with audiences eating out of their hands. Perhaps I just wasn't skilled enough at argumentation or adept enough at apologetics.

But here's a reality check: that's not usually how it works. Dramatic conversions like that are the overwhelming *exception*, not the norm. Yet these are the stories we usually hear or read about. We rarely hear of all the people who never came to truth through our arguments and were perhaps even turned off by them, or who took years to slowly surrender to the reality of God's love through the patient discipling of a humble Christian friend.

People are generally not argued into truth, despite all the time we spend training ourselves in apologetics (which seem to convince ourselves more than others). This is all the more true in societies that place a premium on pluralism, maintaining that all perspectives are equally valid and true. That's the spirit of the age in the Western world. The only people who are not to be tolerated are those who are intolerant. Certainty means oppression.

I remember a conversation during one of our missional community gatherings where TC, mentioned before, shared some reflections on a book I had written. He said he liked it, but in his endearing way, he smiled and added, "You wrote with a little too much certainty for my liking though. How can you be so sure about your views?"

It might be tempting for us to discount such reflections, assuming they come from a person who just doesn't want to commit to anything. And only God knows if that's true. But I also understand them.

It reminds me of a disturbing story Rob Bell quotes in his book *Love Wins*. It comes from Renée Altson, who begins her book by detailing how she was abused as a child, much of which was spiritual abuse. "I don't mean new age, esoteric, random mumblings from half-Wiccan, hippie parents," she writes. "I mean that my father raped me while reciting the Lord's Prayer. I mean that my father molested me while singing Christian hymns."[1]

It gives me the shivers just thinking about it, leaving me utterly sick. This is obviously a tragic version of religion gone awry, but is it any wonder people like Altson would struggle with religious certainty and would perhaps gravitate to more pluralistic expressions of faith?

For so long, dogma has been used as a club by the powerful to beat people into conformity. It has been used to justify abuse. Divergent viewpoints and questions haven't been welcome and have often been punished, leading to unsurprising pushback and dissent.

This is the precise point Lesslie Newbigin makes in his aptly named book *The Gospel in a Pluralist Society*. "Part of the reason for the rejection of dogma," he writes, "is that it has for so long been entangled with coercion, with political power, and so with the denial of freedom—freedom of thought and of conscience." The results have been devastating, as he goes on to explain. "When coercion of any kind is used in the interests of the Christian message, the message itself is corrupted."

This doesn't mean we should bury or diminish the gospel. We just need to present it humbly and in its proper context. "We must affirm the gospel as truth, universal truth, truth for all peoples and for all times, the truth which creates the possibility of freedom," Newbigin continues. "But we negate the gospel if we deny the freedom in which alone it can be truly believed."[2]

That last phrase—"*truly* believed"—is key. We undermine the whole purpose of the gospel if people accept it under duress or through inducement. If we try to leverage anything other than a person's freely exercised agency, we contradict the whole aim of discipleship. God is looking for disciples who freely exercise their will to choose Him, not immature children who are bribed or manipulated into conformity.

I have sat in enough evangelism classes to know the tricks. We were taught how to cue the music right as we slid into the altar call, hoping to play to people's emotions as we invited them to decision.

I remember one evangelist I worked with many years ago who was trying to secure a decision for baptism from a gentleman. The problem was that the man smoked and this disqualified him in the evangelist's mind. So he decided to resort to one of his go-to moves: he visited the man in his house, sat down with him in his living room and placed a pack of cigarettes on top of a Bible. And then in a very dramatic voice, he started into his pitch. "What are you going to choose, brother?" he asked him, "God or these cigarettes? The Bible or these cigarettes?" I don't remember what ended up happening with the guy, but the moment—even way back then—felt uncomfortable and manipulative to me.

To be clear: I don't at all doubt the evangelist's sincerity, and I quite liked him. I don't even doubt that these types of methods should perhaps be used at times to call people to decision. But I just came to the place where I'd rather err on the side of freedom, avoiding anything that could be mistaken for manipulation or pressure.

No-one's eternal destiny rests that firmly in my hands anyway. Jesus died so that I didn't have to be anyone's saviour. And the cross shows us that the only tactic God uses to win people is non-coercive love. He appeals to people's agency, trying to draw and attract, rather than trying to compel and intimidate. Manipulation and pressure are fundamentally at odds with God's character as revealed at the cross.

In the current landscape, where many people in the West look suspiciously at anyone who appears to have a hidden or self-serving agenda—be they slick televangelists or the Bible-thumping Christian next door—we can't afford to be anything but fully respectful of people's freedom and agency.

FUNCTIONAL PLURALISM

As I navigated the missional landscape, I came to realise God was inviting me to take on the posture of a *functional* pluralist. I didn't become a *philosophical* pluralist, believing that every viewpoint is equally valid or that all religions basically teach the same thing and offer equal insight into God. But I began sitting with people with a posture of humility, giving up my inclination to prove them wrong or argue them into truth.

Like Paul, to the pluralists I became a pluralist, that I might win the pluralists. But I still *fully* subscribed to the gospel and all its multifaceted truth.

In fact, I didn't become a functional pluralist *despite* my belief in the gospel but *precisely because of it*.

I came to realise that the more grounded and secure I was in Jesus, the less I felt threatened by different perspectives. I didn't need to prove anyone wrong because my security didn't come from being right. This was a critical realisation for me. I began to see that dogmatism in my demeanour was a reflection of insecurity in my heart.

The truth is, the less certain we are in our beliefs, the more combative and argumentative we are. This might seem counterintuitive, but this is what I observed in my own heart—and I'm willing to bet it's true of you too.

The reason we raise our voices and flex our rhetorical muscles to "protect" our beliefs is because we feel they're being threatened, causing us to question—usually subconsciously—their veracity. And for people, especially those within my faith community, who think our security comes from believing the right things and protecting ourselves against deception, it's an uncomfortable and scary thing to feel we might not have it all right. It undermines our feeling of safety and perceived standing with God.

When we're insecure in the gospel, we tend to try to mark our intellectual turf, acting like we know everything. We get our value and worth from being the smartest person in the room and feel threatened by divergent perspectives. Everything becomes black and white and absolute, and we have no room for nuance. But opinionated people are some of the most insecure people in the world. And they are also some of the most annoying—which doesn't lend itself to great missional success.

It was a revelation to me when I came across Brené Brown's comments about the tendency in religion to think in terms of absolutes. "In an uncertain world," she writes, "we often feel desperate for absolutes. It's the human response to fear."[3]

She's not saying, of course—nor am I—that there are no absolutes. She's simply saying fear drives the need for security, to be able to control something. And since we have a hard time controlling what happens outside of us, black-and-white thinking and clinging to absolutes give us some sense of control over our lives.

This is especially true for people who have experienced significant trauma or abuse in their formative years. Unless the trauma is identified and healed, their thinking will tend to be very black and white later in life, giving them some sense of control as a way of dealing with the things done to them over which they had no control.

I used to think the more spiritually mature a person was, the more black and white they'd be. Living with a lot of grey showed a lack of spiritual commitment and maturity. But then I began to realise just the opposite was true.

We see this in the way we develop as humans. Children are only able to think in concrete terms. They can't think in abstracts. In fact, their survival depends on them thinking in black and white. This is why I tell my little six-year-old, Winnie, that she is never, *ever*, *ever* to run onto the street. This is an absolute command, the disobedience of which could end in disaster. She simply isn't mature enough to think abstractly, determining for herself if it's safe enough to retrieve a ball that's rolled onto the street.

But the older we get, the more our brain is able to process abstract concepts and sort through multiple scenarios. We start to understand that the world is complicated and full of nuance, and we need to start living by principles rather than rules. If you went for a run with Winnie in 10 or 20 years' time and you came to a crosswalk and she refused to cross, saying, "My daddy told me to never, *ever* run out onto the street," you would justifiably conclude something had gone seriously wrong with her mental development.

This is the same with our spiritual development. Life in general, and the spiritual life specifically, is a lot more complicated than many Christians understand. That's chiefly because human beings are complicated. We're not machines. And so we need to learn how to navigate the messiness of relationships by applying the principles of God's law of love in ways that are unique to each situation.

It's no wonder that for many Christians, rules-based religion rather than relationship-based religion feels a lot safer. It gives us a much greater sense of control and we feel a lot more secure when we can just do what we're told. It takes the guesswork out. Rules also don't hurt us. Relationships, even the best ones, do.

It makes sense that people who are overly focused on following the rules usually have a hard time with relationships. Such people are not equipped to navigate the complicated and messy world of relationships. No two people on the planet live by the exact same rules. And so if I allow someone into my life who thinks or acts differently than me, my sense of security and control become undermined.

This does not mean there are no absolutes or that anything goes. It just means there are probably a lot *fewer* absolutes than many of us have been led to believe. Much of what we label "absolute" is usually just an extra layer of protection, like the "fence around the Torah," guarding us from going too close to whatever it is that threatens our feeling of safety. The further we can stay away from it, the more secure we feel—like if I were to tell Winnie that she should not only stay off the street but stop 10 feet before the end of the driveway.

When Winnie is 26, she will understand there are in fact occasions when it's OK to run out onto the street. But she will also understand that she should still never, ever jump in front of a moving car. She won't need the "fence around the Torah" anymore because her mental development will have advanced enough to understand the principle behind what Daddy once told her.

What all this means on a practical missional level is that when we're firmly grounded in God's love as our *only* basis for security, we can sit with people with a posture of humility and not feel threatened by anything they might say. If *everything* I need is found in Jesus, I have nothing to lose. He can't be taken away from me. I'm secure in Him. He's my safety, He's my hope. Jesus is my certainty—my dogma is *not*.

We don't need to attack people for disagreeing with us. We don't need to correct them for potentially heretical views. We can feel free to listen more than we need to talk, knowing our humble posture is as much a witness as anything we might say.

This was a big discovery for me. I realised I had based much of my security on believing the right information, which seems to be pretty common within my faith community. I also had a huge fear of deception, worried that one little misstep could start me down the slippery slope to apostasy. But our only safety against deception comes by relating to Jesus as a *Person*, not as a *proposition*. We aren't safe because of *what* we know but because of *Who* we know.

I don't wish to imply a false dichotomy, of course. To know Jesus as a *Person*, we also have to know propositions *about* Him and His word. It also doesn't mean we get wishy-washy with our beliefs or blow whichever way the wind goes. Even as we take a posture of humility, there's still a critically important place for confidence.

But it's a *humble* confidence—a confidence that doesn't stem from being infallibly right but from being infinitely loved. There's a world of difference between the two. A confidence based on being infallibly right is off-putting and unappealing, and it ultimately makes knowledge our saviour. On the other hand, a confidence based on our belovedness is incredibly attractive and wholly disarming, bringing true humility and healing.

NOTHING TO LOSE AND EVERYTHING TO LEARN

Not only do we have nothing to lose when we're secure in Jesus, we actually have everything to learn. This certainly applies to our understanding of God. In fact, it *especially* applies to our knowledge of God. It's a big world out there and the knowledge of even the most brilliant human is exceedingly small.

I know this may come as a shock to some, but God didn't stop revealing Himself to us in 1517 or 1888 or 1915. There is still more to learn. I even get the impression we'll be learning more about God throughout eternity. God is big and the human mind is small, so we will never exhaust God's knowledge.

This should propel us into new understandings and revelations of God. Sometimes these will come through our own study of Scripture, and sometimes they'll come through the mouths of donkeys or atheists.

I know this perhaps sounds scary to some of us who've been led to believe we can't learn anything from sources outside of Scripture or from anyone outside our religious tribe. But I just don't find this to be a scriptural idea at all.

It gives me great pause that the only people ready for the birth of Jesus were the magi, a group of non-Jews "from the East" who some propose observed the Zoroastrian religion. That the people who were supposed to know the Scriptures so well—the Jews—all missed the "signs of the times" announcing Jesus' birth and yet a group of superstitious astrologers was prepared, calls me to a deep place of humility.

Another intriguing example, pointed out by Lesslie Newbigin, is Peter's experience with Cornelius. Peter was originally headstrong and opinionated. He also felt a fair amount of his security came from meticulously following Jewish custom, which prohibited sitting at the table with non-Jews. So when the Spirit invited him to eat with Cornelius, he was apprehensive.

But the experience with Cornelius opened his eyes. He realised the Holy Spirit had come upon the Gentiles also, which was paradigm-shattering for Peter. Thus, as Newbigin points out, while we usually think of this story as the conversion of Cornelius, it's just as accurate to say that it was the conversion of Peter—through the hands of a Gentile.

"It is essential to the integrity of our witness," Newbigin writes, "that we recognise that to be [Christian] witnesses does not mean to be the possessors of all truth." He even goes so far to say that "there is indeed a proper place for agnosticism in the Christian life."[4] This is an agnosticism in the broadest sense of the term—which simply means to not know.

We simply *don't know* everything, and the reality is that this is completely fine. Our security does not come from knowing everything—saying "I don't know" is actually quite endearing.

My own faith community, which often prides itself on feeling we have the fullest knowledge of truth, itself picked up some beliefs along the way from others outside our faith. We learned the idea of the Sabbath from a Seventh-day Baptist, for example!

This doesn't mean *everything* is up for grabs or that we don't share truth. God is certainly inviting us to share with people the hope that is within us when opportunities arise (see 1 Peter 3:15, 16). But when we do share truth, we do so with a spirit of humility. It's more testimony than prescription. We don't attack people or speak in dogmatic terms. We bear witness to the truth as that which has changed us rather than presenting it as objective truth that others *must* accept if they want to avoid eternal damnation or receiving the mark of the beast or whatever looming threat we typically utilise to compel a decision.

I find that people in our post-Christian contexts aren't as closed to the gospel as some would have us believe. And I've yet to find a non-Christian who has been derogatory or demeaning when they've found out I'm a Christian. The response I get is a lot more gracious and curious, usually something more along the lines of, "Oh, you're a Christian? But you're nice."

We just have to be less dogmatic and more humble.

That's the cool thing about pluralism. It is open to all ideas so long as they are presented with humility and grace—so long as we are willing to be *functional* pluralists when we come to the table with our good news.

11

NOT ALL WHO WANDER ARE LOST

Rob Bell begins his book *Love Wins* in a thought-provoking way. He spends the first few pages discussing the tendency within some Christian circles to act as though it's clear who's in and who's out when it comes to salvation.

He recounts a time his church hosted an art show that focused on peacemaking, inviting artists to share work that communicated their understanding of peacemaking. Included in one woman's offering was a quote from Mahatma Gandhi, the Indian dissident who used nonviolent resistance to help liberate India from British rule.

Many people found the quote inspiring, but not all. Someone attached a paper to the woman's work with these words: "Reality check: He's in hell."

In his typically ironic way, Bell responds in the book with incredulity. "Really?" he wonders. "Gandhi's in hell? He is? We have confirmation of this? Somebody knows this? Without a doubt?"[1]

He then spends the next few pages taking pot shots at various versions of Christian salvation fraught with inconsistencies. Much of it is low-hanging fruit, but it's classic Rob Bell, full of more questions than answers, and it's mostly spot-on.

Perhaps my favourite part is when he tackles whether people's salvation is dependent on other people telling them about Jesus. "If our salvation, our future, our destiny is dependent on others bringing the message to us, teaching us, showing us," he wonders, "what happens if they don't do their part?" And then he asks this question, pregnant with ironic beauty: "What if the missionary gets a flat tire?"[2]

This is the liberating truth I always understood theoretically but only fully appreciated practically as I spent more and more time with people who showed little indication they were inching closer to Jesus because of my missional efforts: no-one's eternal destiny is resting in our finite hands. God loves people too much for their salvation to be riding on our ability to explain the gospel in just the right way.

This is an extremely comforting realisation, allowing us to just sit with people in humility without thinking it all depends on us to "seal the deal." We can leave our clever sales pitches behind, freeing us to relate to people as people, not salvation projects.

This is also why we can become *functional* pluralists as we discussed in the previous chapter. Not only do we realise *our* security is not threatened by others' disagreement with us; *their* security is not threatened by their disagreement with us either.

THE OUTSIDERS ARE THE INSIDERS

Of course, Jesus spent plenty of time confronting the salvation schemes of His own day. Listening to Him leaves one with the dizzying impression that no-one can be quite sure who's in or who's out. All human standards of judgment crumble and fall.

One thinks of the people Jesus talks about who did all these impressive religious activities and yet missed the point. As *The Message* puts it: "I can see it now," Jesus says, "at the Final Judgment thousands strutting up to me and saying, 'Master, we preached the Message, we bashed the demons, our God-sponsored projects had everyone talking.' And do you know what I'm going to say? 'You missed the boat. All you did was use me to make yourselves important. You don't impress me one bit. You're out of here'" (Matthew 7:21–23).

Then there's the parable about the Pharisee and the tax collector who go to the temple to pray. The Pharisee boasts of his holiness, thanking God he's not like the wretched tax collector. "I fast twice a week and tithe on all my income," he brags. The tax collector, meanwhile, can't even look up. He's so ashamed and asks simply for God's mercy. The crowd must have been shocked when Jesus dropped the punchline: "I tell you, this sinner, not the Pharisee, returned home justified before God" (Luke 18:9–14, NLT).

And then there's the time Jesus astoundingly tells the religious leaders that "crooks and whores" will enter His kingdom before them (see

Matthew 21:31, *The Message*). Or the story of a man who was left for dead beside the road and a priest and another holy man pass by him, only to have a Samaritan—a despised, hated, apostate Samaritan—come by and help him.

And on and on it goes.

Over and over again, Jesus astonishes His audiences with great reversal after great reversal. He totally flips the script. The insiders are the outsiders and the outsiders are the insiders. As Lesslie Newbigin notes, when it comes to the judgment, in Jesus' teaching, "the emphasis is always on surprise. It is the sinners who will be welcomed and those who are confident that their place was secure who will find themselves outside."[3]

Perhaps the best example of this is the parable Jesus tells about the sheep and the goats, representing the two classes of people on judgment day. The goats don't make it because they failed to minister to Jesus—feeding Him, clothing Him, caring for Him. The sheep, however, do. Neither are aware they've ever had an encounter with Him or the opportunity to serve Him. They're confused. "Truly I tell you," Jesus says to the sheep, "whatever you did for one of the least of these brothers and sisters of mine, you did for me" (Matthew 25:40, NIV).

It's quite astounding really. There are people in this world who are serving Jesus and yet don't even realise it. They are, as Paul says to the Romans, unaware of God's law of love and yet keeping it, because the law is "written in their hearts" (Romans 2:15) by the Spirit.

Simply put, there are people who love Jesus who don't even know they love Jesus.

I think of my friend Howard, who's a classic example of this. I absolutely love Howard. He's one of my favourite people in the world. He's an older Jewish gentleman with a quintessential Brooklyn accent who lives in Bangor. We spend lots of time together and much of it consists of him making fun of me for not believing in evolution, which I take in stride. He studied at Columbia University and then taught high school science for many years, serving also as a Maine state senator. Evolution is his mistress and nature is his god. "When I'm in nature," he tells me, "I feel God."

Not long ago, Howard and I were chatting, when he suddenly got serious and said to me, "You know, I have to tell you, Reverend," using the humorous title he likes to use for me. "I love Jesus. I really do. And I try to be like Jesus. He was really a great man."

Howard doesn't believe Jesus is any sort of saviour, of course, but he greatly admires His message and ministry of love. And I see that in Howard's life. Not that he's perfect, but he loves people, he helps people, and he wants to be a better and kinder person. Every summer he takes off to his cabin, two hours away in the woods, but he returns every weekend—not to go to synagogue but to serve at the Salvation Army soup kitchen. "I might skip synagogue," he tells me, "but I never miss serving at the Salvation Army."

I don't know what's really going on in Howard's heart. But I have a sneaky suspicion his life is a lot closer to the sheep in Jesus' parable than many of us Jesus-followers. And I wouldn't be surprised if on judgment day Jesus said to him, "Well done, good and faithful servant... Enter into the joy of your lord" (Matthew 25:23).

There are many Christians who can't tolerate such a perspective. They think God will keep people out over legalities, insisting only those who *explicitly* utter the name of Jesus will be saved. This will, of course, leave out *lots* of people throughout human history who never even got the chance to hear Jesus' name, let alone utter it.

But in Jesus' words, "Not everyone who says to me, 'Lord, Lord,' will enter the kingdom of heaven, but only the one who does the will of my Father who is in heaven" (Matthew 7:21, NIV). Jesus is not looking for those who *say* the right things or the right prayers; He's looking for those who, to whatever degree they're aware of the principles of selfless, other-centred love, choose to align themselves with them.

After all, John makes this audacious claim: "*Everyone* who loves is born of God" (1 John 4:7). Notice the word *everyone*. That's pretty inclusive. Not that anyone is perfect when it comes to love. But apparently what's most important to God is whether we're growing in our capacity to and practice of love.

The way we treat others is more indicative of whether we've aligned ourselves with the culture of heaven than whether we've said a prayer or been baptised or committed to a list of doctrines. Entrance into eternal life is not some legal paperwork God does, determined by whether we've checked the right boxes. To be sure, we don't earn God's love by the things we do. But when Christ's love truly reaches our hearts it changes us progressively into His image, manifesting in the way we treat others.

I've seen YouTube videos by so-called evangelists who descend upon unsuspecting people on the streets. They'll ask the victims if they think they'll get to heaven, and when the respondents say they think so because they are a "good person," the evangelist will quote a Bible verse, supposedly indicating it doesn't matter how good a person is—if they don't believe in Jesus, they won't pass the judgment.

But I can't imagine God, who wants everyone to be saved, looking my friend Howard in the eye and saying, "Oh, man. So close. *So close.* You were really kind to people and loved and helped so many. But, sorry man, you didn't check the right box off, saying you believe in Jesus. I can't let you in."

This isn't universalism—the belief that *everyone* will be ultimately saved. The verses cited above clearly indicate there will be many who end up on the outside—not because they didn't say the right words— "Lord, Lord"—but because they failed to allow God's love to transform the way they treated others.

While it isn't universalism, it's an acknowledgment that God's love for all is universal, His death was universal, His forgiveness is universal, and His desire for all to live eternally is universal. And He's looking for every excuse to get people in, not keep as many as He can out.

Neither am I saying that Scripture teaches that the things we do have any merit to them, as though our good life curries favour with God. It's simply to say that a life of *true* good works and charity is a reflection of whether faith is active in our hearts—to whatever degree the Spirit has revealed Himself to us.

I was intrigued when I came across this provocative proposal from Ellen White as well. It feels like it does justice to what I see in Scripture. "Those whom Christ commends in the judgment," she writes, "may have known little of theology, but they have cherished His principles. Through the influence of the divine Spirit they have been a blessing to those about them." She adds further, "When the nations are gathered before Him, there will be but two classes, and their eternal destiny will be determined by what they have done or have neglected to do for Him in the person of the poor and the suffering."[4]

THE MISSIONAL IMPLICATIONS

All this has significant missional implications, determining the posture we take when we're discipling others. When we have the impression that a person's eternal destiny is at stake in every conversation we have

101

with them, it's bound to ramp up the intensity of our exchanges. Our conversation can't be one of mutual encouragement and support, and we inevitably spend our time trying to figure out ways to convert the person, rather than sitting with them in humility and disinterested love.

Feelings of superiority, smugness and condescension creep in, which wreak havoc on any relationship. As Lesslie Newbigin astutely notes, "It is almost impossible for me to enter into simple, honest, open, and friendly communication with another person as long as I have at the back of my mind the feeling that I am one of the saved and he is one of the lost."[5]

All this is quite off-putting, undermining the very thing many well-meaning evangelists think they're trying to accomplish.

This is not to say, of course, that we never share the good news of God's kingdom of love, convinced everyone will live forever anyway. We still eagerly proclaim the gospel when invited, bearing witness to the beautiful and unique truth of God's love in Christ. We just do so in ways that aren't demeaning or pressure packed.

I'll never forget one occasion when I was at Bagel Central with my group of Jewish friends, including Howard, and we somehow got to talking about what it means to be righteous. Everyone was offering their opinions, when suddenly one person turned to me and said, "Shawn, how do you think a person can be righteous?"

The table seemed to collapse into silence.

It was quite a moment, as I realised I'd been given an opportunity to explain the gospel to a group of people that would likely never show up to my church.

I carefully explained faith to them—but not in a way that seemed "cheap" and transactional. I pointed out how Abraham believed God and it was accounted to him as righteousness and explained Jesus as the ultimate source of that righteousness.

I don't know if it moved anyone towards Jesus. No-one spoke to me privately after, asking for baptism. But that's not really the point anyway. No-one's eternal destiny was sitting in my hands that morning, which was a liberating thought that freed me to simply testify of Jesus with humility and grace, rather than ramping up the pressure and issuing an altar call.

I'm not saying there isn't a place to call people to decision, of course. But I need to always tread softly in so doing, lest I do more harm than good, supposing I'm anyone's saviour. Jesus is everyone's saviour, and He's simply called me—He's called *all of us*—to live among and intersect with others, seeking to serve, bless and testify of Him, if and when asked, then leave them in His capable hands.

A RADIOACTIVE EXPLOSION OF JOY

Some people might wonder, of course, whether this takes the impetus out of evangelism. After all, what's the point of evangelism if no-one's eternal destiny is on the line?

That's like asking why a grandparent should talk about their grandchildren—which is a silly question, of course! It just comes out! It's the overflow of joy. They can't help themselves.

The challenge is that too many of us approach evangelism from a place of scarcity, trying to gain more people to our team, rather than an outflow from our wholeness. Mission is about commodity acquisition—and with only a limited number of commodities, it becomes a zero-sum game.

I love how Lesslie Newbigin puts it. "At the heart of mission is thanksgiving and praise," he writes. "We distort matters when we make mission an enterprise of our own in which we can justify ourselves by our works.... The Church's mission began as the radioactive fallout from an explosion of joy. When it is true to its nature, it is so to the end. Mission is an acted out doxology. That is its deepest secret. Its purpose is that God may be glorified."[6]

What a powerful and captivating picture! Mission is not about justifying ourselves or saving others. It's an act of worship—the praise that pours from our lips and the love that goes forth from our hearts as we respond with gratitude to the reality of God's love.

I recognise there are many within my faith community who believe our concern is not simply whether people are saved but whether they're prepared to stand in the last days. Our job is to warn people about the coming apostasy, equipping them to resist deception. And since "time is short," we can't afford to sit around, passively journeying with them, peddling a wishy-washy message. We have a unique calling that is a matter of urgency, so the stakes are high.

I don't deny we're living in a unique time in human history, and there's a place to educate others—in broad strokes—about where we find ourselves prophetically. But the way to inoculate against deception isn't by stoking up fear. It is by focusing on Him who is the Truth. It's fear that will cause people to fall in the end, so why do we think we're doing people a service by presenting a message in a way that elicits fear? It makes no sense. The cure we're using to treat them is the same thing that causes the disease.

No less than Ellen White has put it this way: "The shortness of time is urged as an incentive for us to seek righteousness and to make Christ our friend. This is not the great motive. It savours of selfishness. Is it necessary that the terrors of the day of God be held before us to compel us through fear to right action? This ought not to be. Jesus is attractive. He is full of love, mercy, compassion."[7]

I get the impression there will be many surprises when it comes to who ends up on which side in the last days anyway. There will be many people who knew all the prophetic interpretations backwards and forwards, but who will nevertheless end up on the wrong side because they were never grounded in God's love rather than a fear-based message. And then there will be many others who never even heard about the "mark of the beast" but were discipled by the Spirit in the principles of non-coercive love and who will push back against anything that reeks of coercion and fear-based control when things ratchet up.

I'm so glad I can rest in the assurance that God is capable of preparing people eternally and prophetically, realising I can simply live out a humble witness of love and gratitude that doesn't make me anyone's saviour.

GOOGLING GOD

That doesn't mean I always remember this on a heart-level. Sometimes I get possessive with my mission and want to help the Spirit.

This makes me think of Trisha. She was one of the first friends Camille made after we moved to Bangor, having met her at a story time. They fast became friends, getting together for playdates, going out to eat with other girlfriends for "girls' nights out," coming to our house for birthday parties, and joining us regularly at the pool.

When we first met Trisha, her husband was in Asia, stationed there as a part of his military deployment. Since she was basically a single mom, we tried to support her as much as we could. And knowing I do a little photography, when she asked me to take pictures of her reunion with her husband after he returned from his 13-month military deployment, I eagerly agreed. It was such a beautiful and emotional moment to see him coming through those doors at the airport terminal, with his little daughter running up to him and Trisha awash in tears.

It was also an emotional experience when their son was born with a congenital heart defect a year or so later. We drove two hours through a snowstorm to visit them in hospital in Portland just hours after his birth. We prayed with them and promised to continue to pray for them as the little guy fought for his life.

Fortunately, he came through it, living a relatively normal life since then. But unfortunately, not long after he was born, Trisha's husband got deployed to Asia again, leaving her a single mom of two kids, with all the stresses that brings.

A few days after her husband left, Camille and I took Trisha and her kids out to eat, going to a restaurant with outside seating along the riverfront. We wanted to let her know we were eager to help however we could during such a difficult time. She thanked us and put on a brave face, but we could tell she was understandably struggling.

As we waited for our food, the kids ran out onto the grass to play, and while Camille slipped away to the bathroom, Trisha and I continued the conversation. She told me about an interesting experience she'd had with her daughter, who'd just started first grade. "She has a classmate whose father is starting a new church," she said. "So the classmate is talking to her about God. And she came home a few days ago and asked me, 'Mommy, who's God?'"

With an embarrassed look on her face, Trisha told me she had no idea what to say. Trisha had been raised in a nominal Catholic home but hadn't hung on to much of it after her teen years. "So, Shawn," she sheepishly continued, "after she went to bed, I was actually googling God so I could figure out what to tell her."

We had a little chuckle about that, then Camille returned and the food came, and the conversation diverted to another topic. But later that night after I shared with Camille what Trisha had told me, I said, "I think she was opening the door to learn more about God. Maybe you should offer to get together to talk about the story of God."

After some prayerful consideration, Camille reached out to Trisha and offered to come over to her house the next week and start sharing

God's story with her. Trisha accepted the invitation and the next week they got together.

When Camille returned home after a very long visit, she explained how the night had unfolded. After taking some time to introduce Trisha to the broad themes of God's story, Trisha eagerly asked Camille a bunch of religious questions. It was as though she had been stockpiling questions through the years we'd known her, curious about the way we lived. "What's the deal with this Sabbath thing?" she wanted to know. "And does Shawn get more money if he gets more people to come to his church?" And on and on it went for a long time. It was a surreal moment for Camille.

Unfortunately, the good energy they'd experienced didn't gain any momentum. As often happens, scheduling conflicts arose and future meetings got cancelled, reflecting the fact that the journey of discipleship is never a straight line.

And then the story took an unexpected turn: not long after Trisha's husband returned from his second deployment, he got reassigned to Texas. Within a few months they were gone—just like that.

It was a bit confusing to us. We felt so attached to Trisha and convinced God had placed us in her life to lead her to Jesus. We wanted to experience the joy of seeing a child brought into the mission and family of God, recognising the Spirit had clearly started that good work. But we ultimately came to a place of surrender, comforting ourselves with the recognition that it is God's work, and these are God's children, and we're owed nothing. Our part is to simply love and serve and bless for however long God has us in people's lives, grateful for the chance to nudge people a little closer to God's heart through our faithful witness.

But then the story took an even stranger twist. A few months after Trisha moved to Texas, Camille got a frantic phone call from her. Through desperate sobs and tears, she explained that her husband had left her and demanded she move back to Maine with the two kids. Their marriage was over.

It ripped Camille's heart out, as it did mine when she told me, though we were eager to reconnect with Trisha when she returned. We figured the story wasn't over and this was our next opportunity to participate in God's mission to Trisha. But as I said above, the journey of discipleship is never a straight line. Despite Camille's best efforts, she and Trisha never got off the launchpad again.

Before long we started noticing something interesting: Trisha began posting pictures on Instagram from the new non-denominational church the father of her daughter's classmate had started. And then the pictures turned into a weekly occurrence. Soon she was posting how she finally felt like she belonged somewhere. She even began teaching the children's classes.

I must admit, I had mixed emotions when all this began to transpire. I knew that, theoretically, I should just be happy that she'd finally committed to Christ. There's nothing greater than seeing someone surrender to Jesus. But I wanted Camille and me to be the ones to lead her "across the finish line." After investing so much time in her, I wanted her to be a part of *our* family—and each picture she posted of her time with *that* church family pricked my heart a little more with sadness over what could have been.

And what about truth? Shouldn't she embrace *my* truth—not some generic version of it, promoted by a non-denominational church? Wasn't she just being primed for deception, ill-prepared to resist the great apostasy when it arrives? Perhaps we weren't aggressive enough in our proclamation of "truth" to her, I wondered.

It took me a while but I finally came to a place of peace. God got me there. This isn't to say I never have moments of relapse. It's just that I now recognise more fully it's never been our job to save anyone. The Spirit is the ultimate discipler of people and our job, as N T Wright puts it, is to serve as "bit-part players" on the stage of salvation, who "come on for a moment, say one word, and disappear again, proud to have shared [Christ's] stage and, for a moment, been a tiny part of his action."[8]

Indeed, not all who wander are lost—and no-one's salvation rests in our hands, and their growth towards greater faith and understanding does not ultimately depend on us. We can just come alongside them, do our humble part, and trust everyone to God's capable hands.

FAMILY

TOGETHER AT THE TABLE

One of the hardest decisions we ever made was to stop celebrating Thanksgiving with my extended family.

My family—my mother's side—is very close, and we do a lot together. So the thought of forgoing Thanksgiving with them was very daunting.

But as we pondered what it would look like to be family together as a missional community, we began to realise it might mean moving away from our biological family a little and leaning into greater intimacy with our missional community.

It was the first time in 35 years of life I wasn't with my biological family for Thanksgiving. But it quickly became apparent that participating in God's mission doesn't result in loss. Just the opposite. That first year was the best Thanksgiving of my life and has been equalled each year since.

I think especially of our neighbour Dick. He lives across the street from us and we've been friendly ever since we moved into the neighbourhood a decade ago. But just as we started becoming more intentional about participating in God's mission, Dick, who is in his 80s and lives alone, became gravely ill. He was at death's door. Every day, for about a week, I'd go visit him, encourage him, pray with him, talk to him about hope. At that point, despite being raised in a church-going home, he didn't call himself a Christian but was definitely open, especially as death seemed imminent.

Over the course of his illness, we had many, many conversations about Jesus. He said he wanted to believe but just didn't feel worthy enough, concluding there was no way he would make it to heaven. I assured him there was a wideness to God's mercy, and he tried to cling to that hope.

Eventually, Dick made a miraculous recovery and occasionally found himself at our dinner table, with a standing invitation to join us every Friday evening for our traditional meal of vegetarian tacos, which was a new experience for this meat-and-potatoes guy. But he was a good sport, and we continued to do everything we could to look out for him, baking cookies and pumpkin bread for him, and taking him to dialysis at 6.00 am when he needed a ride.

As Thanksgiving approached that year, we invited him to join us. He'd met everyone in the group already, having come for our cookout, as well as seeing Cameron a time or two as a patient of his. But despite his appreciation for everyone, he said he had an old friend he'd enjoyed Thanksgiving with for over 30 years, so he was all set.

Two days before Thanksgiving though, our doorbell rang and Dick burst through the door with tears in his eyes. He blurted out, "I need to join you for Thanksgiving. My friend just dropped dead yesterday and I have nowhere to go."

We welcomed him to our table with open arms and drew him closer into the family. He kept saying throughout the day it was the best Thanksgiving he'd ever had. As I was processing the experience later, it dawned on me that Dick wouldn't have had anywhere to go, much less experienced his best Thanksgiving, if we hadn't decided to forego celebrating with my biological family.*

The next year was no less memorable. We realised our friends Manish and Shivani, mentioned earlier, didn't have anyone to celebrate with either. In fact, we soon discovered they'd never celebrated Thanksgiving with anyone in America, despite being here for over a decade, so we eagerly invited them to our table as well.

It was just as memorable as the year before, with joy and laughter and good food and true thanksgiving. Shivani's sister, Puja, visiting from New York City, joined as well. She has an interesting background: she was raised Hindu, went to Christian and Jewish schools, and married a Muslim. A religious mutt, in many ways, but—like her sister—not quite sure about the whole God-thing. Having recently started in recovery though, she was beginning to commit to the idea of some Higher Power characterised by love, and we had awesome conversations about that.

---

* Sadly, during the editing process of this book, Dick passed away. I'm grateful I was able to visit with him in the hospital the night before his passing and perform his funeral a few days later.

It came as a pleasant surprise when Shivani later shared that Puja was eager to come to our church the next time she was in town. In fact, despite usually flying in to visit Shivani on Saturday mornings, she decided to fly up on a Friday night so she could attend our gathering the next morning. She had been drawn in by our missional community, drawn in by people who were the same but different, wanting to see what propelled our faith.

That's what happens when you invite people to the table.

TABLES, NOT PULPITS

I bet if you were to ask many church people today what symbol best represents the life of the church, many would say the pulpit does. This is understandable and largely justified. Since the Protestant Reformation, when Scripture was translated into the language of the people, the life of the church has been based upon the proclamation of the Word.

Until that point, people couldn't access the Word. They were at the mercy of the church to mediate that Word to them, and often church authorities did so in ways that furthered their agenda but beat down the people with guilt and shame.

One way they did this was by proclaiming that apart from the Eucharist—the bread and the wine that only a priest could distribute—there was no access to God. Through these symbols, which the church held to be the literal body and blood of Christ, the church *possessed* God and the people had to go to the church to access Him.

All that changed when Scripture became available to the people and they started to understand that God could be accessed by each person individually by reading and hearing the Word. They didn't have to go to a priest anymore to encounter God. They could relate to God on their own, with Jesus as their glorious Mediator.

Ever since then, church life—in the Protestant world—has revolved around the pulpit. The sermon is the centre of the church's existence, leaving many with the impression that if they at least hear a sermon each week, they're right with God. Just as receiving the bread and wine prior to the Reformation was the way to curry God's favour, so today hearing a sermon is its own form of gaining God's acceptance.

As important as hearing the Word is, this is not the great symbol of the church, at least according to Scripture. God doesn't dole out points to us for sitting down and listening to someone else talk at us. It doesn't impress Him. In fact, Scripture talks about the dangers of taking that as our primary posture towards God. For example, Paul wrote, "it is not those who hear the law who are righteous in God's sight, but it is those who obey the law" (Romans 2:13, NIV).

Instead, if we paid close attention to the narrative of Scripture, noting particularly the actions of Jesus, we'd recognise the great symbol of the Jesus-movement is not, nor has it ever been, the pulpit. The great symbol of the Jesus-movement is the table, in all its glory and simplicity.

THE SON OF MAN CAME EATING AND DRINKING

The table was where Jesus did more ministry than any other place. We repeatedly read of Him coming alongside people, sharing meals with them and living out and expounding upon God's kingdom.

Tim Chester points out something fascinating in this regard. He notes how the Gospels describe three occasions that the "Son of Man came…" "The Son of Man came not to be served but to serve, and give Himself as a ransom for many," Mark says (Mark 10:45). "The Son of Man came to seek and to save the lost," Luke offers (Luke 19:10). And "the Son of Man has come eating and drinking" (Luke 7:34).

"The first two are statements of purpose," Chester writes. "*Why* did Jesus come? He came to serve, to give his life as a ransom, to seek and save the lost. The third is a statement of method. *How* did Jesus come? He came eating and drinking."[1]

In other words, the way Jesus pursued His mission of seeking and saving the lost, of giving His life as a ransom, was through sitting at the table with people, eating and drinking. As Chester says, Jesus' "mission strategy was a long meal, stretching into the evening. He did evangelism and discipleship round a table…Jesus didn't run projects, establish ministries, create programs, or put on events. He ate meals." He adds that "in the ministry of Jesus, meals were enacted grace, community and mission.…meals are more than metaphor. They embody God's grace."[2] In that sense, "doing lunch was doing theology."[3]

We probably don't fully appreciate just how subversive Jesus was being through such a posture. The rabbis had strict rules of what they called "table fellowship." Devout Jews couldn't just eat with anyone. To sit at a table with someone meant one implicitly approved their behaviour. So when Jesus sat down at the table with sinners and prostitutes and tax collectors, it mortified their religious sensibilities. He was essentially saying they had a place in His kingdom, they were welcome at God's table.

That's why the religious leaders always complained about who Jesus ate with. "This Man receives sinners and eats with them," they'd frequently grumble (see Luke 15:1).

Jesus used food to unite, to draw people in and bring God's love to them. Sharing a meal told people they had dignity and worth, they belonged in the family. Everyone was equal around the table, beloved of God.

It's quite fascinating what eating together does, actually. Eating causes the body to release various hormones, like dopamine and endorphins, which boost feelings of pleasure. Perhaps more significantly, scientists have discovered the body also releases oxytocin when we eat. Oxytocin is the same chemical that bonds a mother to her child, for example, when breastfeeding. Some have dubbed oxytocin the "love hormone" because of its ability to attach people to one another emotionally.[4]

So when we share a meal together, the body literally releases hormones designed to produce feelings of mutual pleasure and connection among the participants. It binds hearts together in an emotional and physiological way!

It's no wonder Jesus used the table as His main form of mission, of sharing life. In so doing, He created mutual feelings of connection and enjoyment, communicating, through embodiment, what God's kingdom of love is all about. It's also why the church of Acts often broke bread together. It was not simply the act of modern communion—eating a stale cracker and a thimble-full of grape juice. This was the early church sitting at the table together, sharing life, embodying the theology of God's radical, all-inclusive grace.

As we began noticing these realities in Scripture, our missional community started prioritising the table more and more, realising its effectiveness in welcoming people into God's family. We started seeing that sitting at the table together isn't something we do in addition to church; it is one of the most foundational expressions of church.

Think about it: welcoming others into your home is one of the most vulnerable and authentic ways you can pursue God's mission. You are opening yourself up to be seen on the most intimate level, allowing people to get a front-row seat to what truly makes you tick and the values that drive you—and sometimes even your dysfunction. They see what's on your bookshelf, how clean your bathroom is, how you treat your children when they're acting up.

In many ways, it's a lot easier to just invite people to a church service than to invite them to your table. You can keep them at arm's length at a church service and mysteriously disappear when it's convenient.

One thing Camille and I have identified when it comes to our own anxiety about welcoming people to our table is the uncertainty that comes with not knowing when people might leave! We've had people stay for hours and hours, and that can sometimes cramp our schedule. But we know God is calling us into deeper alignment with His mission, embodying what it means to be His family to the world.

Of course, the other side of the coin is no less intimidating. In many ways, sitting at someone else's table is even more vulnerable and meaningful. Doing so communicates we trust the people who invited us, despite not knowing what exactly is in any particular dish or just how clean their hands were when they made it. Showing up at their table is the embodiment of bringing God's kingdom of love into every home.

It reminds me of a story Jim Peterson tells about his friend Mario, who was a hardened atheist. The two studied Scripture together for a long time, and after four years Mario finally gave his heart to Christ.

A few years later, they were reflecting on the journey and Mario asked Jim if he knew what made him decide to follow Jesus. Jim thought of all their in-depth discussions and the airtight philosophical arguments he had made, figuring they were most pivotal. But Mario saw it differently.

"Remember that first time I stopped by your house?" Mario asked, "We were on our way someplace together and I had a bowl of soup with you and your family. As I sat there observing you, your wife, and your children, and how you related to each other, I asked myself, 'When will I have a relationship like this with my fiancée?' When I realised that the answer was 'never,' I concluded I had to become a Christian for the sake of my own survival."

Jim remembered the time. But he remembered it a bit differently, recalling his frustration with his children's behaviour and how he had to correct them in front of Mario. It shows that God doesn't require perfection for us to invite people to our table and embody His love.[5]

This gives me great hope. Truly, it doesn't take a lot. The food doesn't have to be gourmet, the house spotless or the children perfect angels.

People will put up with lots of imperfect peripherals so long as they feel they belong. God can take our simple willingness and multiply it for His glory.

THE TABLE I LONG FOR

But truth be told, as we continued our journey, I began to realise I needed to feel I belonged at the table just as much as anyone else. I needed to feel the radical hospitality of Jesus as embodied in His family.

I remember one Friday night when we were all sitting around the living room at Cameron and Ellie's house, devouring the delicious bread Ellie typically made, reflecting on the week we all just had. Ellie is an incredible host who has a heart and a gift for hospitality, and she loves cooking and welcoming people into her home. And this Friday night was no different. But that particular week I had been beaten up and beaten down by people pushing back against the vision we were trying to pursue. The anxieties were weighing heavily on my heart and I was looking for some sympathy.

As I looked at the wider Christian world, I realised I was a man who, to a large extent, didn't belong at anyone's table. While traditional Christianity was pretty obvious in its exclusionary practices, it felt like those with a progressive bent weren't much better. We all draw our lines and exclude people from our tables for various reasons along the philosophical spectrum.

In the case of those who esteemed themselves as "open-minded" and progressive, I felt a lack of passion for the beautiful story of Scripture and the reality of the cross. Jesus was merely a good example, showing us *how* to love, but not a Saviour who came to rescue us with His love.

It thus seemed that for many, sitting at the table was a humanistic mandate, following the *example* of Christ, but lacking anything that really gripped and changed the heart. But this wasn't my experience. I came to believe that scriptural orthodoxy is not at odds with sitting at the table; on the contrary, *true* orthodoxy—beautiful, rich, Scripture-based orthodoxy—is its true source.

I started to feel something deep within me: progressive Christianity—with its cross-less gospel—left me feeling empty; conservative Christianity—with its gospel-less cross—left me feeling beaten down.

It left me longing for a table to which I could truly belong, reminding me of a poignant thought I'd read from Henri Nouwen: "I am the prodigal son every time I search for unconditional love where it cannot be found."[6] I felt like a prodigal without a home and a table, searching for love and acceptance from people who would never give it to me.

As we sat there that night, sharing our hearts, I felt an urge to unburden myself and admit my aloneness, to receive from others the embodied and unrelenting love of Jesus. But I was hesitant to open up, to share the dirty laundry of ministry. After all, pastors are often told to do ministry but not to receive ministry. We can't truly let our guard down and be known by those we lead lest we undermine our ability to serve.

Others seem to think pastors are supposed to be perfect, free from any weakness or struggle. And besides, as someone with my own insecurities, I'm always self-conscious when I feel I'm talking about myself too much.

Sensing I was carrying a heavy burden, Jim spoke up and encouraged me in grace. "Bro," he said, "don't feel like you have to carry this alone. Don't feel like you can't share with us. We're here for you. And if you want to lead us into full, authentic community, you must lead by example."

It reminds me of what Brené Brown wrote in her magnificent book, *The Gifts of Imperfection*. "Until we can receive with an open heart," she says, "we are never really giving with an open heart. When we attach judgment to receiving help, we knowingly or unknowingly attach judgment to giving help."[7] This is staggering. Vulnerability is a two-way street and when we fail to model it ourselves, it undermines our goal of getting others to share their hearts.

Jim's words were the permission I needed. I opened up and felt love wash over me. Everyone around the table spoke grace into my heart. I realised the table was for me no less than everyone else. I realised the unconditional love I was looking for was found in the heart of God and embodied in His family, however imperfectly they were doing it.

Some time later, a friend of mine, who himself longed for a table where he could belong, shared something powerful that captivated my heart and imagination, reflecting what I'd started to experience within the family of God. It was part of a talk by Jeff Chu, entitled "Together at the Table," where he talked about how, growing up in a Chinese family, the table was the most important space they had. He talked about eating family-style, where the diversity of food matched the diversity of those around the table, and how he hoped the church could embody this.

The climax of the talk, though, is what gripped me. It's the part my friend shared, knowing it would resonate deeply with me. And that's exactly what it did. It touched something deep within me, putting in beautiful words what I had only felt viscerally up until then.

I shared it with our missional community as soon as I could, and it gripped them as well. We felt it perfectly encapsulated what we longed to be as a family. So we decided to read it at the beginning of every missional community gathering, taking turns, each reading a paragraph. It became our de facto "mission statement" of sorts.

Perhaps it will also captivate your heart, reaching down to the hidden longings you never realised you had:

> The table I long for, the church I hope for, is a place where we let others see where the spirit meets the wound, and we help heal those wounds.
>
> The table I long for and the church I hope for has the grace of the gospel as its magnificent centrepiece.
>
> The table I long for and the church I hope for is where we care more about our companions than about winning our arguments with them, where we set aside the condescension that accompanies our notion that we need to bring them our truth.
>
> The table I long for and the church I hope for has each of you sitting around it, struggling to hold the knowledge that you, vulnerable you and courageous you, are beloved by God, not just welcome but desperately and fiercely wanted.
>
> The table I long for and the church I hope for is made of rough-hewn humility, nailed together by a Jesus who has given us this ridiculous freedom to be wrong and yet still be made right.
>
> The table I hope for and the church I long for is a place where we love especially when it isn't easy, allowing us to be vulnerable, inviting every voice to join the conversation, pushing us meal by meal towards community, towards communion.
>
> Can we build that kind of table? Can we be that kind of church? I think so.
>
> And at that table, we're going to eat family style.[8]

13

BETTER TOGETHER

Shortly after starting our missional journey, I began noticing a phenomenon that kept surfacing during our missional conversations. It was one that initially perplexed me but began to make sense as I reflected on it more. The phenomenon was this: many of us would share exciting stories of individual mission, yet these relationships never seemed to really go anywhere.

The same people told stories week after week of things they did to bless or serve their co-workers or neighbours, yet there didn't seem to be any indication these efforts were nudging anyone closer to the journey of discipleship.

I realise, of course, these things take time. In fact, they take a *long* time. I recall reading somewhere, though I can't track it down for the life of me, that it takes a person—on average—four to five years to go from having no conscious interest in Christ to being consciously committed to Him. And that's just the average. For many, it will take a lifetime.

This is different than many of us are used to, especially within my faith community. We expect people to be ready to "sign up" for membership at the end of a five-week seminar. And they need to because Jesus is coming soon. We don't have time to waste. Discipleship must get fast-tracked. It's a matter of urgency.

While some certainly do and will come in this way, it's not the vast majority. That's because the people we usually draw in to these seminars are *already* a long way down the road of faith and attend our meetings because they have an existing curiosity about the material we advertise.

But such people are not the majority of the population in secular societies. The number of people sitting in their homes, consciously wondering what the book of Revelation means, is probably a fraction of even one percent in any given city—at least in the secularised context in which I reside. And yet these are basically the only people our traditional evangelism targets, leaving the other 99 per cent unreached.

This is not the type of people our missional community intersects with though. Many of the people we journey with are not even consciously interested in the gospel, never mind our particular understanding of it. It's not a matter of just adding a few Bible verses to their already-developed theology. When we connect with them, they aren't even aware they *have* a theology, let alone anything that resembles a *developed* theology. This means it's usually going to take a *long* time from point of contact to when they actually commit to Christ, if they ever do.

So I get all that. Yet at the same time, as I reflected on the way we were participating in God's mission, I started to realise a key ingredient was missing in our missional efforts: a community.

Simply put, God never intended for us to pursue mission on our own—as solo artists. Mission is a team sport. Jesus didn't send the disciples out to announce and live His kingdom as individuals. He sent them out in community, two-by-two, giving much greater power to their witness.

Lesslie Newbigin calls this the "hermeneutic of the gospel." *Hermeneutic* simply means *interpretation* or *explanation*. He's saying that if people want to know what the gospel is all about, they must look at the Christian community—they must look at the family of God—to understand it. It's as we live in community with one another that the gospel gets people's attention and begins to make sense.

"How is it possible that the gospel should be credible," Newbigin asks, "that people should come to believe that the power which has the last word in human affairs is represented by a man hanging on a cross? I am suggesting that the only answer, the only hermeneutic of the gospel, is a congregation of men and women who believe it and live by it."[1]

So this is the critically important bottom line: our missional witness will only be effective to the degree we pursue it together in community.

THE GOSPEL WE PREACH

Somehow, I missed this teaching in all my reading of Scripture. But there it is, hiding in plain sight in John's account of Jesus' final prayer before the cross. There, Jesus prays for Himself as He's about to die, thanking His Father that He's finished the work given Him. He then prays for His disciples, asking that they be kept from the evil one as they're sent into the world.

And then He comes to all those who would believe because of the disciples' mission in the world. Specifically, He prays that all these believers "may be one, as You, Father, are in Me, and I in You" (John 17:21). That's quite a prayer, quite a calling! Jesus desperately wants all His followers to be one *as* the Father and He are one. The same quality of oneness that He and the Father share is the same quality that He desires for His family.

This doesn't mean, of course, that all His followers should be clones of each other. Oneness and unity do not mean uniformity. We don't all need to look alike, talk alike, eat alike or worship alike. Neither do we need to believe alike on every little detail of Scripture.

The oneness Jesus prays for is that we would be one in our love for and commitment to each other. That we would be united in our desire to pursue His mission and be His family together. That we would be one in our practice of the fruit of the Spirit towards each other and united in our commitment to and belief in God's grand story.

As a matter of fact, our unity is a lot more impressive the more dissimilar we are. After all, if God can take a group of people who come from diverse backgrounds and cultures and unite them under the banner of the cross, that's quite a compelling argument for the believability of the gospel.

And that is precisely the point. Jesus doesn't pray His followers would be one for oneness' sake. Jesus prays that His family would be one so "that the world may believe that You sent Me" (John 17:21). Our experience together as family is actually what gives Jesus' mission credibility. What a mission!

My friend Laurence Burn, who served as a chaplain when I was in college, puts it this is way: "The way we live together is the gospel we preach." I really like that. Participating in God's mission is a lot less complicated than we've made it out to be. It doesn't require light and laser shows or million-dollar facilities or perfectly argued Revelation seminars. All Jesus is looking for is a group of humble followers willing to love each other.

And this is precisely what we see in the early church. According to Acts 2, the church's evangelistic strategy was extremely simple— almost too simple for our modern minds. Luke explains that the early church ate together, prayed together, learned together and shared their possessions with each other. They "did life together"—to use a popular expression today. And what was the result of all this oneness? Check this out: "And the Lord added to the church daily those who were being saved" (Acts 2:47).

For some, the word "and" seems out of place at the beginning of that sentence. Based on our preoccupation with million-dollar evangelistic strategies, with all the dog-and-pony shows we try in the never-ending pursuit of church growth, most of us act as though the word there should be "but" instead of "and." We live as though Luke has just explained that the early church did all these overly simplistic things in pursuit of true community, *but* God was merciful and added to their numbers, despite their pitiful evangelistic methods.

It's an "and" and not a "but" there though. The reason the early church enjoyed such explosive growth was *precisely because* they pursued such radical community under the banner of Christ's self-emptying love. That was their missional strategy. They didn't need all the gimmicky bells and whistles we think we need today. They practiced radical community in the midst of the world, showing the true power and potency of the gospel.

And maybe that's all God is looking for today. Maybe it's as simple as that. Maybe if we just lived out our *sentness* together, practicing radical community before the onlooking world, we'd experience the type of earth-shattering growth the early church did. Maybe we too would be accused of "turning the world upside down" as the early Jesus-communities were (see Acts 17:6).

I like to put it this way: the greatest argument in favour of Christianity is a gospel-centred community, living out Christ's love together. The family of God is God's missional silver-bullet. It's His ace in the hole.

SOLO LOVE?

What this means practically is that mission must be pursued *together*. While there are obviously moments of individual discipleship, we should seek to disciple others *in community*. This is what really gives force to our missional efforts.

Think of it this way: your neighbour or co-worker may be impressed with your selfless love, but if you're just an isolated individual, they could chalk up your niceness to any number of things. Perhaps you just naturally have a kind or friendly personality. But if they intersected with a *whole group* of selfless—though obviously imperfect—people, now *that* is attention-grabbing. It becomes much harder to explain away such a phenomenon.

Or maybe they've never seen forgiveness or reconciliation in real life. In a world starving for love, where many people come from painful homes where the price of reconciliation and forgiveness is too high, how will the truth about a forgiving God make sense to them? How will they ever understand what this means and whether it can be believed?

They will encounter it in the family of God. When they see imperfect human beings transformed by God's love to such a degree that they live it out towards each other, then the gospel will make sense and be believable.

But it takes a community; it takes a family.

This is why our missional community began to get intentional about pursuing mission *together*. We started connecting people with other members of our missional community as soon as we could. And as much as possible, when we attended an event or party that some of our friends put on, we'd bring as many people from our missional community to the event as we could.

ENCOUNTERING THE FAMILY OF GOD

Sarah and her husband Luke, mentioned before, were some of the first friends we made when we moved to Bangor, after Camille met Luke, who was a stay-at-home dad, at a library story time. We spent lots of time with them—getting pizza together, going hiking and swimming and doing all sorts of fun activities. They were completely unchurched and entirely unfamiliar with some of the most basic stories and characters in Scripture.

To be honest, at one point, if you'd asked us which of our friends were the least religiously inclined, we would have mentioned them without hesitation. We had picked up absolutely nothing that seemed to indicate they were the least bit interested in church or Christianity.

But we were entirely wrong, especially in Sarah's case. And it wasn't until much further down the road that a paradigm-shifting concept clicked for me: non-Christians won't hang out with Christians unless they're open to Jesus. It's that simple.

Think about it: why would a person who doesn't consciously believe in Jesus be comfortable hanging out with someone committed to living a Jesus-centred life unless they're actually open to Jesus? If a non-Christian is attracted to a Christian and wants to spend time with them, they're actually attracted to the Christ within and want to spend time with Him—even if they don't realise it (which is often the case).

This realisation is clarifying. It can help us realise the level of interest others might have in God. If we have people in our lives who keep leaning into relationship with us even after they learn we're Jesus-followers, it indicates they're more interested in Jesus than they may even be conscious of.

When this concept clicked for me, it helped me realise Sarah and Luke were a lot more open to Jesus than I had thought. And through a series of conversations, it became even more apparent that Sarah especially was more spiritually curious than I had originally realised.

So we started inviting them into more open conversations about God and connecting them more with our missional community. We would go to birthday parties they put on and our missional community would all show up to track meets their daughters Izzy and Lucy were running in.

A few months after we had the cookout at our house, which they attended, we invited them, along with a number of our other friends, to join us each Saturday afternoon to go through something we called "the story of God." It's a telling of the big teachings of Scripture in narrative form, introducing unchurched people to who God is and what His family and mission are all about.

We would all gather around the living room each week, in a very cosy and non-threatening environment, sipping hot drinks, listening to each other's stories, and then go through God's story.

For the first few weeks Sarah and Luke sat silently, quietly processing what they were hearing. We weren't sure what they thought about it, since it was all so unfamiliar to them. And I couldn't read them for the life of me.

Finally, a few weeks in, Sarah cleared her voice and raised her hand. Seeing her out of the corner of my eye, I turned to her and invited her to speak. I'll never forget what she said. "You know," she started, "I was just telling Luke on our drive here that this is the most loving group I have *ever* been around. And I don't even mean just religious groups. *Any* group."

My heart leapt for joy the minute the words came out of her mouth, realising that the power and credibility of the gospel, incarnated in His loving family, was reaching a searching heart. *This* was the "hermeneutic of the gospel" in action.

And that's what it's all about. Participating in God's mission actually isn't all that complicated, though it requires a lot. It means pursuing community to such a radical degree that it gets the world's attention. And when people encounter it—when they intersect with and observe a truly gospel-centred community—they will be drawn in.

I mentioned before that the church is called to be *missional* and not *attractional*. But this isn't the full picture. The church, when it is true to its calling, is *extremely* attractional. In fact, I'd argue that it is the most attractional organisation in the world.

But this is the point: it is *the church*—as a community of gospel-loving and gospel-living people—that is the attraction. When we live out God's kingdom of love *together* in the world, people will be drawn in and attracted to that.

It's not our nice buildings or exciting programs that give the gospel its attractive and irresistible power. It's the church—the family of God—living out the gospel in everyday life that is the most attractive force in the world.

This—the family of God—is so often the missing ingredient in our gospel witness.

14

THE ALLURE OF PSEUDO-COMMUNITY

I have a friend in another country who's been sharing with me about his struggle to find a church family, a table at which he can truly belong. He probably isn't unique in this regard, but the nature of his struggle is perhaps less common.

Elijah is a single male, who plans to remain that way for the kingdom of God. Elijah, you see, is gay, but has committed to a life of celibacy, putting him in the unenviable position of receiving disdain from people on "both sides of the aisle." Many traditional Christians are repulsed by his sexual orientation and certainly his choice to refer to himself as "gay," while those on the so-called progressive side look down on him for his supposedly prudish and antiquated religious commitments.

It has left him feeling like he doesn't have a true home.

What complicates things even more is the way his faith community, and many religious communities in general, has implicitly glorified marriage and the nuclear family. We talk as though marriage is the height of human existence and singlehood is simply a temporary stop along the way to the ultimate fulfillment of marriage. Church life revolves around the assumption that everyone has a family or will someday have one, and the "singles' ministries" we run are often nothing more than glorified dating services.

So, on the one hand, we tell him he can't get married—at least to someone of the same gender—but on the other hand just about everything we do and all the language we use is geared towards marriage and family life.

What's more, many would look suspiciously at him if he lived with someone from either gender. In traditional Christian faith communities, the idea of two people of the opposite gender co-habiting often raises eyebrows, yet the opposite is also true: if we know that a gay man is living with another man, we assume something uncouth is going on.

Whatever your views on sexuality are, I think we can all agree that the church leaves people like Elijah between a rock and a hard place, struggling with the desire to pursue their Christian convictions, yet feeling a lack of true Christian community that would help them achieve those convictions.

It's no wonder that the first time I asked Elijah what his biggest struggle was, he without hesitation said, "Loneliness."

All this has come to a head as he's looked for a church in a new city he recently moved to. After searching for a while, he settled on one with a more contemporary vibe that left him optimistic. The church had stripped the guise of formalism, ditching fancy clothes and ancient hymns, and emphasised inclusivity and grace. He even sensed the leaders would be accepting of his sexual orientation, which made him feel at ease.

But after a few weeks of attending, something still didn't quite feel right. And then he realised what it was: when the music ended and everyone exited the building each week, *church was over*. That was it. Everyone went back to their homes and spent the rest of the week with their spouses and kids and perhaps even occasionally a few church members when it could conveniently fit into their schedules. But that was it. Church was a two-hour gathering once a week but noticeably absent from the rest of life.

It left him to fend for himself the other 166 hours of the week.

Being friendly and welcoming and kind for two hours each week is good as far as it goes and a lot better than many other churches. But it's not church—and certainly not community—in any true sense of the word.

What Elijah discovered, and I have also seen repeatedly, is that so often a church thinks it has *community* when all it really has is *pseudo-community*.

And pseudo-community isn't really community at all.

In fact, sometimes it's even worse than having none at all, as my friend Elijah has said—because at least it doesn't get anyone's hopes up.

THE COST OF COMMUNITY

I first encountered this idea of "pseudo-community" from M. Scott Peck in his book *The Different Drum*, written in 1987. Peck, who was a psychiatrist, is most famous for authoring *The Road Less Traveled*, but he wrote other works which are very thought-provoking as well.

In this particular book, he describes his own journey pursuing true community, outlining its various stages. The first stage, he proposes, is *pseudo-community*, which is an intoxicating and alluring place to be and one that many organisations, including churches, often settle into, thinking they've arrived. When a person has been a part of a system with no community at all, or has perhaps experienced a toxic or dysfunctional version of it, the experience of pseudo-community can be incredibly captivating.

But when we stay there, failing to advance beyond this stage, community simply serves as an opiate of sorts, providing superficial comfort for our wounds but failing to deliver the fullness of what community truly is. It's like taking aspirin for a headache when a tumour lurks underneath.

Such community is only skin-deep and very cheap.

This is why I like to say it's not enough for a church to be friendly. Any church can be *friendly*. We can put on nice smiles for a few hours each week and deliver polished, grace-filled sermons and music. We can speak kind words but then forget about each other the rest of the week.

Of course, I'd rather step into a building where the people are kind, warm and friendly than into one where they're mean-spirited and judgmental. But the church can't settle for merely being *friendly*; God is calling us to be *family*—with all its messiness, pain and commitment.

This comes at a cost—a steep cost few of us are willing to pay. As Peck says, true "community neither comes naturally nor is it purchased cheaply."[1]

I've discovered that most of us, myself included, want to *receive* community but few of us want to *give* community. We want others to treat us with kindness, inclusivity and undivided attention, but we're

129

temperamental about reciprocating. We want others to drop everything from their schedules to be present with us in our pain, but we want to extend the same to them only when it's convenient for us. We want people to welcome us at their tables but we're hesitant to fully open up ours.

What's more, we want people to mediate unconditional grace to our wearied souls but we don't want them to hold us accountable for the ways in which we've hurt or damaged them—the ways we've undermined and endangered the wellbeing of the community. As Timothy Keller puts it, "Everyone says they want community and friendship. But mention accountability or commitment to people, and they run the other way."[2]

I must confess I have been in love with a sanitised and romanticised picture of community myself, full of middle class 30-somethings dressed in hipster clothes and sipping hot drinks, free from any significant financial or emotional needs. It's all very simple, full of happy times and good conversation.

But I fear I might be guilty of what Dietrich Bonhoeffer so poignantly warns about in his classic book, *Life Together*. "He who loves his dream of a community more than the Christian community itself," he writes, "becomes a destroyer of the latter, even though his personal intentions may be ever so honest and earnest and sacrificial."[3]

SCRIPTURAL COMMUNITY

If the church of Acts witnessed what we called "community" today, they'd likely be quite confused. Community for the early church was an *all-of-life* thing, requiring every corner of their existence.

We thus read that the early Christ-followers "were together, and had all things in common, and sold their possessions and goods, and divided them among all, as anyone had need" (Acts 2:44, 45).

This is staggering to our modern minds—especially for those of us who live in the Western world. This is because the spirit of the modern age is one of gross individualism. Though I don't want to downplay the important contributions of independence and individuality, and there are definitely downsides to communities that obliterate the individual for the sake of the collective, it's remarkable how we've elevated our individualist assumptions to the level of scriptural mandate.

Technology has certainly exacerbated this issue. Each new device that gets invented allows us to exist in our own little world to greater degrees.

A few months ago, this really hit home when we were driving down the highway and I suddenly realised every single family member in the car, including myself, was in our own little world. All three kids had their headphones on, watching various movies on their individual tablets, while Camille was listening to a podcast on her phone, and I was listening to one on mine. We were in the same car, but we may as well have been on different planets. We were together but all alone—assuming this was not only good but also *necessary* for optimal human flourishing.

I'm not advocating we turn back the clock to a pre-technology age. It's simply an illustration of how each new innovation leads to greater and greater isolation, which subconsciously affects our understanding of what it means to participate in the mission and family of God.

I remember hearing someone talk about another assumption that has invaded the Western mind—especially here in America—about our houses. They are huge, keeping us apart from each other, and we take it as self-evident that every child needs to have their own bedroom. This not only drives up the amount of money we think we need to spend to have a good home but also disciples our children in an individualistic worldview.

Once someone gets a house that is 3,000 square feet, there is no way they're going back down to one that is 2,000 square feet (that is, until they retire—if we don't stick them into a nursing home, where we don't have to worry about them cramping our individualist lifestyle).

This rugged individualism has perhaps wreaked the greatest havoc on how we understand discipleship and participation in the mission of God. Even salvation, in our Western world, is very much a private affair, which would have been a foreign concept to the biblical mind.

Today, it's all about having a *"personal* relationship with Jesus," and what seems to be the most pressing concern is whether I—as an individual—will someday live in heaven with Jesus. Any social, relational or communal concerns become optional add-ons to the Christian journey—leaving many with an ambivalence about anything other than whether they're "saved."

For the people of Scripture though, the primary question was how one could be a part of the *people* of God. That's why there's so much about being members of the larger body, with Paul noting how every member has been gifted by the Spirit—not just to build themselves up but to bring the entire body to the "unity of the faith" (Ephesians 4:13).

This is why I like to say that sanctification—growth in Christlikeness—is a team sport. We can't do it on our own, despite what our upbringing may tempt us to believe.

TRUE COMMUNITY

Of course, the reality is, sharing life together was not simply an option for the New Testament church; it was a necessity. Having all things in common was crucial for the Jesus-message and movement to even survive.

Alan Hirsch points out this dramatic juxtaposition, highlighting the difference between how we understand community today and how the New Testament church experienced it. Christian community today, Hirsch notes, has "become little more than a safe, quiet, reflective soul space" or a spiritual buzz "for people trying to recuperate from an overly busy, consumerist lifestyle." He wonders, though, whether "this is [the church's] grand purpose—to be a sort of refuge for recovering work addicts and experience junkies? A sort of spiritual hospital or entertainment arena?"[4]

The early church faced extreme adversity and pressure. The community they experienced wasn't just a nice idea they pursued in their free time. It wasn't like joining a knitting club or Rotary. As unifying as those experiences can be, they fail to bond hearts together to the degree that results in the missional potency God longs for us to experience.

What Hirsch sees in the New Testament church is community that can only be accomplished when "individuals are driven to find one another through a common experience of ordeal, humbling, transition, and marginalisation." This type of community "involves intense feelings of social togetherness and belonging brought about by having to rely on one another in order to survive."[5]

We see this in various parts of the world today where Christians face extreme persecution—like China or the Middle East. Jesus-followers there understand what it means to cling to each other out of necessity. They experience *true* community. If church was merely a two-hour program once a week, they simply wouldn't survive. True Christian fellowship and community are as necessary for their survival as are food and water.

Our middle-class existence in the West has made true community merely optional for most of us, however, and quite hard to attain as we go from soccer practice to soccer practice, spin class to spin class. We can thus exist in our individual castles, leaving their safety once a week for a couple hours to get a little pep-talk and sing a few worship songs, rejoicing about how much community our church provides.

But what if we could see that there are a lot more people—like Elijah—whose survival is actually at stake? What if community was the only hope for many hanging on to the last shreds of their Christian faith? What if we discovered that all of us actually need this vital expression of church in order to survive? And what if what the world is really looking for is not just a bunch of people who get together once a week and share nice Christian slogans and platitudes but who love each other like family?

I have to be honest: it *really* challenges my natural inclinations. I want community to be served *a la carte*—however and whenever *I* want it. I don't want people digging around my life, asking more of me than I've calculated I can I give. I don't want anyone to have unlimited access to me. I want to be able to "swipe left" if I don't like what they're saying. I want people to assure me I'm loved and accepted and that I belong, but I don't want to embody that for anyone else *all the time*.

In short, what I really want—what comes most natural to me—is *pseudo*-community.

But pseudo-community simply isn't going to cut it any longer for the family of God. The gig is up. For nearly two millennia pseudo-community worked in the Western world—or at least we thought it did—because it was just assumed everyone was automatically a Christian by virtue of their birth. But that ship has sailed, and most church people seem unaware of just how dire a situation we find ourselves in.

The great tragedy of the modern church is just how David Bosch describes it. "The church is always in a state of crisis," he writes, but "its greatest shortcoming is that it is only occasionally aware of it."[6]

Are we going to awaken to this harsh reality? Or will we remain in our fantasy of pseudo-community?

THE "DO DROP" INN

One of the most indelible memories from my childhood is walking down the stairs in my house and seeing my mother on the couch, holding Dorene in a huge bear hug.

Dorene was not my biological sister. She was my mother's co-worker who needed a place to stay for a weekend. She grew up in Dorchester, one of Boston's toughest neighbourhoods, in a very abusive home. When she met my mother, she was in dire straits, struggling with drug and alcohol addiction and attempting to run away from her former life. So my parents invited her in for the weekend.

But one weekend turned into two, and then three, and then five years and then a decade. She shared a room with my sister, two decades younger, and joined us on family vacations. My mother went to Alcoholics Anonymous with her and held her for hours at a time when the childhood flashbacks came—there at the end of our couch as I walked by, my young mind wondering what exactly was going on.

Dorene wasn't the only one though. Far from it. She was just one of the many people my parents took in—as they continue to do to this day. In fact, about a decade ago, we calculated how many people my parents had taken in, and we counted no fewer than 100 people who had lived with us for at least three months—almost always free of charge—over the course of my life. That's radical hospitality!

We had people from all walks of life—drug addicts, Abercrombie and Fitch models, murderers. Pretty much, if you needed a place to stay— for a night, for a month, for a year—my parents would take you in, into the "Do Drop Inn," as some people started calling it.

This is because church has never been just a weekend event for my parents. It has always been an all-of-life thing. They admirably recognise that God hasn't called us to fit community into our lives and schedules when it's convenient for us—community *a la carte*. They've seen that the hospitality of God must be radically embodied in His people.

Though she wasn't the only one, Dorene was certainly the longest-tenured adopted member of our family. She lived with us for almost two decades before moving in with my grandmother to care for her after she got Alzheimer's, returning the kindness to my mother when her mother was in need. Eventually my grandmother died, and so did Dorene, leaving us with a hole in our hearts.

But it's not the final chapter. We'll see her again, sharing life together for eternity. Along the way, Dorene left her old life behind and responded to the grace of Jesus as embodied in my parents. She gave her heart to Christ, joined the family of God and participated in His mission in her own humble way.

That poignant scene in my mind—of my mother holding Dorene there on the couch—reminds me of the beautiful picture Henri Nouwen paints of what it means to be wholehearted participants in God's mission and family. "The leap of faith," he writes, "always means loving without expecting to be loved in return, giving without wanting to receive, inviting without hoping to be invited, holding without asking to be held. And every time I make a little leap, I catch a glimpse of the One who runs out to me and invites me into his joy, the joy in which I can find not only myself, but also my brothers and sisters. Thus the disciplines of trust and gratitude reveal the God who searches for me, burning with desire to take away all my resentments and complaints and to let me sit as his side at the heavenly banquet."[7]

What a beautiful picture of *true* community, of sitting at the table together—the stuff that can't be accomplished simply as a weekend gig or only when it's convenient.

I know I'm not totally there yet, and I have a lot of growing to do. But I want to respond to the God who searches for me and join up with Him as He searches for others, inviting them into the experience of *true* community.

15

FULLY KNOWN AND YET FULLY LOVED

The first time I met Peter, he adamantly declared he had no interest in ever joining a church again. He'd been invited by a mutual friend to join our book club and that first day he joined us, he explained he believed in Jesus but had given up on organised religion.

The rest of us, all of whom were Jesus-followers of various stripes, assured him we weren't looking to convert anyone anyway, so that worked out well.

But I guess the Spirit had other ideas.

The next week when we met, only three of us ended up attending: Peter, Cameron and myself. As often happens, we ignored the book and allowed the Spirit to set the agenda.

And this time, that agenda meant learning more of Peter's story.

For the next hour, he shared about his journey—about growing up around the world as a "military brat," about committing to Christ as a teenager. And then he came to the part that was most painful for him: he had gone in hard with a local church in Bangor, serving on the board of deacons and leading men's groups.

And then he fell. He had an affair. And then another.

And just like that, he was driven out of the church, kicked to the curb and never contacted again by anyone in leadership.

As he shared with us, tears welled up in his eyes. He made it clear that what he did was wrong. He didn't try to evade responsibility. What was so hurtful to him was that in his hour of need, no-one reached out to him. He became *persona non grata* to his church.

Cameron and I sat there listening to his story, our hearts full of sympathy and pain. We could tell his hurt was deep and we didn't try to alleviate it through trite platitudes or confront it through calls to repentance. We just listened and sympathised, giving him a safe space to process his religious grief.

And then something funny happened. A few days later, my phone buzzed, alerting me to a text message from Peter. I quickly opened it. "My wife and I were wondering when your church meets," he started. "We'd like to attend sometime."

I couldn't help it: a big smile came over my face. Not because I had accomplished a strategic evangelism plot but because the ministry of listening had unintentionally drawn a searching soul in—despite his adamant intentions otherwise.

THE PATH TO HEALING

It seems utterly counterintuitive to many Christians, but the path to healing and growth goes through the garden of non-condemning love. People don't overcome sin by being confronted but by being embraced. It is, after all, "the goodness of God" that "leads you to repentance," Paul says—not condemnation (see Romans 2:4).

We see this repeatedly throughout the life and ministry of Jesus, perhaps most poignantly in the story of the woman caught in adultery. John recounts how the religious leaders brought a woman to Jesus as He taught in the temple one day, flinging her down in the midst of the crowd and announcing they'd caught her in the act of adultery.

There's a lot to the story, with Jesus masterfully navigating the religious minefield they'd set up for Him, but the punch line is powerful and poignant. After her accusers fled, unqualified to condemn her, Jesus looked down at the trembling woman and announced this liberating truth: "Neither do I condemn you," He said. "Go, and sin no more" (John 8:11).

This is the plain truth: the non-condemning love of God is the only force in the universe powerful enough to set us free. It is the only reality potent enough to fully heal us. We don't become better people through guilt or shame. We become better people when we stop hiding in the dark, allowing ourselves to be seen in the light of God's all-embracing love.

I love the way my friend Ty Gibson has put it. It was one of the most pivotal realisations in my life the first time I read it nearly two decades ago. "There is nothing more healing to the sinful heart," he writes, "than to be fully known and yet fully loved."[1]

We know this to be true biblically and theologically, and we know this to be true psychologically and emotionally. One of the greatest gifts I've received is when I was introduced to the work of Dr Brené Brown, a professor of social work who specialises in shame research.

She talks about the incredibly damaging role shame plays in our lives. We are hardwired for connection, but shame undermines this by nudging our true selves into the dark. We all have a desire to belong, but we trade it for fitting in. "Fitting in," she writes, "is about assessing a situation and becoming who you need to be to be accepted. Belonging, on the other hand, doesn't require us to *change* who we are; it requires us to *be* who we are."[2]

There is nothing fulfilling—or sanctifying—about wearing a mask around all the time, trying to do what we need to do so people will accept us, or being who we think we need to be so others will love us. Hustling for the approval of others is an exhausting exercise, and it just leads to anxiety, loneliness and addiction.

We need to experience self-acceptance and self-compassion, founded on the love and acceptance of Jesus. "Loving and accepting ourselves," Brown writes, "are the ultimate acts of courage."[3]

I have to admit that I used to think this type of talk was silly at best and dangerous at worst. Talking of "loving myself" felt like it was giving me permission to be proud and self-absorbed, despite recognising that Jesus said we are to love our neighbour *as ourselves* (see Matthew 22:39). It felt like it was giving me license to be selfish and sinful.

But it does just the opposite. It allows me to acknowledge the value God sees in me, recognising that "worthiness doesn't have prerequisites."[4] This is the only reality that can launch me into the orbit of true Christlike obedience. Nothing else works.

So I must not reject myself, as I so often do, because God does not reject me. I must not shame myself, because God does not shame me. I must not declare unworthy what Christ gave His life to demonstrate as infinitely worthy. And amazingly, my imperfection does not disqualify me from God's grace. In fact, it is the precise thing that qualifies me for it.

All this has implications for my relationships with others, which is the substance of what the Christian life is all about. Good relationships are the whole point of the Jesus-journey. Yet so many of us have made it about so much else.

But here's the reality: I can only love others to the degree I love myself—loving my neighbour *as* myself, as Jesus put it. I can only have compassion on others to the degree I have compassion on myself. "When we're kind to ourselves," Brown writes, "we create a reservoir of compassion that we can extend to others."[5]

Any unresolved shame I experience has to be offloaded somehow. I was not created by God to carry it. The human instrument was not designed with this ability or capacity. So if my shame is not offloaded onto Jesus, who willingly carried it to the cross, then I will offload it on to others. This is exactly what we see in the story of Adam and Eve, who tried to pass their guilt down the line to everyone else. It has been repeated ever since, as every human tries to evade the overwhelming and soul-crushing sense of shame. As Richard Rohr has famously put it, "If we do not transform our pain, we will most assuredly transmit it."[6]

Similarly, Carl Jung, one of the giants of psychiatry, put it in these astounding terms:

> The acceptance of oneself is the essence of the whole moral problem and the epitome of a whole outlook on life. That I feed the hungry, that I forgive an insult, that I love my enemy in the name of Christ—all these are undoubtedly great virtues. What I do unto the least of my brethren, that I do unto Christ. But what if I should discover that the least among them all, the poorest of all the beggars, the most impudent of all the offenders, the very enemy himself—that these are within me, and that I myself stand in need of the alms of my own kindness—that I myself am the enemy who must be loved—what then?[7]

His closing question lingers in the air, begging sober reflection.

It is for this reason that a few years ago I realised I have to give myself permission to be imperfect. In fact, as scary as it sounds, *God* actually gives me permission to be imperfect, knowing that this is, in fact, the only environment in which true growth can occur. Any environment which expects perfection and condemns imperfection undermines the very goal it hopes to achieve.

I remember I shared this a few years ago when I was leading a group Bible study, and a woman shot her hand right up, immediately demanding I provide chapter and verse. She wasn't having any of it. "Remember what David says," I offered her, "As a father pities his children, so the Lord pities those who fear Him. For He knows our frame; He remembers that we are dust" (Psalm 103:13, 14).

Any good parent knows that condemning imperfection in their children stunts the child's ability to learn, grow and develop. If I had berated my daughter Acadia every time she fell while learning to walk, she would have never learned. She would have deemed sitting to be a safer option because it would never result in condemnation, which is soul-crushing and demotivating.

And so it is with the spiritual journey. Living in an environment where it's OK to be imperfect and it's OK to make mistakes is how we grow in our discipleship, learning to live and love like Jesus to greater degrees.

In fact, Pia Mellody points out that expecting perfection in children actually prevents them from being spiritual when they are adults. "When children live in families that expect perfection, they learn to lie (to avoid the pain and shame of frequent failure)," she writes. "And this means these children can't be accountable and spiritual as adults, since they cannot tolerate *seeing* the mistakes and sabotaging behaviour in their own lives."[8]

As is true with our biological children, so too with those who are children spiritually.

This is why something Henri Nouwen says in his marvellous book *The Return of the Prodigal Son* resonated so deeply with me when I first read it:

> For a very long time, I considered low self-esteem to be some kind of spiritual virtue. I had been warned so often about pride and conceit that I came to consider it a good thing to deprecate myself. But now I realise that the real sin is to deny God's first love for me.... Because without claiming that first love....I lose touch with my true self and embark on the destructive search among the wrong people and in the wrong places for what can only be found in the house of my Father.[9]

God invites me into His house, assuring me that I can both be seen and loved, without fear of condemnation or disconnection. I don't have to be perfect to be worthy.

THE POWER OF STORY

But we are creatures who need not only to *hear* the good news of God's non-condemning love, we need to actually *see* it embodied in the family of God.

I remember one time when a shame-attack came over me a few years ago. I was feeling it bad. I tried to quote all the Bible verses I could and assure myself of God's love, but it quickly became apparent I needed more than that. I needed to hear it in the voice of another human being and see it embodied in their life.

So I called up Jim, mentioned before, and shared my story with him. Beautifully, mercifully, wonderfully, he mediated God's forgiveness to me, assuring me of my belovedness, which turned God's grace from an abstract concept into an embodied reality.

In his amazing book on Christian community called *Life Together,* Dietrich Bonhoeffer explains that so often in a church community there is a kind of fellowship that doesn't resolve loneliness or produce healing because people are not allowed to fully bring themselves into the light. "Many Christians are unthinkably horrified when a real sinner is suddenly discovered among the righteous," he writes. "So we remain alone with our sin, living in lies and hypocrisy."[10]

As embodied people, though, the very thing we need in order to fully experience the healing love of Jesus is the proclaimed and lived-out Word among the fellowship of Jesus-followers. It doesn't become real to us, and reach us on an emotional level, until it is acted out among God's people. And this is precisely the point Bonhoeffer makes that was so revolutionary to my thinking:

> A man who confesses his sins in the presence of a brother knows that he is no longer alone with himself. He experiences the presence of God in the reality of the other person. As long as I am by myself in the confession of my sins everything remains in the dark, but in the presence of a brother the sin has to be brought into the light.[11]

And then this was the real clincher: "The assurance of forgiveness becomes fully certain to me *only* when it is spoken by a brother in the name of God."

It must be so! Not in some quasi-Catholic way that requires human confession in order for God to forgive us, but in order for it to fully penetrate our psyches and convince us of its reality. God did not design us to be closed-loop systems. He created us as relational creatures, dependent on others to fully encounter His love and to help us grow in our likeness to Jesus. It's no wonder James invites us to "confess your sins to each other and pray for each other *so that you may be healed*" (James 5:16, NLT, emphasis added).

We need to be safe people for others to share their stories with. When they come to us with their pain, trauma and shame, it's a sacred moment. It's a gift from that person and it's a gift from God. Brené Brown notes that shame requires three things in order to grow out of control in our lives: secrecy, silence and judgment. But it "loses its power when it is spoken."[12]

I used to think that listening to people earned me the right to "witness" to them later. But then I realised that in a world full of self-absorbed and judgmental people, *listening itself is the witness.* It is a critically important gospel work that cannot be neglected if we want people to experience God's grace. It helps them feel validated, heard and loved, which is incredibly healing and yet tragically uncommon.

So many of us are unsafe people though. We're quick to judge, advise, critique, shame and to try to convert. We think people need our Bible verses when all they really need is our listening ears. When we listen, we're embodying the very Bible verses we think we need to quote.

Attempts at converting people usually have the opposite effect anyway. They build walls and create distance. They push people farther away, which undermines the very thing we're trying to accomplish.

M Scott Peck notes this fascinating paradox in *The Different Drum*. "Most of our human attempts to heal and convert prevent community," he notes. He then shares this really provocative thesis: "Human beings have within them a natural yearning and thrust towards health and wholeness and holiness," he says, noting how all three words come from the same root. This "natural yearning," which I would actually ascribe to the universal work of the Holy Spirit, is often "enchained by fear" and "neutralised by defenses and resistances" though, as we seek to shield ourselves from the judgment of people we deem to be unsafe. But then here's the punchline: "But put a human being in a truly safe place, where these defenses and resistances are no longer necessary, and the thrust towards health is liberated. When we are safe, there is a natural tendency for us to heal and convert ourselves."[13]

The idea of "converting ourselves" is really the work of the Spirit, I believe, but his point still stands and is incredibly important. If the non-condemning love of Jesus is what leads us to repentance and conversion, then it can only do its full work when it is embodied in the family of God. The Spirit is already working on everyone's heart, bringing conviction and inviting them into greater "holiness," as Peck puts it. But our failure to provide the safe community they desperately need, where their "defenses and resistances are no longer necessary," inhibits the very task of making disciples we are attempting to pursue. "Paradoxically," Peck adds, "a group of humans becomes healing and converting only after its members have learned to stop trying to heal and convert."[14]

That is quite a staggering statement, but one I believe carries incredible gospel and scriptural truth.

This doesn't mean there is no need for practical instruction or loving encouragement in righteousness, of course. The Spirit also uses the Jesus-community to speak words that people may only sense on a visceral level. And it certainly doesn't mean we don't set boundaries or promote holiness or have hard conversations. Jesus did also say to the woman caught in adultery to "go, and sin no more."

But we should be extremely patient with people, allowing them to learn how to listen to the Spirit for themselves, armed with the guidance of Scripture, and refuse to be their consciences for them. It's only as we've earned people's trust that we have the right to go anywhere near offering them advice or admonishing them in holiness. The reason Christ could tell the woman to "go, and sin no more" is because He had first announced the healing message of His non-condemning love.

Until we have convinced people of this healing message, we have no business advising them on their conduct. Failing to do so actually sets them up for failure, which then spirals them back into more shame and disobedience.

BECOMING A SAFE COMMUNITY

What our missional community began to realise is that we needed to provide a safe space for people's stories to be heard. If what brings healing is to be fully known and yet fully loved, then people need the space to be fully known—not just by a God they can't see, but through God's family who they can see.

I put it this way: we can only feel loved by others to the degree we feel known by them. Which means we can ultimately only feel loved by God to the degree we feel known and loved by God's family. Think about the implications of this carefully.

That's why, to repeat what I shared in the previous chapter, it's not enough to simply be a *friendly* church. Friendly churches don't get down into the mud. They don't provide safe places for people to open up the closet where the skeletons hide. They can make a person feel loved, but it's a shallow love because it's a shallow relationship.

When a random person walks through the doors of our building some weekend, we *should* be kind, friendly and welcoming. But until we learn their story in all its depth and messiness, our kindness will only reach as far as our understanding of that person. They will appreciate the warmth but may have lingering doubts, wondering if our acceptance would continue if we learned their full story.

Right from the very beginning with our missional community, we made it a practice for one person to tell their story each week, sharing with us those parts of their lives they felt shaped who they were. This quickly became a critical and precious part of our time together.

It was a fascinating exercise on many levels. It's quite amazing how little we really know about each other. We can sit in a pew next to a person for decades and yet not really know them.

Unfortunately, so much of traditional church life is not conducive to being fully known and therefore fully loved and fully healed. Most of it is shallow and skin-deep—especially when we make a big corporate gathering the main expression of community life.

But there's an incredible energy when people open up and share their story. It's truly a work of the Spirit. When someone honours us with their story, we are standing on holy ground. It's a sacred trust we can't take lightly or betray.

BECOMING A SAFE CHURCH

I remember our friend Rachel stopping me in the hallway after one of our church gatherings a few years ago. She shared how she'd spoken to a good friend and mentioned that she was a part of this new church she really loved. The friend was pretty shocked, knowing how Rachel had struggled with previous church experiences and had seemingly given up hope that she'd find a place she felt she belonged.

"Thank you," Rachel said to me. "This church is making such a big impact."

It was so gratifying to see Rachel lean more deeply into our church family, feeling she'd found a place to truly belong.

I know for some, including my younger self, it might sound like our church is nothing but Christianity-lite—like all we do is sit around in big, overstuffed chairs, sip hot drinks, talk about our feelings, share group hugs and affirm everything about everyone. But that's simply not true. We talk about holiness, we passionately study Scripture together, we discuss Christ's call to a costly obedience, and we try to share truth in all its varied and confronting facets.

But we give people the space and the time to grow into these things at the *Spirit's* pace, not our arbitrary, man-made schedules. Every person is unique and comes from a different place and goes at a different pace. There's no "one-size-fits-all" formula, developed by well-meaning people somewhere at a school of evangelism. We believe it's the *Spirit* who primarily extends the altar call, not us.

I think of what Preston Sprinkle says when it comes to our need to embrace all God's children and lovingly listen to their stories. "People will gravitate to where they are loved the most," he writes. "And if the world out-loves the church, then we have implicitly nudged our children away from the loving arms of Christ."[15]

Our church is far from perfect in the way we experience and pursue God's call, and we're always seeking to more faithfully align ourselves with the high standards of Scripture. We know we don't have it all figured out. And truthfully, sometimes we probably err on the side of being too lax and permissive.

But when dealing with people—God's precious children made in His image and for whom Jesus died an agonising death—we ought to be very, very careful just how bold we get in our discipleship. I'd rather stand before God and hear Him tell me I was too easy on His precious children than too harsh.

So I'm learning how to just listen well, allowing people to be fully known and fully loved, setting them up to experience healing through the Spirit's hands. This is God's high calling for His family.

16

WOUNDED HEALERS

A while back, I was invited by Jim to join him at a meeting he was leading. With nothing else on my schedule, I eagerly accepted his invitation and ventured out into the cold January night, making my way across the river from Bangor into Brewer, to a white Congregational church. There were only a few cars in the parking lot.

After discovering that the front door was locked, I raced around the dark church and found the back door open. Seeking shelter from one of the coldest nights of the year, I quickly stepped into the old building and made my way down the rickety stairs. The meeting was being held in the basement. It was a recovery group.

When I entered the large fellowship hall, I found more people than the cars seemed to predict, and they were sitting around tables, chatting before the meeting officially began. Jim introduced me to the group as his special guest while I found a seat on the side.

I quickly sized everyone up, recognising that they probably weren't from the same side of the tracks as I was. But they welcomed me, hardly bothered by my intrusion.

When it was time for the meeting to begin, Jim quieted the room and explained that this meeting, and the following week's, weren't going to be typical. He'd been asked by the leaders, who were on vacation, to teach the group about co-dependency. This met with a few laughs, which were compounded when Jim invited everyone to share their name and then estimate, on a scale of 1–10, what they knew about co-dependency. "Not," he said, "how co-dependent you are." Everyone laughed again.

As the introductions proceeded, the full spectrum of understanding was revealed. "I'm Holly, and I'm a three." "My name is Mindy, and I'm a seven." "My name is Mike. I'm a 10, and I should be leading this group." Laughter again. Coming to me, I introduced myself and revealed I was probably about a seven.

With that, Jim launched into his presentation on co-dependency, asking questions, soliciting interaction and gently steering the group towards understanding, sprinkling it all with occasional humour.

Ten minutes into the meeting, the back door flung open and in walked another young man. He charged towards the empty seat next to me as a number of people eagerly greeted him. "John! It's been so long!" one of the girls said from across the room. "Where have you been?"

Jim stopped and acknowledged John's presence, and then asked if he wanted to introduce himself. "I think I know everyone here," John replied, "except for this guy." He pointed at me. I introduced myself, and John then told us that he'd walked all the way to the meeting, about three miles (five kilometres) from his home. When he came upon the parking lot and saw only a couple of cars, he said he felt like he'd die if the church was locked, since it was so cold and he couldn't imagine turning around and walking all the way back home. He was clearly relieved to see everyone—and to be inside.

After bringing John up to speed, Jim continued explaining co-dependency—about how it happens when we find our value outside ourselves, how we think our happiness is dependent on other people's happiness with us. As he described the characteristics of co-dependency, I could see the lights turning on in the minds of those sitting in the old church basement.

"Oh," one young lady blurted out, "that is so me. I am co-dependent with my son."

"My ex-husband . . ." another cried out. "This was our relationship."

Before long, Jim shared his final words, then invited the audience— all of whom came from some type of faith-background—to join him in prayer. After the final amen, as everyone shot up and started to disperse, I asked John where he was going next. "Just heading back to Ohio Street," he replied. "I'm actually going to Leadbetter."

Leadbetter is a convenience store in Bangor just a few blocks from my house but a whole world apart. It's "ground zero" for Bangor's junky world—a place I'd never even thought about stopping at, much less frequenting. I'd seen plenty of people walking in there but never anyone I'd known as a human being.

Despite my apprehension about Leadbetter, and the realisation that I didn't even know John, I quickly responded, "Why don't I give you a ride?" It was, after all, freezing outside.

But then another person yelled across the room, "John, do you need a ride? I'm going to Ohio Street to drop off Mike and Janel."

John looked back at me. "Oh, uh. Well, he had offered me a ride."

I quickly tried to alleviate his mind, "If you would rather go with them because you know them, that's totally fine."

He thought about it for a minute. "No," he yelled to the woman. "That's OK." Looking back at me, he continued, "I can get a ride with him."

As the group emptied the basement and we walked out into the cold night towards my car, I confirmed with him, "So, Leadbetter?"

"Yeah," he responded. "Thanks."

I pulled out of the parking lot and started making my way back towards the lights of Bangor, just across the river. I quickly struck up a conversation with him about his life, where he was from, what he did. He was just a year older than me.

"Man," he said as he rubbed his hands—with tattoos of small crosses along the knuckles—together, "my brain is just spinning right now. I haven't been to one of these meetings forever."

As we crossed the long bridge that spans the Penobscot River, connecting Brewer to Bangor, I thought about John crossing it on foot just an hour before. He'd braved the wind and cold—all to get to a meeting that offered a little community and perhaps a little hope.

We made it up the hill to Leadbetter and I pulled into the parking lot, alongside a stretch limo. A few people were standing outside the store in the freezing cold, puffing on cigarettes. I slid the car into neutral and left it idling for a second.

John expressed his appreciation and we exchanged farewells, shaking hands. He then slipped out into the cold and made his way into the store, where he was hoping to find a cup of coffee, since he didn't find any at the meeting.

As he slowly made his way into the dingy store, I wondered if I'd see him again. And then suddenly a thought occurred to me: there's a human going into Leadbetter.

RECOVERY

As I reflected on that meeting and my brief visit with John, I realised I'd been with a group of people who were refreshingly aware of and honest about their insecurities, their fears, their dysfunction. There were no pretentions. They knew they had problems, and they freely admitted them. "Of such," I recalled Jesus' words, "is the kingdom of heaven."

What a stark contrast, I mused, to every prayer meeting or Sabbath school class I'd ever attended.

And I realised that this was borne out of their common pursuit of recovery—of giving up on themselves and depending on a power outside themselves for sobriety. As someone has remarked, there is usually more real church going on in church basements than in the sanctuaries above them.

It didn't take long for my mind to start connecting the dots. If we were going to invite others into God's family to pursue the journey of discipleship, this idea of recovery *had to be* an integral part of the process. People cannot become God's full image-bearers without pursuing recovery. Our problems are not merely intellectual and theological; they're very much emotional and relational.

For those who might not be familiar with the idea of recovery, let me try to explain it. Essentially, when people talk about recovery, they mean that human beings not only sin but also suffer wounds and experience deep pain. We not only act upon others, but others act upon us, leading to immeasurable damage, brokenness and hurt.

This starts from the moment we come out of the womb—and even before, actually. From conception on, we encounter people who are sinful, damaged and broken, and they act in ways that are hurtful to others—all in an attempt to protect themselves from further pain. We thus go through life trying to alleviate the feelings of hurt, shame and loneliness we experience using coping mechanisms, which often lead to addictions—some more visibly destructive than others.

Most of us turn to "clean addictions" though, so we remain unaware of our need for recovery. One of the more popular "clean addictions" many of us turn to, which Jim pointed out to me, is actually religion. Many of us use religion as a way to avoid having to process, feel and deal with our pain.

I've seen this over and over again. I've had a lot of parishioners who were well-versed in the nuances of Scripture but who were emotionally stunted. And these are good and sincere and godly people who have a fairly robust grasp of the *theory* of the gospel. But that theory is never connected to their deeper wounds. It's applied in shallow ways that allow them to avoid the true pain inside.

When we use Bible verses to trivialise our emotions, giving pat biblical answers to more deep-rooted issues of woundedness, we're placing a very low ceiling on our capacity to be shaped into Christ's image—in all of its emotional dimensions. I know of many people who are kind and loving and friendly, as far as those things go. But their love is one-dimensional, lacking all the contours of empathy and emotional availability that fully reflect the image of God.

It seems to me that the average Christian doesn't need more Bible knowledge; what most Christians need is more *emotional* knowledge.

I also know many other Jesus-followers who have a strong grasp of the theory of the gospel but are angry, impatient and unkind. They know all the right answers, but they lack emotional depth and empathy for others. As I've learned their stories more, having put them together piece-by-piece because of their unwillingness to delve too deeply into their pasts, it has become apparent that they've suffered a great many wounds throughout their lives but were never given the skills to process them.

This is largely because, for many of us, religion has solely been an intellectual pursuit. We keep it all up in our heads. It's a lot easier and safer to stay in our heads, high above the pain that storms below, than to get down into the pain.

Of course, one of the biggest challenges is our inability to even recognise that the pain exists at all. Many of us are so out of touch with our own inner emotional life, failing to realise the critical part this plays in our discipleship and growth in Christlikeness, that we've become highly skilled at avoidance techniques. But we've had to do this because we never learned the skills to process our pain in a healthy manner.

This is why recovery is so important. Recovery allows us to take the mask off and acknowledge our brokenness. It helps us see that the way we act is not simply because something is wrong with us, though we're certainly sinners who act upon others in hurtful ways, but because things have been done *to* us. Before we ever made a conscious choice as newborns, people started acting towards us in ways that we were never supposed to be acted upon, even in the healthiest of families.

As my friend Ty Gibson likes to say, God created us with the capacity to *only* ever experience love. Humans were not designed to receive anything other than kindness and grace. The whole universe was made this way, in fact, operating on the principle of unselfish, other-centred love. Its optimal functioning and flourishing can only be achieved when these parameters are in place.

But that's not been the story of humankind, ever since the fall. Self-centeredness replaced selflessness in the human heart and every person who enters the world quickly becomes the recipient of abuse and trauma, on some level. That's basically what sin is: acting in abusive ways towards others in an attempt to exploit them for our own ends.

Of course, very few people actually understand that this is all going on down below the surface. We are so skilled at survival that we don't even recognise when we're doing it.

But recovery helps us slow down. It helps us give up on ourselves and process our pain. It helps us to stop blaming others for the things that have been done to us and realise that, by God's grace, we can stop the cycle of trauma and abuse.

THE CRACKS THAT LET THE LIGHT SHINE THROUGH

When it comes to figuring out who is truly a part of our missional family in Bangor, I am less concerned about whether people have the right answers or even the same ones as I do. What's most important, from where I sit, is whether people have given up on themselves and acknowledged their brokenness, wanting to experience healing at any cost.

When I read Scripture, these were the people God was most easily able to work with. It wasn't the people who had all the answers or who thought they knew everything. It wasn't the people who boasted of their strength and perfect holiness—or even those who knew Scripture inside and out. It was the people who were acutely aware of their weaknesses and wounds—who, like Paul, recognised that Christ's strength was made perfect in weakness. "For," as Paul said, "when I am weak, then I am strong" (2 Corinthians 12:10).

God can work much more effectively with people who are empty than with those who are full—with those who are hungry than with those who are satisfied. This is why Jesus, when He launched His public ministry, shocked His listening audience with the astounding declaration, "Blessed are the poor in spirit, for theirs is the kingdom of heaven" (Matthew 5:3). He completely flipped the script, highlighting the strength of the weak and vulnerable rather than the mighty and strong. "Blessed are those who hunger and thirst for righteousness," He added, "for they shall be filled" (Matthew 5:6). Thus, as James K A Smith puts it, "Discipleship is more a matter of hungering and thirsting than of knowing and believing."[1]

Our brokenness does not disqualify us from participating in God's mission; it's actually a prerequisite—and then an ongoing requirement. We don't have to be perfect to join His family or to continue in His mission, we just have to be willing to give up on ourselves, knowing that He will recover His image in us, as we continuously respond to His grace.

What is missing from most churches, I believe, is an atmosphere of recovery. People don't have permission to be imperfect and to merely be *on* the journey, rather than having already arrived. Even in my church, with as many strides as we've made, Jim will sometimes say to me after someone has shared their story or preached a sermon, that it was "good, but there wasn't much recovery in it."

What he means by that is that the person spent a lot of time explaining the *theory* of the gospel but no time applying it to their own pains or hurts or weaknesses. They didn't pull back the curtain on their own brokenness, revealing how the gospel has addressed it in their lives.

What I have explicitly started communicating to my church with regularity is that, quite literally, we could *all* use some good therapy. As alarming as it might sound coming from a pastor, there are many things about our emotional health that simply can't be healed by studying the Bible or praying really hard. The things that have been done to us, the traumas we've experienced, don't magically stop affecting us because we've fasted or prayed. That's not how God works. We may think they don't affect us because we aren't always conscious of them, but pain that is not processed *always* shows up in our lives—often affecting every relationship we have.

The truth is, God doesn't want us to heal in ways that bypass our participation anyway. That would be short-changing the process, preventing us from growing in the really awesome—though painful—ways that equip us to minister to others in their pain. God has no interest in doing for us that which we can do for ourselves, because most of the joy with Christ comes through participation.

Just as a person doesn't lose weight simply by reading the Bible or praying but by exercising and eating better, neither do we experience emotional healing by simply praying or reading the Bible. It requires real emotional work.

This is one of the reasons why I believe Jesus said that if we wanted to "enter the kingdom of heaven" we needed to "become as little children" (Matthew 18:3). This is what we do when we remember, acknowledge and process the things that have been done to us. What we experience as little children, when we are the most vulnerable, has the biggest impact on who we become later in life. It sets the whole trajectory for our identity and self-understanding—and ultimately shows up in the ways we treat others.

So when we "become as little children," we revisit the pains we weren't able to process at the time—because we didn't have the necessary tools or skills at that point—trying to recapture the innocence which was lost. In so doing, we cooperate with God in trying to recover His image in us, which we buried beneath layers of rubble as we tried to protect ourselves from more pain and hurt.

It goes without saying that this is part of the important work of being God's family together. We have all experienced pain and hurt from our original families—even ones that were highly functional, since every family is composed of imperfect and sinful people. Everyone does the best they can, of course—which is an important acknowledgment in our journey of recovery. But this side of heaven, it will always fall short, causing hurt and pain that has to be processed and offloaded.

So in our own journey with our missional community, as we tried to become family together, we tried to give each other space and safety to process our stories of pain. We wanted to allow people to be fully known so they could feel fully loved.

Many tears were shed, and much healing happened.

This doesn't mean we neglected Scripture during our time together, of course. On the contrary, Scripture so often became the launching point to help us recognise the realities that were going on deep within us. In that sense, Scripture became three-dimensional for us—not just speaking to our heads but also nurturing our hearts and healing our wounds.

BY HIS WOUNDS WE ARE HEALED

Sometimes our journey of recovery goes down a single-lane road for a little while, however, with another trusted friend coaching us. This has been my experience at times.

A few years ago, I decided to engage more deeply in my own story. To be honest, part of the impetus for this was a rather strange and perhaps somewhat funny phenomenon: I have a hard time crying. During our nearly 15 years of marriage, Camille has seen me cry probably twice—much to her chagrin. I didn't even cry when any of our children were born.

This was just one reason I decided to explore my own inner life more. But the main impetus was my desire to become more emotionally safe and available for others. That, to me, is what discipleship is all about—learning to love well, just as Jesus did, so that others, including my wife and children, can learn to love well through me.

I started reading a lot of books and doing more journalling. I spoke frequently with Jim, who provided feedback and encouragement. I also decided to start going through the 12 Steps of Alcoholics Anonymous, despite having never drunk a drop of alcohol in my life.

One of the first things this particular version of the 12 Steps has you do is write down all the people who ever did anything hurtful to you during your childhood, noting what they did. This is obviously a very laborious and sometimes painful task. But it quickly helps you realise how much shame you still carry from long ago.

At one point, I came to one painful memory that I realised had cast its shadow over much of my life. It has been my constant companion. And suddenly I was transported to that scene—sitting in that room, feeling helpless and alone, wanting to cry but no tears coming out. As I sat there on my bed, recalling the moment, my eyes started welling up with tears, and I suddenly found myself crying. And then I wept and wept and wept. The tears kept coming. It felt good and it felt overwhelmingly sad, all at once.

It occurred to me as I was crying that I was crying for that little boy—that little boy who sat there feeling all alone, who didn't know how to cry for himself. I wanted to put my arm around him and tell him it was OK to feel sad and it was OK to cry, and that everything would be all right. I wanted to tell him that he didn't have to carry the shame for the rest of his life because, in the words of Bryan Stevenson, "each of us is more than the worst thing we've ever done."[2]

It was such a healing moment for me, and though I still have a long way to go on my journey—as it goes with recovery—I hope it has made me even just a little more compassionate and emotionally available for others. I still don't cry very much, but I like to think I'm getting there.

A half-century ago, Henri Nouwen wrote a classic book with a seemingly paradoxical title, which was course-setting in its vision. The book was entitled *The Wounded Healer*, focusing on the call for Christian leaders to embrace their woundedness as a way to embody God's healing love to the world. "Jesus is God's wounded healer," Nouwen later wrote. "Through his wounds we are healed. Jesus' suffering and death brought joy and life. His humiliation brought glory; his rejection brought a community of love. As followers of Jesus we can also allow our wounds to bring healing to others."

This is the task of the family of God. We are all wounded. We are all broken. But it is out of this woundedness that we can mediate God's healing grace.

"Nobody escapes being wounded," Nouwen writes. "The main question is not 'How can we hide our wounds?' so we don't have to be embarrassed but 'How can we put our woundedness in the service of others?' When our wounds cease to be a source of shame and become a source of healing, we have become wounded healers."[3]

The choice is before us: will we embrace the invitation to become wounded healers—or will we take the less painful route and try to make one-dimensional disciples whose ceiling stops far below being God's full image-bearers?

17

WHY IT ISN'T ENOUGH TO BE "NOT RACIST"

One of the most surprising and sobering discoveries I've made as I've sat at the table and listened to others' stories is just how racist I am.

This may sound like an alarming admission to some. Or perhaps a silly one to others. But our missional community started forming on the heels of the Black Lives Matter movement. Racial tensions were once again heating up in America—or, more accurately, coming to more prominent light—and it forced me to examine my thinking.

Having a few persons of colour within our group, the topic inevitably came up—not because it was an interesting issue to discuss, but because they felt those tensions personally on a visceral level. It was crushing their souls. So we provided a safe space for them to process their anxiety and grief.

I say that we "provided a safe space" because that's what we intentionally had to do. We committed to listening to each other's stories without criticism or pushback, without giving in to the temptation to invalidate anyone's story. This is not an easy task.

I have to admit that, in the past, I considered myself to be fairly racially sensitive. But it soon became apparent that I prided myself on merely being what Ibram X Kendi calls "not racist," which actually isn't really a thing. When we're merely "not racist," we take a passive posture about racism, generally liking black people and priding ourselves that we have "black friends." But we don't do much to directly confront issues of racism, because they don't really affect us personally.

What's more, as Christians, we like to say that these issues are not a "skin problem" but a "sin problem," insisting we shouldn't spend time focusing on the symptom of racism but should instead focus on the root of the problem, which is sin. "Just focus on the gospel," we say, "and everything else will take care of itself. Don't get caught up in these social justice issues."

But it wasn't simply preaching the gospel that emancipated enslaved people in America. It required good people to directly call out racism and work towards abolishing slavery politically in order for it to be annihilated. Simply preaching the gospel wasn't enough.

So we can't merely be "not racist," Kendi submits. Being "not racist" is usually just an excuse to leave the status quo unchallenged. We must be "anti-racist," which is an active posture. We should proactively speak out about racial inequalities and injustices and do what we can to rectify them.[1]

As I sat in our missional community gatherings and listened, refusing to push back, I learned a lot. I learned that however much I wanted to pretend that racism ended in America 50 years ago, our black brothers and sisters still feel its debilitating sting. I have no business telling a person of colour how they should feel about their experience because I've never walked in their shoes. Their experience is their experience and it's not mine. We can't invalidate another's story.

Instead, we should sit with people in their pain, recognising that the picture is much larger than our limited viewpoint can grasp.

And if we're going to pursue true community, seeking to proclaim and live out the gospel, we must realise that addressing racial injustice is at the heart of this task.

It's not an optional issue we can discuss if we have time and everyone is feeling up to it. These conversations are a fundamental part of the gospel—and they're a fundamental part of what it means to participate in the mission and family of God.

WHICH GOSPEL?

It wouldn't be an exaggeration to say that if we stripped away racial concerns from the New Testament we wouldn't even have the New

Testament. We wouldn't have Paul's letters to the Galatians or to the Ephesians; we wouldn't have much of Romans or parts of Colossians.

When Paul sat down to write his epistles, he wasn't simply writing about abstract theological concepts. Paul wasn't doing systematic theology, waxing eloquent about the esoteric mysteries of God. He wasn't even explaining to his readers how they could be saved so that they could one day go to heaven.

At the heart of Paul's agenda was a very practical issue that was wreaking havoc on the churches and threatening to tear apart the young Jesus-movement: how should Jews relate to non-Jews? The question started brewing soon after the movement began and took off with a vengeance.

Perhaps the most poignant example of this tension is evident in Paul's letter to the Galatians, which many scholars feel is one of the first letters of Paul's we have. The whole letter is basically a treatise debating how Jewish non-Jews had to become in order to enjoy fellowship within the Christian community.

Right from the beginning, Paul pulls no punches, reprimanding the Galatians for turning to "a different gospel" than the one he'd proclaimed. "There are some who trouble you and want to pervert the gospel of Christ," he writes, before telling them that anyone—even an angel—who tries to preach any other gospel than the one he first proclaimed should be "accursed" (Galatians 1:6–8).

It wasn't simply an abstract gospel that concerned Paul. He didn't want to assure the Galatians that if they just believed in Jesus they could someday go to heaven. There are many Christians for whom this is the totality of the "gospel." This is what it's fundamentally about. Just believe in Jesus and one day you can go to heaven. All the bad things you've done can be forgiven by God because Jesus got you off the hook by His death. And nothing else really matters.

But at the heart of the gospel is restored relationships—bringing all into the one family of God. This isn't a passing concern. This is foundational to the gospel Paul proclaimed, foundational to the reality of God's kingdom of love.

Paul thus moves in his letter to describe an issue within God's family involving Peter. Apparently, Peter, still learning how to navigate his new religious reality, which included both Jews and non-Jews, willingly sat at the table and ate with non-Jews, extending fellowship to them. But when Jewish representatives from Jerusalem showed up on the scene, Peter quickly withdrew from sitting at the table with the non-Jewish Christians, afraid of how it might look to his fellow Jewish believers.

At the heart of this issue was the attitude the Jewish believers had. They had finally gotten to the point where they believed that non-Jews could be a part of God's covenant-people, but they firmly maintained that these non-Jews had to essentially become Jewish—especially through the rite of circumcision—in order to be full members of God's family.

And the table was the main battleground for this dispute. Non-Jews could not sit at the same table as Jews. Their lack of circumcision disqualified them from full participation. For a Jew to sit at the same table as a non-Jew was to undermine the belief in Jewish uniqueness and superiority.

All this infuriated Paul, angering him so much that when Peter came to Antioch, he "had a face-to-face confrontation with him because he was clearly out of line" (Galatians 2:11, *The Message*) calling him a "hypocrite" (verse 13). It wasn't simply that Peter was acting like a hypocrite. What infuriated Paul was that by keeping Jews and non-Jews at separate tables, Peter and those who followed him had "deviated from the gospel" (Galatians 2:14, HCSB).

Don't miss this critical point. Paul, point blank, tells Peter that refusing to sit at the same table as non-Jews is to deviate—to depart—from the gospel. The whole purpose of the gospel, Paul submits, is to bring everyone to a single table, acting as a single family.

Based on what we read in Paul's epistles, the gospel is not primarily concerned with making Jesus our "personal Saviour." It's about bringing together everyone into one family.

This is the point N T Wright makes, reflecting on Paul's ambitious project. "Paul's emphasis," he writes, "is on the fact that the Messiah has one family, not two, and that *to deny this is to deny the gospel itself*, to suggest that the Messiah did not need to be crucified."[2] Wright goes on to explain elsewhere that this Christian experiment, "the idea of a single community *across traditional boundaries of culture, gender, and ethnic and social groupings*," was unheard of in the ancient world. "Unthinkable, in fact," he adds. "These communities, small at first, but growing, were an experiment in a way of being human, of being human *together*, that had never been tried in the world before."[3]

Simply put, there is no gospel apart from its racial implications. We cannot separate the two unless we want to do violence to the gospel. And we have not truly experienced the gospel if we're not actively pursuing racial reconciliation. Pursuing racial reconciliation is a fundamental gospel work.

ASSIMILATION AND UPLIFT SUASION

The racial tensions Paul addressed in his letters are actually a perfect example of the subtle and insidious forms of racism that plague us today—both within and without the church. In his book *Stamped From the Beginning*, which traces the history of racism in America, Ibram X Kendi notes that when it comes to racism, there are three basic categories that everyone falls into.

The first two categories are quite obvious and conspicuous. There are those who are segregationists, maintaining that persons of colour are inherently inferior and largely responsible for their own troubles. Then there are those who are anti-racists. They propose that every race has implicit worth and value, and that the inequalities blacks and other persons of colour have suffered are due to the inhuman and racist policies and practices of white people.

Any attempt to lay blame on the doorstep of black people for their own troubles is victim-blaming, ignoring the racist policies and practices that started long before America even became a nation. And any racial progress in the future will come not as the result of persons of colour changing themselves. Instead, it will come through white people recognising the inherent worth of black culture and identity and working to rectify the inequalities that have been in place from the beginning.

The third category is a lot more subtle and inconspicuous—and has, in Kendi's estimation, wreaked more havoc on the racial landscape than outright segregationists. This third category is what he calls "assimilationists." This attitude lays the blame for racial inequalities on both white people *and* black people, maintaining that if black people would just assimilate to white culture, they could be fully accepted at the table.

Kendi proposes that many activists throughout American history who fought for equality and civil rights were themselves, in some fashion, assimilationists. He notes that "assimilationists constantly encourage Black adoption of White cultural traits and/or physical ideals" in order to justify their place at the table.

He cites the work of Nobel Laureate Gunnar Myrdal as a classic example. Myrdal was a Swedish economist whose study of race relations in 1944 was influential in the civil rights movement. "It is to the advantage of American Negroes as individuals and as a group," Myrdal wrote, "to become assimilated into American culture, to acquire the traits held in esteem by the dominant white Americans."[4]

Kendi also introduces the idea of "uplift suasion" which further puts the onus on black people to work for their own acceptance in white society. If black people could just become educated enough, wealthy enough or moral enough, this would persuade others they deserve to be equals. He demonstrates that this type of thinking has been prevalent—and continues to be prevalent—even within the black community itself, with many blaming themselves for their own defeats and disadvantages.

As I write this, America is reeling from yet another tragic example of this unfortunate idea. A young black male, Ahmaud Arbery, was gunned down in broad daylight while running in a wealthy Georgia neighbourhood by a white father and son who acted as a couple of vigilantes. They claimed there had been a number of break-ins in their neighbourhood prior to the incident, and Arbery supposedly fit the description of the burglar. So they decided to chase him down with their truck, loaded guns in hand, as he went for a run in the neighbourhood.

When he refused to comply with their demands, trying to run around their truck as it idled in the middle of the road, the son came around to the front of the vehicle, meeting up with Arbery. They then got into a short tussle. The son shot Arbery twice in the chest, and he tumbled to the ground, his life over.

Neither the father nor the son were arrested for two months after the incident. It took the leaking of a video of the incident for them to be charged. Astute commentators noted that it wasn't the fact that authorities saw the video which led to the father and son being charged, since authorities had access to the video two months earlier. It was because *we* saw the video that they were finally charged.

Sadly, that's often what it takes for white men to get charged for the murder of black men in America.

There was a lot of arm-chair quarterbacking after the incident, of course. Arbrey shouldn't have approached the son, some say. He should have just kept running.

A few days after the father and son were charged, someone else leaked a video of Arbery apparently snooping around a house being built in the neighbourhood. Many white people, myself included, observed that this is something we've all done before, and it never led to our murder. Yet, what if what Arbery had done by looking around a construction site *was* unique and illegal? Would such behaviour justify two white men taking matters into their own hands, serving as judge, jury and executioners? Who empowered them to decide the fate of a young black man, even if he had committed a crime? Would he not deserve the same treatment every white person in America enjoys under the same circumstances?

It all speaks, of course, to the continued belief in the minds of many white people in America that black people are still subjugated to white rule. This was chillingly evident when, a few days after the arrest of father and son, a group of self-proclaimed Christians started a Facebook group, with 20,000 followers, trying to raise support for these two "God-fearing men" who "were only trying to protect their neighbourhood." The description of the group explained that there had been a number of break-ins in the neighbourhood and that Arbery "fit the description," and—most horrifying of all—"did not comply with the simple commands."

What a way to articulate it! Apparently black people are supposed to "comply with the simple commands" of white strangers, as though they are still enslaved—and if they don't, violence and murder are apparently justified. Black people must obey white people if they want a place at the table, the thinking goes.[5]

Of course, very few of us are conscious of our implicit racial biases and we would passionately push back against the idea that we were racist, hiding behind the "not racist" title. But I've found that my racism is often unconscious and surfaces in unexpected ways.

BACK TO PAUL

This is exactly what Paul confronted head-on in his letters. The Jewish Christians insisted that the non-Jews had to *assimilate* to Jewish culture in order to have a place at the table, to be equal members of the family. Non-Jewish culture was implicitly inferior and non-Jewish behaviour—refusing to be circumcised, for example—made them second-class Christians.

I have to candidly admit that this type of thinking is all too common in my own head and heart. I like to comfort myself with the thought that I am not racist because I believe that every race has inherent worth. And yet in the same breath I'll also think that if black people just dressed the right way or presented themselves with enough sophistication—as my culture defines sophistication—they would be treated with the proper respect. But this is nothing more than assimilationist thinking.

Likewise, it's assimilationist thinking when we say that if Trayvon Martin had simply not worn a hoodie, he wouldn't be dead right now. Or if black people spoke with proper English grammar, instead of using Ebonics, we would take them more seriously. In other words, if they lived by *our* standards, we would accept them—and until they do, we're justified in withholding our respect.

What is even more troubling is when we do this within a religious context. We may claim we're not racist, but then say that we have a problem with the way black people preach or the way they worship—the music they perform—implying they are spiritually inferior and not as scripturally faithful. If they would just tone it down and get in line with God's standards of worship, we maintain, then they'd be as spiritually enlightened as us.

It's funny, of course, how what we deem to be scripturally faithful worship bears a striking resemblance to our traditional white European sensibilities. What an incredible and fortunate coincidence that God likes and sanctions the exact same music we feel comfortable with!

It's actually quite a tragedy, and reason for repentance on my part, how racist our views on music often turn out to be. I've used the arguments in the past: drums are evil because they came from voodoo rituals in Haiti, imported from devil worship in Africa. Or something like that.

Never mind the fact that such arguments are historically dubious. Never mind the fact that Paul said that "an idol is nothing in the world" (1 Corinthians 8:4) and anything used in their service does not therefore become inherently unholy. And never mind the fact that there is not a single line in Scripture that prohibits the use of drums—quite the opposite is in fact the case.

The whole argument is an example of what Ibram X Kendi says about the pathology of racism: contrary to popular belief, racist ideas don't lead to racist practices and policies. It's the exact opposite. Racist practices and policies lead to racist beliefs, as we try to come up with reasons to justify why our policies are superior, all in an attempt to maintain control.

In the case of music and worship, we committed ourselves to traditional white liturgy because it was what we were used to. And when others came along with a different style that made us feel uncomfortable and threatened our control, we started looking for ways to explain why their music and worship were wrong and evil—which led to racist theories of music and worship.

The long and short of all this is that I have committed myself to a posture of humility when it comes to my journey with our black brothers and sisters. There is a lot of pain, a lot of delegitimising of their stories, a lot of "whitesplaining" that I get tempted by. And I just need to shut my mouth and listen. I must be a safe person to those who have felt unsafe in America ever since its inception.

The reality is, if I ever have to make the statement that I am "not racist," I've already lost the battle. The fact that I think I have to make this claim is likely evidence that I am, in fact, racist. It's sort of like insisting that I'm humble. If I'm truly against racism, it will be obvious to all—especially to my brothers and sisters of colour. They won't have to guess where I stand. And I won't find myself having to make the claim.

An integral part of what it means to be missional is pursuing the reconciliation of all peoples. The Father sent Jesus "to reconcile all things to Himself" (Colossians 1:20), Paul explains. I cannot be reconciled to God and yet not be reconciled to my brothers and sisters of all the various races, ethnicities and nationalities. I cannot sit at God's table, be a part of God's family, and maintain any level of racial or cultural superiority. Nobody has to adopt white culture in order to prove their spiritual maturity.

I know the pushback, of course. "Just talk about Jesus," people will say. "Don't talk about issues that divide us." But here's a newsflash: Jesus didn't just talk about Jesus. He talked about bigotry and oppression and injustice, calling them out. He said He didn't come to bring peace but a sword, setting a man against his father, a daughter against her mother, and a daughter-in-law against her mother-in-law (see Matthew 10:34–36).

If the price of calling out racism is that it divides the family of God, then so be it. We can't afford to pursue pseudo-peace and pseudo-community if it comes at the cost of subjugating any of God's children to continued inequalities, simply because of the colour of their skin or the customs of their culture. Committing to anti-racism is a critical and uncompromising part of participating in God's mission in the world.

THE KINGDOM COME

Sadly, it's hard to keep up with the constant assault on black and brown bodies. No sooner did I put (what I thought were) the finishing touches on this chapter, when another black man was murdered in broad daylight by police on the streets of Minneapolis.

With the country still reeling from what happened to Ahmaud Arbery, four police officers pinned a helpless black man, George Floyd, to the ground, claiming he had resisted arrest on suspicion of forgery. One of the cops knelt on the back of his neck as he screamed that he couldn't breathe. It was all caught on video by bystanders who did all they could to urge the cops to get off him.

Their pleas were to no avail. Over the course of the nine-minute video they recorded, Floyd could be seen eventually losing consciousness, unable to breathe anymore. By the time the paramedics came to attend to him, all that remained was a limp body that they haphazardly threw onto a stretcher and hauled off.

Life is so cheap in our world. And black and brown lives are even cheaper.

I watched the whole video. I wanted to feel the sadness and the outrage and the anger. I listened as another black man yelled at the police from the sidewalk, demanding they get off Floyd's neck. He used every curse-word imaginable. Somehow, I imagined it was Jesus speaking through him, cuss-words and all. If that sort of thing doesn't elicit Jesus' anger, I don't know what will.

A few days later, as the collective ire of many Americans rose to dizzying heights, I listened to one of my favourite songs. The third verse of U2's famous song "I Still Haven't Found What I'm Looking For" spoke poignantly to my heart, speaking of believing in a kingdom to come, where all the colours will bleed into one.

I couldn't fight back the tears as I thought of Floyd lying there, pleading for his life, and then thinking of the day when that kingdom comes, and we will see everyone from every nation, kindred, tribe, tongue and people, sitting at the same table together—not as "colour blind" people, but celebrating and rejoicing in all the wonderful diversity God made.

I don't know what it's going to take to get us all there. But I do know that I want to be a part of God's kingdom of love *today*, living in the reality of His self-emptying, other-centred love which welcomes everyone—from all nations—to the table.

18

GOD HAS LEFT THE BUILDING

There's a particular event seared into my memory from childhood that resurfaced a few years ago when we started grappling with what it means to be the church. For some reason, the experience never left me.

It was a Saturday morning and we were gathered together for worship. I guess I had slipped into boredom because I remember lying down on the pew, putting my head on my mother's lap and having her stroke my hair to pass the time. I seem to remember this being a fairly common occurrence during the church service. I didn't think anything of it, and she didn't think anything of it either—but apparently someone else did.

Right after the church service ended, and everyone was mingling in the lobby area, a well-meaning gentleman walked up to me, grabbed me, stared intently into my eyes and very firmly said, "Never, *ever* do that again. *Never* lie down in the pew in the sanctuary during the worship of God."

To say I was shaken would be an understatement. I felt incredibly ashamed and embarrassed, which is why I still remember the incident more than three decades later.

The experience was part of a larger religious framework emphasised (not so much by my parents, but by others) when I was a kid that elicited fear and trembling. The church is the house of God, the messaging went, and we needed to behave accordingly. As soon as we set foot in the sanctuary, voices needed to be lowered, walking needed to be slowed, and "reverence"—whatever that exactly meant—needed to be practised. God was in the room—and apparently not in any other room—and we needed to adjust our behaviour in light of that.

In fact, children all over the world in my faith community are taught to "walk softly in the sanctuary." We knew this mantra by heart. It was practically the 11th commandment.

Looking back all these years later, I can't help but realise just how much theology was packed into this simple directive—most of it subconscious and unprocessed. Think about it. If by entering into the presence of God—stepping foot into His special room—I have to be quiet, walk softly and fight off boredom, then I would probably be justified in concluding that God really isn't all that interesting a Person to be around—and likely Someone to be feared.

Simply put, if entering into God's presence means that the fun stops as an eight-year-old, then I might be tempted to run the other way.

And would you blame me?

Of course, the implications of this "theology of sacred space" go far beyond the concerns of an eight-year-old, as critically important and perhaps eternally course-setting as those might be. As I began grappling more with what it means to participate in the mission and family of God, I started to see just how much this "theology of sacred space" works against the very things we're trying to accomplish as God's missional people.

WHAT IS GOD'S HOUSE?

There's an enlightening exchange in the Old Testament that informs this discussion in a thought-provoking way. In 2 Samuel 7, the writer recounts a conversation King David has with the prophet Nathan about his desire to build God a permanent house. As David dwells in his big, expensive palace, it suddenly occurs to him that he is living in luxury while God has been stuck in a tent ever since the beginning of Israel's history.

Initially, when David broaches the subject with Nathan, he gets the green light to start his building project. But later that night, God visits Nathan in a dream with a different message. He notes that throughout Israel's history, He moved around with Israel wherever they went, dwelling in a tent rather than a house. And then He wonders: "Did I ever say to any of their rulers whom I commanded to shepherd my people Israel, 'Why have you not built me a house of cedar?'" (2 Samuel 7:7, NIV). The answer to the rhetorical question is obvious.

God wants to know where David came up with this idea to build Him a house! It certainly wasn't His suggestion. God was perfectly content with His portable arrangement, able to travel with Israel wherever they went.

Interestingly, I recently came across another thought from a writer outside Scripture that takes it a step further. Even though God had asked Israel to build Him a moveable sanctuary soon after they left Egypt, so that He could "dwell among" His people (see Exodus 25:8), this itself was a concession. It wasn't God's original intent to limit His presence by walls or physical spaces. "Accustomed as they had been in Egypt to material representations of the Deity, and these of the most degrading nature," Ellen White offers, "it was difficult for them to conceive of the existence or the character of the Unseen One. *In pity for their weakness*, God gave them a *symbol* of His presence, 'Let them make Me a sanctuary,' He said, 'that I may dwell among them.'"[1]

This is a fascinating proposal. Not only was God not interested in being restricted to one location, as He would be with an immovable temple, He didn't even want to be equated with physical space to begin with. It was a teaching tool. He wanted His people to know that *wherever* they went He was with them. He didn't want them thinking, as the heathen nations around them thought, that they had to go to a specific place in order to access Him. As the almighty God of the universe, present in all spaces and places, He could be accessed and related to anywhere. It was only because of Israel's *weakness* that He allowed them to build a physical structure—as a symbol of His presence.

The story with David takes another fascinating turn. A few verses after God explains to David—through Nathan—that it's not His idea to have a house built, God actually turns the tables and declares that, instead, He would build *David* a house.

But it's not the kind of house David expects. "When your days are over and you rest with your ancestors," God explains, "I will raise up your offspring to succeed you, your own flesh and blood, and I will establish his kingdom.... Your house and your kingdom will endure forever before me; your throne will be established forever'" (2 Samuel 17:12, 16, NIV).

Don't miss this point! The house God promised He'd build David wouldn't be a physical structure, made of wood and stone. It would be a kingdom, a dynasty, a people. It would be the "house of David," from which the Messiah would eventually come. It would be the family of God, established forever by Jesus Himself.

This is such a crucial point. What God has always been interested in doing is not dwelling in a physical structure, bound by space and limited to a location. God has been looking to dwell in a people—in a *family*—through which the world could encounter His love.

The New Testament echoes all this, of course, spelling it out in even more explicit language. In His ministry, Jesus makes it clear that He is transferring divine significance from the physical temple in Jerusalem to Himself. After explaining that He would "destroy this temple" and "in three days" raise it up again, John explains that He was "speaking of the temple of His body" (John 2:21). And what is true of Christ is true of His people, since He stands as our representative.

Thus, when we come to Paul's writings and he refers to God's temple, nowhere does he attach any significance to the temple in Jerusalem—or any other earthly temple. While there is a temple in heaven (see Hebrews 8:1, 2), the only references to any temple on earth relate to the bodies of each individual believer (see 1 Corinthians 6:9) and the collective family of God (see 2 Corinthians 6:16).

I love this second reference especially because after explaining to the Corinthians that "you are the temple of the living God," Paul evidently combines a number of Old Testament passages and quotes God as saying, "I will dwell in them, and walk among them. I will be their God, and they shall be My people."

This makes me excited, I have to be honest! This is what we call a "high ecclesiology." It elevates the significance of the church—not as a building, but as God's people. Scripture has a high view of the church, the family of God. If we want to encounter God—to visit where He lives, to walk where He walks—then we should step into the presence of His family, whenever and wherever they are. We don't go to some building, made of brick and mortar, and subject to decay. We journey with His people.

And if we want to beautify God's house or expand it, we don't start a fundraising campaign to raise millions so we can build an addition or renovate the foyer. We disciple the family of God in the gospel so we can beautify our characters with love and grace and draw people into *our* presence, thus drawing them into His.

Indeed, as Stephen proclaimed, raising the ire of his audience, "The Most High does not dwell in temples made with hands" (Acts 7:48).

But somehow we've missed all this.

DEMYTHOLOGISING CHURCH BUILDINGS

Somewhere along the way, Jesus-followers got to thinking that God still dwells in buildings—that He has temples and houses and sacred spaces. Some may not think this idea is all that significant, but such a perspective has wreaked havoc on how we participate in God's mission and experience His family.

Not long after we restarted our church, I remember conversations we had with some of our members—who came from a more traditional mindset—about some of the decisions that troubled them. One of the things we decided to do for our restart was to completely revamp the way we gathered together as a church on Saturday mornings and the physical space in which we met.

As a way to promote more connection and community, which is a critical element of what it means to be God's people, we decided to have a more informal gathering that fostered greater communal participation. So we got rid of the rows of chairs in our "sanctuary," rolled in round tables and set them up in the room, inviting attendees to sit with one another, looking at each other's faces, rather than the backs of one another's heads.

We also cut the overhead lights and set up a few standing lamps in the corners, which created an atmosphere of intimacy. It's actually quite amazing how much our physical environment affects the way we gather and the messages—and theology—we communicate. And yet very few of us give it much thought.

The other thing we decided to do was serve refreshments at the beginning of our time together. We even set up a classy refreshment cart in the back corner of the room, replete with snacks and non-caffeinated beverages, recognising that eating together is a typical and important element of forming bonds and experiencing community.

To the uninformed onlooker, it could appear we made these changes in an attempt to be a "cool" church or to attract non-believers. I probably would have thought the same thing myself 20 years ago.

But nothing could be further from the truth. We weren't attempting to be attractional, trying gimmicky methods to bring people in. We wanted to harmonise our values of discipleship and community with the way we gathered together. We recognised that if we were going to be connected as a family and disciple one another whenever we were together, then we couldn't sit in straight rows, staring at the backs of one another's heads. We couldn't just be passive consumers of religious programming. We needed to be in intimate spaces that facilitated connection.

Not everyone saw it this way, of course. Some were troubled. I remember one couple refused to set foot in the room, never attending a single worship gathering. Instead, they'd leave after an informal Bible study, which they held in another room. A few months later, they moved.

I remember someone else saying that the first time he set foot in the room, he thought he was in a night club. I figured we were either a pretty pathetic version of a night club or the person had never actually been in one.

I don't wish to demean anyone's perspective. I get it. Change is hard and so many of us have been raised with the idea that our security with God is partially dependent on us participating in a certain version of "church." After all, if the church building is the "house of God" and we must be quiet and reverent when we're there, how will God react when we fail to take this posture?

But that's precisely my point: I became very sad when I realised that so many of us judge the seriousness of people's faith based on their behaviour in a building which we've labelled "God's house." We've implicitly communicated that what takes place *in that building* is more important than what takes place *outside* that building. If our deportment in that room doesn't reflect sombreness, seriousness and sobriety, that's supposedly some significant insight into our level of spiritual maturity and commitment.

We can literally be standing in a spot, acting a certain way that we deem to be acceptable, but move three feet into "God's house" and suddenly that same behaviour is now unacceptable. It doesn't make sense. And it's kind of funny to me that many of us feel that certain buildings, which were made with human hands, are somehow more sacred and holy than nature, which was made by God's hands.

A classic example of this, of course, is what a person wears when they "go to church." Somehow, wearing jeans in the parking lot of a church building is acceptable but moving a few feet and wearing them into

"God's house" now means we're being disrespectful. Where did we get the idea that God cares at all about what we wear when we're in certain buildings? Why do we think He likes ties more than t-shirts? I haven't found *a single line* in Scripture that says anything at all about what a person should wear when they gather with God's people.

Quite ironically, such a perspective, based solely on arbitrary standards of decorum, is what the pagan gods surrounding Israel cared about. If a supplicant wanted to avoid the wrath of their god during worship, the person had to approach the god in just the right way, lest they stir up their fury. It was all superstition and magic—nothing the God of Israel wanted anything to do with.

As seen most clearly in the face of Jesus, the God of Scripture doesn't require arbitrary and superficial standards of outward deportment. The things God looks for when we approach Him are of a *moral* nature. "Who may ascend into the hill of the Lord? Or who may stand in His holy place?" David asks. "He who has clean hands and a pure heart" (Psalm 24:3, 4). I don't read anything about certain attire or styles of music or the decibel level of our voices. God asks us, when we gather, to come just the way we live out the rest of our lives—with openness, honesty and purity of heart, not trying to cover ourselves up with impressive clothes that make us look like someone other than who we are the rest of the week.

I know this might not seem like a big deal to some, which I've been told numerous times. But I remain convinced that a faulty theology with this leads to disastrous outcomes. And, ironically, the people most likely to say we shouldn't make such a big deal of this are often the same ones who become extremely troubled when we try to move away from a traditional approach. I've concluded that it's not really a big deal to people until it is. As soon as we disagree with them about it, all hell breaks loose.

It's actually really fascinating to me. Over the course of my ministry, I have preached on lots of serious and somewhat controversial topics without much pushback. But I quickly discovered that nothing—and I mean literally *nothing*—stirred the pot like questioning the way we gather together as God's family. It is the definition of a sacred cow, leading me to conclude that people *really* draw a lot of security from a traditional worship routine. And in that sense, I realised that the quicker we could expose this reality, the better.

I don't mean to sound insensitive or calloused. But if we're stuck in a mentality which says that God resides in a single building somewhere, and as soon as we set foot in that building we need to act differently—we have to be really quiet, dress up in fancy costumes and play "reverent" music—then we're undermining the gospel. We're giving some people a false sense of security based on something other than the gospel and alienating others through a picture of a wrathful God who apparently needs to be approached with fear and trembling.

THE NEED FOR SOLITUDE

Of course, I would also add this: I get that there is within the human spirit a desire for sacred and special spaces. We like to attach meaning to places that are significant to us. In fact, we *crave* this. That's why places like Notre-Dame in Paris or Saint Basil's Cathedral in Moscow, both places I've been to, inspire awe and wonder. Even worship. And it's why we're so deeply moved when disaster strikes them, like with Notre-Dame a few years ago.

But this is true of many spaces, not just "churches." I've felt that same sense of awe when I've visited Buddhist temples or Islamic mosques. I feel the same way about Cameron and Ellie's house, which has beautiful and inviting architecture and is where we've had so many amazing experiences with God as a missional family together. It's a "sacred" and special place to me. And if it burned down tomorrow, I'd feel that a little part of me—a *sacred* part of me—was lost.

I also understand that we want to have places that engender quiet reflection and careful contemplation. This is how people have related to church buildings for so long. They have been little safe havens where people can quietly meditate on the divine—little outposts of solitude.

But if all we want is a place we can go that promotes quiet reflection, do we need to invoke God for that? Libraries and museums seem to have figured it out just fine.

The truth is, God doesn't need us to be quiet—but maybe our fellow congregants sitting next to us do. I get that. In a world full of constant noise and distractions, where all of us are on our smartphones watching TikTok videos or scrolling through Facebook incessantly, we're in desperate need of quiet spaces that facilitate thoughtful reflection.

But let's separate our need for these things from God's. Any time we bring Him into the equation, claiming He requires certain behaviours, we suddenly elevate everything to a much more serious level, setting people up to experience religious shame over requirements that God Himself never promotes.

There is a place for having important conversations about the way we conduct ourselves in certain buildings. We just need to demythologise those buildings before we have those discussions.

GETTING OUT OF THE REAL ESTATE BUSINESS

It's not just those who have a more traditional view of "sacred space" that are in danger of idolising church spaces. The classic attractional church model places a disproportionate amount of focus on real estate as well.

I remember a church just down the road from where I used to pastor in New Hampshire that had an incredible and beautiful facility. It was a newly constructed building that looked like a giant red barn. They'd put millions of dollars into it. I wasn't terribly surprised though when a colleague told me after I moved that the church was barely scraping by now. They had gone from a few hundred attendees to fewer than 100, partly due to the massive financial demands the facility required.

More recently, a large non-denominational church in Bangor completed a $10 million fundraising campaign to expand its campus. They had been growing by leaps and bounds and quickly ran out of space to hold all the many hundreds of people who were showing up each Sunday. After a drawn-out fundraising campaign, they finally completed the project, only to have their grand opening scheduled for the first Sunday that every church in Maine had to be shut down due to coronavirus.

I know a few people who are a part of the church, including the pastor. They're all very nice people who love Jesus. And though I haven't picked their brains about what transpired, I'd imagine they were sweating a bit as a $10 million building sat empty for three months, with no way to collect an offering for a very expensive mortgage.

And even though they were eventually allowed to start meeting in person again, it leaves me thinking that perhaps it's not advisable to get into the real estate business anytime soon as a church, especially since these types of issues may surface with greater frequency in the future.

Maybe this whole pandemic is God's gracious gift to wean us off relying on buildings and programs. Maybe it's a practice run—an opportunity to get down to our fighting weight so we can take the world by storm as we hit the final stretch. Perhaps it's God's merciful invitation to put our money into people rather than building projects and to recognise that church is, in the words of Tim Chester and Steve Timmis, "a network of relationships,"[2] not a building made of brick and mortar.

When it is true to its calling, the church is the most attractive and powerful force in the world. When we recognise that church is a family, called by God into the world to live out the gospel in everyday life, we take our focus off buildings and locations and turn it to the *real* house of God—His people.

It's not simply the new megachurches that need to have their gazes reoriented, of course. Whether traditional or contemporary, when physical space captures too much of our missional imagination and finances, we neglect the real substance of what it means to participate in the mission and family of God—which has always been, and ever will be, about people.

All this reminds me of Francis Chan. At one time he pastored a huge church in California, which he started, and was one of the most popular pastors in America. But one day, he suddenly realised something was seriously broken. Church for him had become about everything other than what it should really be about. So he quit, packed up his family and moved to San Francisco, where he started a house church movement, called "We Are Church." He was, it seems, a man ahead of his time.

In his book, *Letters to the Church*, he recounts the journey that led him to this conviction. He recalls the many years of explosive growth in his church, when they kept having to build larger facilities to accommodate everyone. They'd have massive fundraising campaigns and jump through hoops to convince city officials to let them expand. Each time he kept saying to himself, "There's no way Jesus would do it this way!" But he couldn't imagine anything different.

It was always a hustle, stressing about raising enough money, and then stressing about filling all the seats to pay for the massive mortgage, and then stressing that he might compromise on the gospel to ensure people would keep showing up and paying. It was an endless religious rat race.

And then something hit him one day: what would he do if God called him to start a church in the middle of a city—where real estate prices are astronomical? He started doing the calculations and realised the megachurch model simply doesn't work in big cities, where most of the world's populations reside. The megachurch movement is essentially a middle-class, suburban model of mission (if one can call it "mission" in the true sense of the term). You might be able to construct *one* church building for millions of dollars in a massive city like New York, but what about the millions of people that couldn't be served by that single church? One can't just keep investing in more real estate, costing millions of dollars, in order to reach everyone.

And then it dawned on him: "Everyone has a home," he writes. "If it's possible for a church to fit in a home, then we have an infinite number of potential churches no matter where we go. Going small is our best shot at getting big."[3]

And so it is. For too long, churches—traditional churches, megachurches, *all* churches—have been location-centric and inward-focused.

But a new day has come.

God has left the building and He's wandering through the streets of our neighbourhoods, and the halls of our homes.

The question is, will we follow Him there?

RESTARTING

19

RAISING THE DEAD

There are a lot of really crazy ideas that go through my head, but this one was probably the craziest of them all. I remember the moment well. I was sitting on my bed on a Saturday morning, praying and preparing myself emotionally for the church service I was about to lead, when suddenly a thought came to me: *Maybe we should have a funeral for our church. Like, literally, a funeral. Let's just bury the whole church and start over again.*

You have to understand the context to fully appreciate how my mind reached that morbid place. It was January, 2018, and we had been going strong with this missional thing for about two years. After our church-planting team transitioned to become a missional community, choosing not to start a whole new church but to work within the existing structure, our missional life exploded. Many of these stories I've recounted in this book took place within that two-year span, and life as a Jesus-follower in general and a pastor specifically had never been more fulfilling.

But then there was the rest of the church—and I don't mean the individual people, whom we dearly loved and appreciated. I mean the system and the programming and the culture of the collective group. And especially the Saturday morning worship service. *That* was draining and boring—and anything but life-giving.

Yet there we found ourselves, torn between two worlds. Most everyone in our missional community was energised by the mission we were pursuing the other six days of the week together as a family, but found it increasingly difficult to sit through a lifeless program each Saturday morning and continue to invest in the larger church, which lacked direction and energy.

What's more, many of the people we were discipling in everyday life started asking us about where we'd "go to church." This was an anxiety-inducing question. Many Christians know this feeling all too well. Inviting a friend "to church" just isn't an option because you're not sure what they'll encounter. It might be more traumatic than edifying, pushing them farther away from Jesus rather than nudging them closer.

So all this was going on in my head and heart, and it was reaching a boiling point—which the other members of our missional community were feeling as well. There was incredible cognitive dissonance going on, and we weren't sure how much longer we could take it. It felt a lot like how John Pavlovitz describes it, when "the difference between the Church you dream of and the one you're experiencing is taking its toll."[1]

To be honest, there were actually quite a few moments when Camille and I started having conversations about a topic I never dreamed possible: quitting paid ministry. I felt so convicted about the direction God had taken my ministry that I couldn't imagine pursuing any other type. The genie was out of the bottle and there was no way of putting it back in. Once you've experienced something so rich and powerful and fulfilling—and once you feel like you've finally found your calling—you can never settle for anything less. I felt like I had seen a whole new world and I couldn't un-see it.

I'm also a person who is big on authenticity. I've never been a "fake it till you make it" kind of guy. I can't just go through the motions or participate in an activity or organisation out of habit or obligation. I need good and thoughtful reasons for anything I do. As a creative person, I'm huge on originality and can't just inherit a system or set of practices and carry them out without knowing the reasons behind them. To do something because "it's always been done this way" is frustrating and draining to me.

I realise, of course, that it's not all about me. Sometimes you do what you have to do, even if you don't understand it. And I know that the life of a Christian in general and of a pastor specifically calls for great sacrifice. It won't always be balloons and ice cream. It won't always be happy times.

But I also came to the conviction that God doesn't want us to be *miserable* in our calling either. And sometimes the discontent in our hearts is the Spirit's way of telling us that something isn't quite right—that God wants something so much more for our lives and for our ministries and for our communities. Indeed, sometimes God is desperately trying to tell us through the discontent in our heart that all the failure we've experienced is a giant billboard, pointing us to the fact that something has to change.

And so there I was on my bed that Saturday morning, overwhelmed with this feeling that I couldn't shake: it was time for a funeral.

TRYING SMARTER

It occurred to me though that a church can't simply have a funeral for itself and then show up a week later and do the exact same things it did the week before. What would be the point of burying a church if it would simply be business as usual after the funeral?

So I realised that if we were going to have a *funeral* then we also needed to have a *resurrection*. We needed to have something better in place if we were going to move on from the past.

It's a *lot* of work to change the culture of an organisation, especially a church that has been around for 90 years. There's so much inertia to contend with. That's why many pastors say it's easier to give birth than to raise the dead. In other words, it's much easier to start a new church than to try to change the culture of an existing one.

But I was naïve and didn't know any better—and I felt like this was my only option.

So I came up with a plan: I would reach out to individuals in the church and visit them one-on-one, pitching the idea of restarting the church. I was completely willing to trash the whole idea if it became apparent there was no desire for it. This was a big point of surrender for me, because I tend to think that my ideas are the best and any sort of rejection of them feels like a rejection of me. Again, I have a lot of growing to do.

I quickly formulated a list of people to reach out to, starting that very morning with Warren and Michelle, a couple who weren't part of our missional community but were nevertheless resonant with the vision. I quickly fired off a text to them, giving a broad overview of what I was thinking and asking if we could visit that week. To my surprise, they immediately responded they that thought it was a great idea and excitedly welcomed me into their home a few days later to hear more about it.

After I visited with them, I scheduled a visit a few days later with another person. Again, much to my surprise, that person responded with enthusiasm. And then the next person and the next person and the next person. Over the span of about a month, I visited with about 20 of the most active stakeholders in the church and every single one of them agreed that something drastically different needed to happen with our church.

To be completely honest, I was shocked. I figured there'd be a handful of people who thought we needed to change, but I didn't think *every* single person would agree.

Soon after I visited with the major stakeholders, I invited key leaders—most of whom comprised the church board—to start meeting regularly to pray about and plan our next steps. When I had visited with the individual members, I didn't pitch any specific vision as to what a restarted church would look like. I simply gauged their level of interest in the general idea and explained that we would be taking one step at a time.

For about a month, I met with those key leaders and we talked and prayed, building momentum and excitement. Somewhere along the way, a number of them started really asking what exactly a "restart" would look like. What did I mean by that, they wanted to know.

I found myself in a dilemma. I wanted to make sure it wasn't just me driving the bus. But I also realised I'd been privileged to have many years of formal theological and pastoral training, as well as—perhaps more significantly—a number of years of very focused study on what it means to be the church, living God's mission. For the past two years, I had been eating, breathing and dreaming about this stuff non-stop, and I felt convicted that God had equipped me to cast a vision and invite others to give their feedback.

So I tried my hand at it and invited the leaders to imagine a scenario: what if they moved away from Bangor and returned in 10 years. What would the church they returned to look like?

Then I painted a picture of what I imagined it could be like if we made changes now. It went something like this: they'd discover a church that was made up of missional communities. This was the primary expression of church—everyone involved in a missional community, living together as family. When people thought of "church," they thought first and foremost about doing life together in these smaller communities. They would be the engine that ran the church.

They would also see a church full of disciple-makers, everyone seeking to become more like Jesus and inviting others into the same journey. They would view everyday life as the place to be and make disciples, developing authentic relationships with their neighbours, co-workers and anyone else God placed in their paths.

What's more, they would encounter a safe church. Every circle people entered would be a safe place to grow in grace at the Spirit's pace. The church would not be one that majored in minors or one that ostracised people on the basis of their viewpoints. It would be a church that was wholeheartedly committed to the beautiful story of God and the scriptural teachings of our community of faith. As a result, it would be theologically generous, refusing to exclude anyone who sincerely and humbly wanted to wrestle with their faith.

Lastly, it would be a church where everyone was in recovery in some fashion or form, admitting their imperfection and weakness and seeking to continuously grow in all areas of life—emotionally, spiritually, intellectually, physically.

This was the vision I shared with those leaders. And I was moved that it spoke to their hearts—even bringing some to tears. They so much wanted to experience a church like that and they eagerly wanted to share the vision with the wider church.

So after more prayer and conversation, we decided it was time to invite the whole church into the conversation. We picked a date for a church business meeting and invited the members to a Sunday morning brunch at a local hotel. One person volunteered to foot the bill to rent out a conference room and to pay for all the catering. We determined that for such an important occasion, we would go big.

And so on a Sunday morning at the end of March, the church gathered to hear the vision. Nearly 40 people showed up—which was about twice as many as any other business meeting we'd had in the recent past. There we were, gathered around tables, enjoying fellowship, eating good food and talking about what God had in mind. And then I invited a couple of people to share how their hearts had been moved by God's call to mission. Following their stories, I stood up and presented the same vision I'd shared with the leaders.

I then explained that we would form a steering committee to prayerfully plot out a course to implement the vision, which we would then bring back to the whole church for final approval at a future date.

We weren't exactly sure how we'd form the steering committee though. To be completely honest, my inclination was to just hand-pick a number of people who I knew would be resonant my agenda, so things could just move forward as quickly and as seamlessly as possible. But a few leaders pushed back on this approach, insisting that if we were trying to be a church that practiced inclusivity, then we needed to practice it right from the beginning and thus invite *everyone* to participate in the steering committee.

Despite my reluctance, I agreed. I announced that beginning a few weeks later we would start an eight-week steering committee process and everyone was invited.

I had no idea who would show up that first week and I was quite nervous about what course we would take. I honestly had no idea how to proceed, having never led out in such a process. Things got even crazier when, shortly after the meeting began, one person raised his hand and volunteered to chair the committee. He then came up front and proceeded to write on the white board all these steps that he'd learned in his many years in business, using terms that didn't make sense to most of us, myself included. What's more, it was apparent he didn't really get the missional concepts and was instead steering us back towards a traditional model of church.

When he finished, he put the marker down, looked me in the eye, and told me it was up to me if I wanted him to chair the committee. It was in my hands.

I didn't know what to do. My head was spinning. Always conscious of not wanting to wield unilateral authority, I wasn't sure how to proceed. But we got to the end of the meeting and I told the gentleman I would call him to chat more.

I was due to travel a few days later to present at a conference, and during a layover in Detroit I gave him a call. We talked for about 45 minutes as I tried to get a better handle on where he was coming from and tried to explain to him what I was thinking. And then something remarkable happened: I actually decided it might be best to have him chair the committee. I figured if the Spirit was really leading then we had nothing to fear. God could work in the process no matter who was chairing.

But this was the really remarkable thing: at the very moment I came to that conclusion and made the offer to him, he reached the opposite conclusion. He seemed to realise that the church as a whole was really intent on going a different direction than he hoped to steer it, and so he withdrew his offer at the same time I accepted it.

When the steering committee met the next week, we began our planning in earnest. Over the next eight weeks, about 20 people participated in the process. For the first two weeks, we re-familiarised ourselves with the gospel and God's story, recognising that the gospel is the foundation to everything. It's only as we understand the reality of the gospel that we can understand the purpose and mission of the church. If we're not clear on the gospel, we won't be clear on why we exist and what our calling is.

We then spent a few weeks focusing on what it means to be God's people, whose primary task is to make disciples. This, again, is foundational to everything we do. And if we're not clear on this then we won't be clear on how to organise ourselves. So many churches don't know why they exist and wander aimlessly, putting on random programs that don't seem to contribute to a cohesive vision.

Eventually, we came to the trickiest part: actually planning what the church would look like from day-to-day, week-to-week, as we participated in God's mission. This was another area I was unsure how to lead. Again, I didn't want to unilaterally set this vision, but I also knew there weren't very many people in my congregation who travelled in the world of ecclesiology or who had the imagination to think beyond what they already knew.

So I decided to come the next week with a proposal of what it could look like, inviting feedback and reflection.

The proposal had three parts: first, we would become a larger church of smaller communities. Second, we would organise our gathering on Saturdays to facilitate our values of disciple-making and community. What this would look like on a practical level was going informal—setting up tables and having a simple worship service that included singing, sharing and a teaching. It also meant that we would discontinue our adult Sabbath school (Bible study) time and hold our children's Sabbath schools during the worship gathering, right after we were done singing. And third, we would reorganise our leadership structure to focus on these two areas alone. We wouldn't have any other positions besides those focusing on running these two pursuits—our missional communities and our simplified Sabbath gathering.

After a few weeks of discussion, the committee agreed on these proposals and we set a date to bring it to the whole church for final approval. I remember the date well: July 17, 2018, the date of Camille's and my anniversary.

As the date approached, I got increasingly nervous. I caught wind that one of the few members on the steering committee who wasn't entirely happy with all the proposals had started calling around to inactive members, trying to rally them to attend the meeting. All I could imagine was showing up to the meeting and seeing 30 people we hadn't seen in a decade, and them undermining all the hard work we'd done. I wrestled with God a great deal as I thought about this possibility, but finally came to a place of peace on the morning of the meeting.

And when I showed up, I realised my fears were unfounded. It quickly became apparent we would have more than enough people in favour of all the proposals. Within short order we voted on each one, receiving at least 80 per cent approval for all three of them.

We then set a date for our official restart—September 15, 2018—and closed the meeting.

I let out a huge sigh of relief when the meeting ended. I felt so incredibly satisfied. It felt like the culmination of a very long journey. We never got to holding a funeral for what had been, but a process of rebirth was underway. I had felt God's invitation for our church family to step into a radically new way of participating in His mission, and all our hard work had paid off. I slept very well that night, dreaming of what was to come.

PREPARING TO RE-LAUNCH

Over the next few months, we kicked into high gear as we prepared to officially restart. We formed a new leadership team, which came together quite amazingly and providentially and quickly. We also completely redecorated the church building, aligning it with our vision and values. We repainted classrooms for the children's Sabbath schools and started forming new missional communities. We also made a beautiful promotional video, featuring a number of members reciting the "The Table I Long For" reading that our missional community reads at the beginning of each gathering.

A few weeks before our official restart, we posted the video to our Facebook page and it sort of went viral—at least by our very modest standards. It struck a chord with so many people. I remember our friend Shivani telling me after she watched it that we surely made the video just for her. She said she would definitely be at our first worship gathering, despite having never come to one of our church services before. She just had to be there.

September 15 eventually came, after much preparation and planning, and so did the crowd. We were bursting at the seams with people that first week. The atmosphere was electric. The crowds came again the next week and the week after.

One of the reasons the atmosphere was so electric was because we started having a lot of people from various religious backgrounds— or no religious background at all—leaning in and participating in community life. This was partly because we made a conscious effort to only use language that non-members could understand. We banished all "insider" language that would be confusing to the uninitiated.

I also think one of the most enjoyable features we introduced, which some remarked was our "secret sauce," was the story time we'd have each week, where one person shared their story, through whatever twists and turns it took. This became everyone's favourite part of the gathering and we came to know each other more deeply, moving beyond the friendly pleasantries.

We also went down a full decade in our average age. This was largely due to our children's Sabbath school group, which saw a 400 per cent increase in participation over the first few months, and a 200–300 per cent increase over the course of the first year. The church went from being composed largely of older people to being mostly a church of younger families. And this was mostly because we started gaining younger families, not because the older people decided to leave, although unfortunately a few did.

And lastly, our giving went up by nearly 50 per cent in the first full year, despite the fact that—or perhaps because—we decided to stop collecting an offering during our gathering, choosing instead to believe the Spirit's ability to disciple people in giving.

While, predictably, the initial excitement and energy wore off a bit after a few months, it didn't take long for the church to take on a completely different vibe and culture. The best way I can describe it is that it felt like the church went from being full of people who thought they had it all figured out, to being full of people who realised they didn't but who wanted to continuously grow. It was OK to not be OK and to not have all the answers. I remember our friend Shivani saying a few months later that gathering with our church gave her such a huge sense of peace, which means a lot coming from someone who is not a Jesus-follower but who is searching.

Not that we've arrived, of course. Our church is far from perfect and it's not like we have yet reached a point where we're overcrowded and having to turn people away. And all of us, myself included, have to be continuously reminded of what it means to be family together, pursuing God's mission every day and not just once a week. We have to constantly learn and re-learn what it means to truly be the church, living as a missional people together in all our lives.

Similarly, a worldwide pandemic took its toll on us, as it did for everyone, just as we were hitting our stride. So, in some ways, as we collectively pray for life to finally return to some level of "normalcy," we find ourselves having to "re-start" our re-start again, trying to recapture some of the momentum we lost as a result of humans not being able to get skin-to-skin with each other for so long. But we take comfort in Paul's words that "he who began a good work in you will carry it on to completion until the day of Christ Jesus" (Philippians 1:6, NIV).

As I tell people, the past five-plus years have easily been the best years of my life, and certainly the best years of my ministry. I wouldn't trade them for anything. God works in strange and mysterious ways. I thought all my hopes and dreams had come crashing down when I received that last rejection letter from Harvard, but I have come to discover that God had something so much better for me—which, ironically, included a recent acceptance into the part-time PhD program at Oxford University. (God certainly has a sense of humour and gave me a good consolation prize.) I've learned so much about God, about faith, about what it means to be the church and to participate in God's mission. And I've learned so much about myself.

More importantly, we've experienced such rich joy and fellowship and mission. We've sat at the table together and tasted what it means to be the church. And it is good. So good.

APPENDIX A:
FINDING A "PERSON OF PEACE"

One of the things I've discovered about the average Christian is that many—if not *most*—Christians don't have any friends who are not already Christians. This is especially true in my own faith community, the Seventh-day Adventist Church, in which many Adventists live in towns and communities that are clustered around an Adventist institution, like a university or hospital. They can live much of their lives without ever having to really spend much time with anyone outside the "tribe."

So what do you do if you feel called to engage a community incarnationally, yet don't know anyone who doesn't already know Jesus?

You find a "person of peace."

Missionaries in other parts of the world have long known about this concept, but missionaries in the West are just beginning to catch on. The idea is based on Luke 10, where Jesus sends the 72 out to proclaim the gospel in the surrounding villages, preparing them for His ministry. He told the apostles that if a "son of peace" welcomed them into his home, feeding them and looking after them, the apostles were to "remain in the same house" and to not "go from house to house" (Luke 10:7). Essentially, they had found a "person of peace" who resonated with their mission, and the apostles were to stick with them instead of spreading themselves around to everyone else. They were to think in terms of micro-mission rather than macro-mission, focusing on the few rather than the many.

This is what we can do as we join God's mission. Instead of thinking about reaching the masses and focusing on quantity, God invites us to slow down and just find that *one person* who welcomes us into their lives, focusing on quality. All it takes is one.

But what you will soon discover is that when you slow down and focus on just *one person*, that person almost always represents scores of other people. No man or woman is an island, after all. So just meeting and journeying with one person is a "gateway" of sorts to meeting a whole bunch of other people.

Many people have written about this "person of peace" concept, and there are many different layers to it, but the person who was most clarifying for me was Alex Absalom in his book *The Viral Gospel*. In that book, Absalom outlines the basic characteristics of a "person of peace." He notes that (1) they welcome you, (2) they receive you, (3) they serve you, (4) you intentionally invest in them, and (5) they operate as a gatekeeper to a larger relational network. Essentially, a "person of peace" is someone who likes you and you like them, and you decide to spend time together. It's really as simple as that.[1]

For me, I never really set out to have a "person of peace," but looking back, I realise that my friend Ben served in that role to some degree. He was a city councillor in Bangor and served as mayor for a few years, and we somehow met on Twitter. That eventually led to a friendship in real life, and he introduced me to scores and scores of people. In fact, I've lost track of the number of people in Bangor that Ben has introduced me to—and many of those introductions have led to deep friendships as well. I could diagram a whole "friendship tree," with Ben at the top, that demonstrates the vast network of people I've become friends with, all because I met Ben.

For example, after Ben joined our book club, he invited his friend Jason. Jason then introduced me to Mike (the Mike mentioned earlier who played football), and Mike introduced me to Fred (who, it ends up, had gone to high school with two young ladies who are already a part of our church family). All three of these men—Jason, Mike, and Fred—are important people in my life now, and I am regularly meeting with them, praying with and for them, and providing whatever spiritual, relational and emotional support I can. This is also how I met Peter, who I mentioned earlier. Ben invited Jonathan to our book club, and Jonathan then invited Peter.

Essentially, I went from knowing almost *no-one* in the community and having zero impact on anyone outside my small and cloistered church world to knowing lots of people in my city. All because I met and became good friends with Ben.

To be clear: that is not *why* I became friends with Ben. Meeting him was not a calculation. I like Ben for Ben—whether or not he ever introduces me to anyone else. But Ben also knows I have a heart for people and a desire to positively impact our city, so over the years he has intentionally sought to connect me to people he knows.

The bottom line is that if you have a heart for people—if you want to bless others in ways that are meaningful and long-lasting—find a person of peace. *Just one person.* If they like you and start leaning more and more into life with you, stay with them. Don't try to reach the masses; focus on one; go deep rather than wide. You will be amazed at how that opens up such significant, satisfying and meaningful opportunities.

APPENDIX B: THIRTEEN PRACTICAL WAYS TO BE MISSIONAL IN YOUR CITY OR TOWN

In Appendix A, I described the importance of finding one "person of peace" that you can journey with. But some people don't even know where to begin or how to find a single person they can naturally strike up a friendship with. Approaching random strangers at the store and asking them if they want to be your friend probably won't have the effect you're looking for (unless the effect you're looking for is a really mortified look).

So how and where do you meet people? And how do you live a life of incarnational mission, rather than just putting on programs or providing services for the random and nameless masses? (Remember: being missional, in the truest sense, is not just about putting on occasional services for people, no matter how "humanitarian" they are. Being missional is about going *and* staying; it's about entering into life with people and blessing and serving them as you embody the gospel in their midst.)

As mentioned in Chapter 4, the key is to enter into missional rhythms that naturally bring you into frequent and repeated contact with the same people. Here are some practical suggestions about how you can get out of your "bubble" and into life with people and participate in the life of your community:

1. Throw a Christmas party or summer cookout and invite all your neighbours.
2. Bake or cook for your neighbours.
3. Have a garden and give extra produce to your neighbours and co-workers.
4. Invite a co-worker to join you for lunch.
5. Join a sports league—for example, soccer, hockey, basketball.
6. Coach a children's sports team.
7. Join a club—for example, running, language, photography.
8. Participate in programs your local library offers—for example, kids' story times, book clubs.

9. Attend city/town events—for example, parades or other holiday events and volunteer to serve at them.
10. Get involved in your local government—for example, attend City Council meetings, serve on a parks and recreation committee, join a community garden project.
11. Join a local civic organisation—for example, Rotary, Lions Club, Kiwanis.
12. Walk or run regularly in your neighbourhood and/or join a gym.
13. Volunteer at non-profits—for example, Salvation Army, homeless shelters.

No doubt there are many people who already participate in these types of things, so it's just a matter of now participating in them with gospel intentionality, listening to see where the Spirit is already working, and inviting people into our lives. There may be others who have never stepped out of their bubble or joined a group that wasn't overtly Christian-based and the thought of participating in such pursuits seems like a waste of time or lacking any type of gospel-urgency. But remember: Christ has called us to be "salt," meeting people where they are and patiently incarnating the gospel in their midst. The life we live is the Bible study we give—and it's not until we live a life of humble service, without agenda, that people will start to lean into life with us and want to hear what's important to us.

APPENDIX C:
HOW TO START A
MISSIONAL COMMUNITY

One of the questions we get asked most frequently is how to start a missional community. In some ways, it's extremely simple; in other ways I guess it's complicated, and we're still trying to work out the kinks.

It's first of all important to keep in mind what a missional community is and what it isn't. It's not simply a weekly meeting, a Bible study, or a support or activist group. While a missional community will certainly *include* a number of these ingredients, that is not what it is foundationally. We need to think of a missional community more as an organic group of Jesus-followers who are seeking to become family together and *together* join up with God's mission in our neighbourhoods, cities and towns. This will mean, of course, that we regularly meet together to study Scripture, to pray, to eat, and to encourage and disciple one another in the gospel. We will also prayerfully consider and plan ways to bless and serve our friends and neighbours, inviting them into God's family. But a missional community, first and foremost, is a group of people who are seeking to "do life together" and participate in God's mission.

So how do you start a missional community?

The first step is to prayerfully ask God to show you others in your life who might be open to sharing life together and pursuing His mission in the world. When you feel impressed, approach another person or two, or another couple or two, and share the burden that's on your heart about how God can grow you in the gospel together and how you can bless, serve and disciple others in the gospel.

If anyone responds, next figure out a time when you can regularly— preferably weekly—spend time together to eat, study Scripture and prayerfully ask God who He's calling you to bless and serve. While a missional community is so much more than a weekly meeting, it is not less than one. So having a regular, weekly meeting is critically important to setting a solid foundation as you try to go deeper with one another.

The format of the weekly meeting is not terribly important, but having regular time for the study of Scripture, prayer and learning one another's stories in a safe environment is critical. You also need to prayerfully discuss these questions as you figure out how to be family together and participate in God's mission:

- What do you need to do to progressively become family for one another? Spend holidays together? Go on vacation together? Eat together once a week? Twice a week?
- What is your common mission? Serving one person's neighbourhood? Blessing a specific demographic—like single mothers or immigrants? And what would it look like to embody and incarnate the gospel *together* for these people? Mowing their lawn? Babysitting their kids? Inviting them to a weekly meal?
- Who are you mentoring to eventually send out in 12–24 months to start another missional community so that you can multiply God's family and mission? This is a critically important ingredient—and one that you should be mindful of and intentional about from the very beginning. The goal is to create ever more circles that can bring others into God's family and mission.

Eventually, as you find people in your broader community who are leaning into life with your missional community, you can invite them to join you for more explicit spiritual conversation and discipleship. You can invite them to your missional community gatherings, where you have fostered a very safe and open environment that doesn't major in dogmatism and respects all perspectives (even while unapologetically maintaining allegiance to the gospel). You may even want to go over the "Story of God," which is an eight-week telling of the grand story of Scripture (see Appendix E for a citation of this resource) that is very relevant and relatable to those who don't consciously know Jesus.

BUT WHAT ABOUT THE CHILDREN?

One of the questions that most frequently surfaces when it comes to missional community is what to do with children. In asking this, most people assume that a missional community is nothing more than a weekly meeting. But a missional community is an all-of-life family. So just as your children are a part of your family, they are a part of your missional community as well. They can—and should—participate in most of the life of the community. They can eat with everyone else, serve with everyone else, do life with everyone else, pray with everyone else and even study Scripture with everyone else.

With that being said, there are definitely times in which a missional community may have—or want—adult-only times of meeting and fellowship. This is especially true if you have stay-at-home-mums (or dads) who crave a little kid-free time and adult conversation.

There are no simple answers when it comes to navigating this dynamic. If you want to have a regular meeting with just adults, there are really only a few options: either you take turns as adults providing other programming for the children while the adults meet, or you hire a babysitter (and split the cost among everyone), or you have your meeting when all the kids are in bed (which means either all the kids go to bed in whatever house you're meeting in or are left at home with another caregiver).

As I said, it can be a bit tricky. I've heard of people who have tried various approaches, and a lot of it depends on how much you want to prioritise meeting together. I have plenty of friends who don't put their kids down to bed until late at night, and they don't care if their kids are playing while the adults are meeting. I know others who cannot have an ounce of peace until their kids are sleeping. I've heard of others still who have said they are so committed to pursuing mission and family together with others that not having their kids sleeping soundly in their own beds is a sacrifice they're willing to make.

We've tried various approaches in our missional community with varying degrees of success. For the bulk of its existence, we've put our children down to sleep at Cameron and Ellie's house when we meet on Friday nights at 7 pm. We then wake them up at 10 or 11 pm when we're done meeting and then drive home. While this approach works for our two families, it makes things a little more difficult for other families who have kids—some of whom might not put their kids to bed until much later than ours. Consequently, it's been hard for people who have small kids to regularly participate in our Friday night meetings, because they either have to put them to sleep at Cameron and Ellie's house (which no-one has done) or leave them with a babysitter or another family member. This has been a point of wrestling for us all along.

The bottom line is that we need to first remember that a missional community is more than a meeting and that children should participate in the vast majority of what we're doing together as a missional community. But when it comes to adult-only time, each missional community needs to figure out whatever works best for their context. And sometimes sacrifices have to be made—whether that's kids' sleep schedules, or adults missing a meeting every few weeks to provide programming for children, or everyone chipping in to pay for a babysitter.

APPENDIX D:
ELLEN WHITE ON BEING MISSIONAL

I'm hesitant to do this, because I think our views should be based solely on Scripture, but I also realise that many of the readers of this book will likely be from my faith community and some may be concerned about how these views align with those of our church's co-founder and prolific author, Ellen White. Others may simply find these views so outside the bounds of traditional Adventist orthodoxy that they aren't sure what to make of them.

A whole book could be written to respond to such concerns but suffice it to say that I believe the views I've offered are completely harmonious with traditional Adventist orthodoxy and Ellen White's understanding of the gospel and mission. In fact, Ellen White's writing was as influential in my "missional rebirth" as anything or anyone else. As I've said before, Ellen White was ahead of her time and was "missional" about 100 years before anyone knew what "missional" was. Just read the book *The Ministry of Healing* and you will encounter her missional posture and views.

I thus thought it might be helpful to share a sampling of her writings that speak to the importance of contextualising and incarnating the gospel, trying new methods, and not being bound to tradition and what we've always done in the past. Obviously, anytime one selects quotes and shares them without their full context there's always the risk of grossly misrepresenting the author's true intent. But I feel that these selected quotes accurately reflect Ellen White's overall emphasis and hermeneutic. In short, contrary to what some might think, she was very forward-thinking, innovative and, dare I say, progressive in her understanding and application of the gospel and mission.

I thus present a very small sampling of a much larger body of material that reflects her forward-thinking and incarnational posture:

ON THE IMPORTANCE OF TRYING "NEW METHODS"

"God selects his messengers, and gives them his message; and he says, 'Forbid them not.' New methods must be introduced. God's people must awake to the necessities of the time in which they are living. God has men whom he will call into his service,—men who will not carry forward the work in the lifeless way in which it has been carried forward in the past" (*Review and Herald*, September 30, 1902).

"God would have men cultivate their abilities, that they may have broader ideas in planning and executing his work.

"God has different sets of workman for the different branches of his cause. When those whom he has called to do a certain work, have carried that work along as far as they can with the ability he has given them, the Lord in his providence will call and qualify other men to come in and work with them, still making advance moves, that together they may carry it farther, and lift the standard higher.... There must be no belittling the men who God has accepted as his workmen.

"There are some minds which do not grow with the work, but allow the work to grow far beyond them, and they find themselves tired and worn before they comprehend the circumstances. Then when those whom God is qualifying to assist in the work, take hold of it in a little different way from that in which these responsible men have tried to do it, they should be very careful not to hinder these helpers, or to circumscribe the work. Since they did not see the work in all its bearings, and did not have the burden which God has specially laid upon others, why should they say just how that work should be done? Those who do not discern and adapt themselves to the increasing demands of the work, should not stand blocking the wheels, and thus hindering the advancement of others....

"The weary, worn minds of all the older brethren do not take in the greatness of the work in all its bearings, and are not inclined to keep pace with the opening providences of God. Therefore the responsibilities of the work should not rest wholly with them, as they would not bring into it all the elements essential for its advancement, and thus the work should be retarded....

"Much ability has been lost to the cause of God because many in responsible positions were so narrow in their ideas, that they did not discern the increasing responsibilities....

"The Lord has presented before me that men in responsible positions are standing directly in the way of the workings of God upon his people, because they think that the work must be done and the blessing must come in a certain way they have marked out, and they will not recognise that which comes in any other way....

"The Jews, in Christ's day, in the exercise of their own spirit of self-exaltation, brought in rigid rules and exactions, and so took away all chance for God to work upon minds, until mercy and the love of God were entirely lost sight of in their work. It was this which caused rulers to lay upon the people the heavy burdens of which they justly complained, which our Saviour condemned.

Do not follow in their track, Leave God a chance to do something for those who love him, and do not impose upon them rules and regulations, which, if followed, will leave them destitute of the grace of God as were the hills of Gilboa, without dew or rain" (*The Ellen G White 1888 Materials*, pages 107–113).

"We are to study the field carefully and are not to think that we must follow the same methods in every place....Whatever may have been your former practice, it is not necessary to repeat it again and again in the same way. God would have new and untried methods followed. Break in upon the people— surprise them" (*Evangelism*, page 125).

ON THE DANGERS OF TRADITION AND FORMALISM

"The ministry of Christ was in marked contrast to that of the Jewish elders. Their regard for tradition and formalism had destroyed all real freedom of thought or action. They lived in continual dread of defilement. To avoid contact with the 'unclean,' they kept aloof, not only from the Gentiles, but from the majority of their own people, seeking neither to benefit them nor to win their friendship. By dwelling constantly on these matters, they had dwarfed their minds and narrowed the orbit of their lives. Their example encouraged egotism and intolerance among all classes of the people" (*The Desire of Ages*, page 150).

"The leaders of Israel professed to be the expositors of God's word, but they had studied it only to sustain their traditions, and enforce their man-made observances. By their interpretation they made it express sentiments that God had never given" (*The Desire of Ages*, page 257).

"Priests and scribes and rulers were fixed in a rut of ceremonies and traditions. Their hearts had become contracted, like the dried-up wine skins to which He had compared them. While they remained satisfied with a legal religion, it was impossible for them to become the depositaries of the living truth of heaven. . .

"[T]he scribes and Pharisees had no desire for the precious new wine. Until emptied of the old traditions, customs, and practices, they had no place in mind or heart for the teachings of Christ. They clung to the dead forms, and turned away from the living truth and the power of God" (*The Desire of Ages*, pages 278–279).

"[Christ] did not hesitate to break down the wall of traditional requirements that barricaded the Sabbath" (*The Desire of Ages*, page 286).

"It is through false theories and traditions that Satan gains his power over the mind. By directing men to false standards, he misshapes the character" (*The Desire of Ages*, page 671).

"The Jewish people had been made the depositaries of sacred truth; but Pharisaism had made them the most exclusive, the most bigoted, of all the human race. Everything about the priests and rulers—their dress, customs, ceremonies, traditions—made them unfit to be the light of the world. They looked upon themselves, the Jewish nation, as the world. But Christ commissioned His disciples to proclaim a faith and worship that would have in it nothing of caste or country, a faith that would be adapted to all peoples, all nations, all classes of men" (*The Desire of Ages*, page 819).

"There are many at the present day thus clinging to the customs and traditions of their fathers. When the Lord sends them additional light, they refuse to accept it, because, not having been granted to their fathers, it was not received by them. We are not placed where our fathers were; consequently our duties and responsibilities are not the same as theirs. We shall not be approved of God in looking to the example of our fathers to determine our duty instead of searching the word of truth for ourselves" (*The Great Controversy*, page 164).

"The effort to earn salvation by one's own works inevitably leads men to pile up human exactions as a barrier against sin. For, seeing that they fail to keep the law, they will devise rules and regulations of their own to force themselves to obey. All this turns the mind away from God to self. His love dies out of the heart, and with it perishes love for his fellow men. A system of human invention, with its multitudinous exactions, will lead its advocates to judge all who come short of the prescribed human standard. The atmosphere of selfish and narrow criticism stifles the noble and generous emotions, and causes men to become self-centred judges and petty spies.

"The people partook largely of the same spirit, intruding upon the province of conscience and judging one another in matters that lay between the soul and God. It was in reference to this spirit and practice that Jesus said, 'Judge not, that ye be not judged.' That is, do not set yourself up as a standard. Do not make your opinions, your views of duty, your interpretations of Scripture, a criterion for others and in your heart condemn them if they do not come up to your ideal. Do not criticise others, conjecturing as to their motives and passing judgment upon them" (*Thoughts From the Mount of Blessing*, page 123).

ON THE IMPORTANCE OF EXEGETING CULTURE AND CONTEXTUALISING THE GOSPEL

"While He ministered to the poor, Jesus studied also to find ways of reaching the rich. He sought the acquaintance of the wealthy and cultured Pharisee, the Jewish nobleman, and the Roman ruler. He accepted their invitations, attended their feasts, made Himself familiar with their interests and occupations, that He might gain access to their hearts, and reveal to them the imperishable riches" (*The Ministry of Healing*, page 25).

"Though He was a Jew, Jesus mingled freely with the Samaritans, setting at nought the Pharisaic customs of His nation. In face of their prejudices He accepted the hospitality of this despised people. He slept with them under their roofs, ate with them at their tables,—partaking of the food prepared and served by their hands,—taught in their streets, and treated them with the utmost kindness and courtesy. And while He drew their hearts to Him by the tie of human sympathy, His divine grace brought to them the salvation which the Jews rejected" (*The Ministry of Healing*, page 26).

"When the practices of the people do not come in conflict with the law of God, you may conform to them. If the workers fail to do this, they will not only hinder their own work, but they will place stumbling blocks in the way of those for whom they labour, and hinder them from accepting the truth" (*Review and Herald*, April 6, 1911).

ON THE CRITICAL IMPORTANCE OF BEING INCARNATIONAL

"The world needs today what it needed nineteen hundred years ago—a revelation of Christ.... Christ's method alone will give true success in reaching the people. The Saviour mingled with men as one who desired their good. He showed His sympathy for them, ministered to their needs, and won their confidence. Then He bade them, 'Follow Me.'

"There is need of coming close to the people by personal effort. If less time were given to sermonising, and more time were spent in personal ministry, greater results would be seen. The poor are to be relieved, the sick cared for, the sorrowing and the bereaved comforted, the ignorant instructed, the inexperienced counselled. We are to weep with those that weep, and rejoice with those that rejoice. Accompanied by the power of persuasion, the power of prayer, the power of the love of God, this work will not, cannot, be without fruit" (*The Ministry of Healing*, page 143).

"This was Christ's method. His work was largely made up of personal interviews. He had a faithful regard for the one-soul audience. . . We are not to wait for souls to come to us; we must seek them out where they are" (*Christ's Object Lessons*, page 229).

"The badge of Christianity is not an outward sign, not the wearing of a cross or a crown, but it is that which reveals the union of man with God. By the power of His grace manifested in the transformation of character the world is to be convinced that God has sent His Son as its Redeemer. No other influence that can surround the human soul has such power as the influence of an unselfish life. The strongest argument in favour of the gospel is a loving and lovable Christian" (*The Ministry of Healing*, page 470).

"Our influence upon others depends not so much upon what we say as upon what we are. Men may combat and defy our logic, they may resist our appeals; but a life of disinterested love is an argument they cannot gainsay. A consistent life, characterised by the meekness of Christ, is a power in the world" (*The Desire of Ages*, page 141).

"As Christ is the channel for the revelation of the Father, so we are to be the channel for the revelation of Christ. While our Saviour is the great source of illumination, forget not, O Christian, that He is revealed through humanity. God's blessings are bestowed through human instrumentality. Christ Himself came to the world as the Son of man. Humanity, united to the divine nature, must touch humanity. The church of Christ, every individual disciple of the Master, is heaven's appointed channel for the revelation of God to men" (*Thoughts From the Mount of Blessing*, page 40).

"The greatest deception of the human mind in Christ's day was that a mere assent to the truth constitutes righteousness. In all human experience a theoretical knowledge of the truth has been proved to be insufficient for the saving of the soul. It does not bring forth the fruits of righteousness. A jealous regard for what is termed theological truth often accompanies a hatred of genuine truth as made manifest in life. The darkest chapters of history are burdened with the record of crimes committed by bigoted religionists. The Pharisees claimed to be children of Abraham, and boasted of their possession of the oracles of God; yet these advantages did not preserve them from selfishness, malignity, greed for gain, and the basest hypocrisy. They thought themselves the greatest religionists of the world, but their so-called orthodoxy led them to crucify the Lord of glory.

"The same danger still exists. Many take it for granted that they are Christians, simply because they subscribe to certain theological tenets. But they have not brought the truth into practical life. . . Men may profess faith in the truth; but if it does not make them sincere, kind, patient, forbearing, heavenly-minded, it is a curse to its possessors, and through their influence it is a curse to the world" (*The Desire of Ages*, page 309).

ON THE IMPORTANCE OF MISSIONAL COMMUNITIES

"Why do not believers feel a deeper, more earnest concern for those who are out of Christ? Why do not two or three meet together and plead with God for the salvation of some special one, and then for still another? In our churches let companies be formed for service. In the Lord's work there are to be no idlers. Let different ones unite in labour as fishers of men. Let them seek to gather souls from the corruption of the world into the saving purity of Christ's love.

"The formation of small companies as a basis of Christian effort is a plan that has been presented before me by One who cannot err. If there is a large number in the church, let the members be formed into small companies, to work not only for the church members but for unbelievers also" (*Review and Herald*, August 12, 1902).

"Christ sought the people where they were and placed before them the great truths in regard to His kingdom. As He went from place to place, He blessed and comforted the suffering and healed the sick. This is our work. Small companies are to go forth to do the work to which Christ appointed His disciples" (*Review and Herald*, April 12, 1912).

"Many of the members of our large churches are doing comparatively nothing. They might accomplish a good work if, instead of crowding together, they would scatter into places that have not yet been entered by the truth. Trees that are planted too thickly do not flourish. They are transplanted by the gardener, that they may have room to grow and not become dwarfed and sickly. The same rule would work well for our large churches. Many of the members are dying spiritually for want of this very work. They are becoming sickly and inefficient. Transplanted, they would have room to grow strong and vigorous.

"It is not the purpose of God that His people should colonise or settle together in large communities. The disciples of Christ are His representatives upon the earth, and God designs that they shall be scattered all over the country, in the towns, cities, and villages, as lights amidst the darkness of the world. They are to be missionaries for God, by their faith and works testifying to the near approach of the coming Saviour.

"The lay members of our churches can accomplish a work which, as yet, they have scarcely begun. None should move into new places merely for the sake of worldly advantage; but where there is an opening to obtain a livelihood, let families that are well grounded in the truth enter, one or two families in a place, to work as missionaries. They should feel a love for souls, a burden of labour for them, and should make it a study how to bring them into the truth. They can distribute our publications, hold meetings in their homes, become acquainted with their neighbours, and invite them to come to these meetings. Thus they can let their light shine in good works" (*Review and Herald*, June 30, 1903).

APPENDIX E: FURTHER READING

There are many great resources that expand on the missional ideas I have proposed in this book, as well those that talk about recovery and emotional health. Unfortunately, aside—ironically enough—from Ellen White, I have found there to be a real lack of material within my faith community that fleshes out these incarnational ideas. But there are many within the broader Christian community that have taken up Ellen White's mantel—without realising it—and applied the missional paradigm to our current context. I share some recommendations below.

I have also taken it for granted in this book that everyone reading it started with a strong gospel-foundation. But that may be a wrong assumption. I am continually amazed and saddened by how many Jesus-followers I encounter for whom the gospel is like a foreign language. But the gospel must be our foundation. Living a missional, recovery-oriented life is the outflow of the gospel. If we don't know the gospel, these concepts will either turn into a humanistic endeavour or they will threaten our sense of security—which is often based on tradition and perfectionism.

So I first share some recommendations to further acquaint yourself with the gospel, begging you, at all costs, to get to know it intimately before anything else.

BOOKS ON THE GOSPEL

I'd first recommend two books I've written: *Pursued by a Relentless God* (Pacific Press, 2011) and *There's More to Jesus* (Signs Publishing, 2016). It's also critically important, especially in our current age, to understand the gospel within the framework of God's grand story. The gospel is not simply a list of ideas; it is a narrative that God invites us into. To that end, I have written a small booklet called *God's Story and My Story*, which is available on Amazon. This is also what we use for "The Story of God," which I mentioned in Appendix B.

I also highly recommend anything my friend Ty Gibson has written but especially *See With New Eyes* (Pacific Press, 2000) or *An Endless Falling In Love* (Pacific Press, 2003). Another book that has been as transformational as any other for me over the past few years is Henri Nouwen's *The Return of the Prodigal Son* (Image Book, 1992). Though a little more intellectually rigorous, I'd also recommend anything by N T Wright to understand the larger framework of the gospel, for example, his book *The Day the Revolution Began* (HarperOne, 2016).

Ellen White's works on the gospel and the life of Christ are absolutely foundational, including *The Desire of Ages* (Pacific Press, 1898), *Thoughts From the Mount of Blessing* (Pacific Press, 1896), *Steps to Christ* (Pacific Press, 1892) and *Christ's Object Lessons* (Review and Herald, 1900).

BOOKS ON MISSIONAL CHURCH AND DISCIPLESHIP

Anyone who has heard me talk about my "missional rebirth" over the past few years knows that the most influential book in setting my whole journey in motion was Jeff Vanderstelt's *Saturate* (Crossway, 2015). It put into words what I had been sensing in my heart in the months that led up to my reading of it. Tim Chester and Steve Timmis's *Total Church* (Crossway, 2008) was also influential, as was Caesar Kalinowski's *Small Is Big, Slow is Fast* (Zondervan, 2014). Francis Chan's *Letters to the Church* (David C Cook, 2018) is a critically important book on discipleship, and Dave Ferguson's *Hero Maker* (Zondervan, 2018) highlights the critical role of multiplying leaders and disciples. A little farther afield, Dietrich Bonhoeffer's classic *Life Together* (HarperOne, 1954) is such a beautiful and inspiring exposition on how to form and be community together.

There are some other really important works that approach the missional concepts from a theoretical standpoint, providing a theological and philosophical basis for the ideas. These books are thus for the less faint of heart. The British missiologist, and former missionary to India, Lesslie Newbigin, is generally considered to be the "grandfather" of the missional movement. His books *The Open Secret: An Introduction to the Theology of Mission* (Eerdmans, 1978) and *The Gospel in a Pluralist Society* (Eerdmans, 1989) are seminal works and incredibly thought-provoking and paradigm-shifting. His book *Proper Confidence: Faith, Doubt, and Certainty in Christian Discipleship* (Eerdmans, 1995), is also an incredibly important work when it comes to how to approach faith in ways that aren't characterised by the type of thinking that the Enlightenment imposed on the world for a long time. Beyond Newbigin, Alan Hirsch's revised edition of *The Forgotten Ways* (BrazosPress, 2016) and the revised edition of his book with Michael Frost, *The Shaping of Things to Come* (Baker Books, 2013) are extremely helpful works on the theory of missional church.

It should also be mentioned that Ellen White, in *The Ministry of Healing* (Pacific Press, 1905), anticipated the missional movement about a century in advance.

BOOKS ON RECOVERY AND EMOTIONAL WORK

As I shared in Chapter 16, I believe that processing and dealing with our wounds and brokenness is a critical part of experiencing wholeness and becoming fully matured disciples. The gospel will remain one dimensional in our experience, and we will have a hard time truly entering into the thoughts and feelings of others, until we engage in "inner work," as some people call it. We can't be fully missional and provide the inclusive spaces and circles that non-religious people crave until we process our own pain and trauma (which we all have). This is thus not optional in my mind, if we are to mature to the point that God wants us to mature to.

Reading anything by Brené Brown is a good start. She talks a lot about vulnerability, authenticity and shame. Many of her books are similar but *The Gifts of Imperfection* (Hazelden Publishing, 2010) is a good and succinct place to start. Prior to Brené Brown, John Bradshaw was perhaps foremost in talking about shame and vulnerability. His book *Healing the Shame that Binds You* (Health Communications Inc., 2005) is a must-read. Pia Mellody's *Facing Codependence* (HarperOne, 2003) is eye-opening and heavy but so critically important, and anything by Harriet Lerner, like *The Dance of Intimacy* (Harper, 1989), is really good. For a couple of books that are a little heavier, Bessel van der Kolk's *The Body Keeps the Score: Brain, Mind, and Body in the Healing of Trauma* (Penguin Books, 2014) and *A General Theory of Love* (Vintage Books, 2000) by Thomas Lewis, Fari Amini and Richard Lannon, are excellent. Lastly, for a practical book that can be utilised for recovery groups, *The Twelve Steps for Christians* (Recovery Publications, 1988) is really good.

ENDNOTES

Chapter 1
1   <https://twitter.com/Benjaminlund/status/1256839330229653504>.

Chapter 2
1   Lesslie Newbigin, *The Open Secret: An Introduction to the Theology of Mission* (Grand Rapids, MI: Eerdmans, 1995), pages 1, 2.
2   Variations of this quote can be found in various places, but see <http://standrewschurch. org.in/newsletter/Andrews_newsletter_Sep_2017.pdf>.

Chapter 3
1   Caesar Kalinowski, *Small is Big, Slow is Fast: Living and Leading Your Family and Community on God's Mission* (Grand Rapids, MI: Zondervan, 2014), page 25.
2   Jeff Vanderstelt, *Saturate: Being Disciples of Jesus in the Everyday Stuff of Life* (Wheaton, IL: Crossway, 2015), pages 39, 86.
3   <https://relevantmagazine.com/god/ragamuffin-legacy/>.
4   <https://twitter.com/alanhirsch/status/517667468245233665>.

Chapter 5
1   Lesslie Newbigin, *The Open Secret: An Introduction to the Theology of Mission* (Grand Rapids, MI: Eerdmans, 1995), pages 33, 35.
2   Lesslie Newbigin, *The Gospel in a Pluralist Society* (Grand Rapids, MI: Eerdmans, 1989), page 136.
3   Newbigin, *The Open Secret*, page 127.
4   <https://twitter.com/bobrobertsjr/status/1255895973219500035>.
5   Tim Chester and Steve Timmis, *Total Church: A Radical Reshaping around Gospel and Community* (Wheaton, IL: Crossway, 2008), page 78.
6   Jeff Vanderstelt, *Saturate: Being Disciples of Jesus in the Everyday Stuff of Life* (Wheaton, IL: Crossway, 2015), page 182.
7   Ellen G White, *The Desire of Ages* (Mountain View, CA: Pacific Press, 1947), page 141.

Chapters 6
1   Thomas Lewis, Fari Amini, and Richard Lannon, *A General Theory of Love* (New York: Vintage Books, 2000).
2   Ellen G White, *Thoughts From the Mount of Blessing* (Mountain View, CA: Pacific Press, 1928), page 40.

Chapter 7
1   Tim Chester, *A Meal With Jesus: Discovering Grace, Community, and Mission around the Table* (Wheaton, IL: Crossway, 2011), pages 82, 83.

Chapter 8
1   Cited in Lilianne Doukhan, *In Tune With God* (Hagerstown, MD: Review and Herald Publishing Association, 2010), page 291.
2   Todd Engstrom, "Why Small Groups Won't Work," <https://youtu.be/kvWnXYSELF4>.

3   Lesslie Newbigin, *The Gospel in a Pluralist Society* (Grand Rapids, MI: Eerdmans, 1989), page 144.

4   Larry W Hurtado, *Destroyer of the Gods: Early Christian Distinctiveness in the Roman World* (Waco, TX: Baylor University Press, 2016), page 10.

5   Hurtado, *Destroyer of the Gods*, page 8.

6   Jay Y Kim, *Analog Church: Why We Need Real People, Places, and Things in the Digital World* (Downers Grove, IL: IVP, 2020), page 12.

7   Francis Chan, *Letters to the Church* (Colorado Springs, CO: David C Cook, 2018), pages 186, 187.

Chapter 9

1   Alan Hirsch, *The Forgotten Ways: Reactivating Apostolic Movements*, rev. ed. (Grand Rapids, MI: BrazosPress, 2016), page 133.

Chapter 10

1   Quoted in Rob Bell, *Love Wins: A Book About Heaven, Hell, and the Fate of Every Person Who Ever Lived* (New York: HarperOne, 2011), page 7.

2   Lesslie Newbigin, *The Gospel in a Pluralist Society* (Grand Rapids, MI: Eerdmans, 1989), page 10.

3   Brené Brown, *Daring Greatly: How the Courage to Be Vulnerable Transforms the Way We Live, Love, Parent, and Lead* (New York: Avery, 2012), page 176.

4   Newbigin, *The Gospel in a Pluralist Society*, page 12.

Chapter 11

1   Rob Bell, *Love Wins: A Book About Heaven, Hell, and the Fate of Every Person Who Ever Lived* (New York: HarperOne, 2011), pages 1, 2.

2   Bell, *Love Wins*, page 9

3   Lesslie Newbigin, *The Open Secret: An Introduction to the Theology of Mission* (Grand Rapids, MI: Eerdmans, 1995), page 173.

4   Ellen G White, *The Desire of Ages* (Mountain View, CA: Pacific Press, 1947), pages 637, 638.

5   Newbigin, *The Open Secret*, page 173.

6   Lesslie Newbigin, *The Gospel in a Pluralist Society* (Grand Rapids, MI: Eerdmans, 1989), page 127.

7   Ellen G White, *Lift Him Up* (Hagarstown, MD: Review and Herald, 1988), page 98.

8   N T Wright, *Justification: God's Plan and Paul's Vision* (Downers Grove, IL: IVP Academic, 2009), page 27.

Chapter 12

1   Tim Chester, *A Meal With Jesus: Discovering Grace, Community, and Mission around the Table* (Wheaton, IL: Crossway, 2011), page 12.

2   Chester, *A Meal With Jesus*, pages 13–15, 89.

3   Chester, *A Meal With Jesus*, page 21, quoting Conrad Gempf, *Mealtime Habits of the Messiah* (Grand Rapids, MI: Zondervan, 2005), page 133.

4   See <https://www.healthline.com/health/happy-hormone#sunlight>.

5   Tim Chester quotes this story in *A Meal With Jesus*, pages 95, 96.

6   Henri J M Nouwen, *The Return of the Prodigal Son: A Story of Homecoming* (New York: Doubleday, 1992), page 43.

7   Brené Brown, *The Gifts of Imperfection: Let Go of Who You Think You're Supposed to Be and Embrace Who You Are* (Center City, MN: Hazelden Publishing, 2010), page 20.

8   Adapted from Jeff Chu, "Together At the Table." <http://byjeffchu.com/together-at-the-table/>.

Chapter 13

1   Lesslie Newbigin, *The Gospel in a Pluralist Society* (Grand Rapids, MI: Eerdmans, 1989), page 227.

Chapter 14

1   M Scott Peck, *The Different Drum: Community Making and Peace* (New York: Simon and Schuster, 1987), page 21.
2   <https://twitter.com/timkellernyc/status/970743366349721601>.
3   Dietrich Bonhoeffer, *Life Together: The Classic Exploration of Christian Community* (New York: HarperOne, 1954), page 27.
4   Alan Hirsch, *The Forgotten Ways: Reactivating Apostolic Movements*, rev. ed. (Grand Rapids, MI: BrazosPress, 2016), page 165.
5   Hirsch, *The Forgotten Ways*, page 163.
6   Quoted in Hirsch, *The Forgotten Ways*, page 169.
7   Henri J M Nouwen, *The Return of the Prodigal Son: A Story of Homecoming* (New York: Doubleday, 1992), page 86.

Chapter 15

1   Ty Gibson, *See With New Eyes: The True View of God's Character* (Nampa, ID: Pacific Press, 2000), page 55.
2   Brené Brown, *The Gifts of Imperfection: Let Go of Who You Think You're Supposed to Be and Embrace Who You Are* (Center City, MN: Hazelden Publishing, 2010), page 25.
3   Brown, *The Gifts of Imperfection*, page 30.
4   Brown, *The Gifts of Imperfection*, page 24.
5   Brown, *The Gifts of Imperfection*, page 61.
6   <https://cac.org/transforming-pain-2018-10-17/>.
7   C G Jung, *Modern Man In Search of a Soul*, trans. W S Dell and Cary F Baynes (London: Kegan Paul, Trench, Trubner & Co Ltd, 1933), page 271.
8   Pia Mellody, *Facing Codependence: What It Is, Where It Comes From, How It Sabotages Our Lives* (New York: HarperOne, 2003), page 194. Emphasis original.
9   Henri J. M. Nouwen, *The Return of the Prodigal Son: A Story of Homecoming* (New York: Doubleday, 1992), page 107.
10 Dietrich Bonhoeffer, *Life Together: The Classic Exploration of Christian Community* (New York: HarperOne, 1954), 110.
11 Bonhoeffer, *Life Together,* 116, emphasis added.
12 Brown, *The Gifts of Imperfection*, page 40.
13 M Scott Peck, *The Different Drum: Community Making and Peace* (New York: Simon and Schuster, 1987), page 69.
14 Peck, *The Different Drum*, page 69.
15 Preston Sprinkle, *People to Be Loved: Why Homosexuality is Not Just an Issue* (Grand Rapids, MI: Zondervan, 2015), page 140.

Chapter 16

1   James K A Smith, *You Are What You Love: The Spiritual Power of Habit* (Grand Rapids, MI: BrazosPress, 2016), page 2.
2   Bryan Stevenson, *Just Mercy: A Story of Justice and Redemption* (New York: Spiegel & Grau, 2015), page 17.
3   Henri Nouwen, *Bread for the Journey: A Daybook of Wisdom and Faith* (New York: HarperOne, 1997), July 8.

Chapter 17

1   Kendi discusses these concepts in his two books *Stamped From the Beginning: The Definitive History of Racist Ideas in America* (New York: Nation Books, 2016) and *How to Be an Antiracist* (New York: One World, 2019).

2   N T Wright, *The Day the Revolution Began: Reconsidering the Meaning of Jesus's Crucifixion* (New York: HarperOne, 2016), page 242. Emphasis added.

3   N T Wright, *Paul: A Biography* (New York: HarperOne, 2018), pages 91, 112. Emphasis original.

4   Kendi, *Stamped From the Beginning*, page 3.

5   <https://www.news4jax.com/news/local/2020/05/08/social-media-group-garners-support-men-who-shot-and-killed-unarmed-jogger/?outputType=amp>.

Chapter 18

1   Ellen G White, *Education* (Mountain View, CA: Pacific Press, 1903), page 35. Emphasis added.

2   Tim Chester and Steve Timmis, *Total Church: A Radical Reshaping around Gospel and Community* (Wheaton, IL: Crossway, 2008), page 59.

3   Francis Chan, *Letters to the Church* (Colorado Springs, CO: David C Cook, 2018), pages 184–186.

Chapter 19

1   John Pavlovitz, *A Bigger Table: Building Messy, Authentic, and Hopeful Spiritual Community* (Louisville, KN: Westminster John Knox Press, 2017), page 49.

Appendix A

1   Alex Absalom, *The Viral Gospel: How Finding Your Person of Peace Accelerates Your Mission* (Exponential Resources, 2014), Ebook.

ACKNOWLEDGMENTS

It goes without saying that these types of projects cannot be done alone. Indeed, the journey this book details was really a group effort. Though I would never claim they'd endorse everything I've written in this book or have come to believe, I've learned more from the fellow disciples in my church, and those in my broader community, than any book I've read or seminar I've attended or podcast I've listened to.

That starts with my dear wife, Camille, who has processed all these ideas, ad nauseum, with me over the past five years. But more importantly, she has been a constant encouragement when I've gotten down and discouraged and full of doubt—which, as she will tell you, happens with great frequency. But she has been my biggest cheerleader, constantly reminding me of my belovedness, and to not listen to the critics.

Besides her, my church family and missional community have been so incredibly supportive and encouraging. Truly, I am so blessed to have such an amazing church. But chief among those who've been at the front of this journey of discovery with me have been Cameron and Ellie Trubey—whose love and support have been unsurpassed—and TC and Avery (you know who you are), and especially my brother, Jim Mello (and now Alice!). I truly would have given up long ago without you guys.

More broadly, and at the risk of forgetting people, our church has gone where it's gone because of the critical participation from people like (in no particular order) Warren and Michelle Brown, Jeff and Debbie Verrill, Robin Hamilton, Stan and Paula Hartin, Josh and Courtney James, James and Jennifer Moors, and Ben and Alyssa Verrill. There are many, many others, of course, and my apologies for missing people. But thank you for sticking with me all these years!

I'm also grateful for those who may not show up every week to our gatherings, but who have nevertheless been extremely supportive and helpful along the way—either closer to home, in Bangor, or farther afield and cheering from a distance. I'm thinking especially of Mike DeVito, Ben Sprague, Nathan Stearman, Ty Gibson, Chris Irrgang, Jarod Thomas and my extended family (my parents especially included), who have all at times been the tragic recipients of some of my crazy thinking and living. I'm also especially grateful for the support I've received from my administrative mentors as we've experimented with some of these ideas: Bob Cundiff and Ted Huskins have taken many chances on me and our church in Bangor, and for that, I'm eternally grateful.

Second to lastly, I'm extremely appreciative to Signs Publishing for their willingness to take on this project. You are truly wonderful to work with, and the editorial oversight that Lauren Webb and Nathan Brown provide are insightful and refreshing. Thank you!

Lastly, I'm grateful to God. To quote the apostle Paul, "To me, who am less than the least of all the saints, this grace was given, that I should preach among the Gentiles the unsearchable riches of Christ" (Ephesians 3:8). I'm grateful that God not only loves me, but He *likes* me—which is truly the only thing that keeps me going.

Shawn Brace pastors in Bangor, Maine, where he lives with his wife, Camille, and their three children, Camden, Acadia and Winslow (all named after locations in Maine). Over the past few years, their ministry has shifted from being inward-focused to incarnating the gospel in their neighbourhood and city, and leading their church into greater relational and missional awareness. This led to the replanting of their church in 2018, centring it on the gospel, mission, discipleship and community.

Beyond his local ministry, Shawn is also an author, having previously written three books, and he frequently contributes to various publications, including a regular column for *Adventist Review*. He was also recently accepted into the DPhil program at the University of Oxford, which he will pursue part-time, studying 19th-century American Christianity.

A native New Englander, Shawn and his family love spending time in the outdoors, especially going hiking, swimming and downhill skiing. More than anything, they love people—and often invite their friends and missional family along on their adventures. Shawn also enjoys photography and videography, some which you can see on Instagram @shawnbrace. You can also hear more about their missional life and musings via their podcast, Mission Lab, and by signing up for Shawn's newsletter at <shawnbrace.substack.com>.